Taste *of* Home

MEDITERRANEAN
MADE EASY

TASTE OF HOME BOOKS • RDA ENTHUSIAST BRANDS, LLC • MILWAUKEE, WI

Visit us at **tasteofhome.com** for other
Taste of Home books and products.

International Standard Book Number:
978-1-61765-891-4 (Paperback)
978-1-61765-975-1 (Hard Cover)

Library of Congress Control Number:
2019947876

Executive Editor: Mark Hagen
Senior Art Director: Raeann Thompson
Editors: Amy Glander, Christine Rukavena
Art Director: Maggie Conners
Designer: Jazmin Delgado
Copy Chief: Deb Warlaumont Mulvey
Editorial Intern: Daniella Peters

Cover
Photographer: Mark Derse
Food Stylist: Josh Rink
Set Stylist: Melissa Franco

Pictured on front cover:
Mediterranean Shrimp Orzo Salad, p. 270

Printed in China
7 9 11 10 8 (Paperback)
9 11 13 12 10 (Hard Cover)

24

38

211

312

CONTENTS

AT-A-GLANCE ICONS

Icons throughout the book indicate
five-ingredient, slow-cooked,
freezer-friendly and quick-to-fix fare.

MORE WAYS TO CONNECT WITH US:

Bring Color, Flavor & Flair to the Table!

You might not be able to jet off to Greece or Italy tonight, but with *Mediterranean Made Easy*, you can savor the flavors of the renowned coast right at home.

It's never been so simple to set the table with irresistibly light and refreshing food as it is when you have *Taste of Home*'s all-new cookbook, *Mediterranean Made Easy*, as your culinary tour guide.

In fact, this sensational collection of tried-and-true recipes makes it a snap. That's right! You'll find an array of favorites, from Spain's Hearty Paella (p. 150) to refreshing Chopped Greek Salad (p. 159). Each of these 321 recipes comes from the treasured files of today's family cooks who have happily adopted lively Mediterranean cuisine in their own homes and want to share all this delicious goodness with you.

The best part is that not only does Mediterranean food taste amazing, it's good for you, too! It's easy to eat well every day of the week with full-flavored dishes that make the most of fresh veggies, seafood, nuts, legumes, beans, olive oil, whole grains and other light, everyday ingredients.

In addition to these recipes, nutrition facts, gorgeous full-color photos, and prep and cook times make this one of the best cookbooks in your collection!

117

"Perfect in its simplicity! A tasty salad that is quick and simple to prepare. I used red wine vinegar instead of white. Loved the flavor boost from the sugar! This is a perfect accompaniment to any seafood dish."

— CAST_IRON_KING, TASTEOFHOME.COM

259

"This chicken was very tasty, and also easy to prepare. I didn't use capers, but we loved the olives with the chicken! We enjoyed it, and I'll definitely make it again."

—KITTIECATT, TASTEOFHOME.COM

"I've made this several times and always had success! On the advice of my nutritionist, I cut the sauce ingredients in half and used a light mayonnaise and it was just as good as the original recipe."

—PFONTES, TASTEOFHOME.COM

72

 WINE PAIRING

A Match Made in Heaven

Balancing the flavors of food with the perfect wine can be challenging. Fortunately, you don't have to be a sommelier or even a wine aficionado to find the right vino to enjoy with your meal. Just look to our wine pairing suggestions throughout the book.

BLT GRAIN BOWLS,
PAGE 8

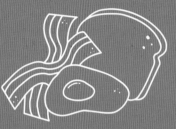

GOOD MORNINGS

Start your mornings right with a colorful parfait, no-fuss oatmeal or an impressive omelet. These feel-good dishes get you ready to take on the day—every day!

DATE OATMEAL

You can prepare this hearty oatmeal in a flash, and if you don't have dates available, try substituting raisins. Either way, everyone will love this filling breakfast.

—*Patricia Kaliska, Phillips, WI*

- -

Takes: 10 min. • **Makes:** 2 servings

- 2 cups apple juice
- 1 cup quick-cooking oats
- ½ cups chopped dates
- ¼ tsp. ground cinnamon
  Dash ground nutmeg
  Milk
  Shredded coconut, optional

In a saucepan, bring apple juice to a boil. Stir in oats; cook 1 minute. Remove from the heat; stir in dates, cinnamon and nutmeg. Cover and let stand for 5 minutes. Serve with milk and sprinkle with coconut if desired.

¾ cup: 395 cal., 3g fat (1g sat. fat), 0 chol., 10mg sod., 88g carb. (56g sugars, 8g fiber), 7g pro.

BLT GRAIN BOWLS

I absolutely adore a BLT with sliced avocado and an egg. Recently, I've been trying out grain bowls, and I thought the flavors of my favorite sandwich would work really well. My family agreed!

—*Elisabeth Larsen, Pleasant Grove, UT*

- -

Prep: 15 min. • **Cook:** 20 min.
Makes: 4 servings

- 1 cup quinoa, rinsed
- 4 Tbsp. olive oil, divided
- 2 Tbsp. minced fresh basil
- 2 Tbsp. white wine vinegar, divided
- 1 Tbsp. lemon juice
- 4 large eggs
- 8 oz. cherry tomatoes
- 3 cups fresh arugula
- 1 small ripe avocado, peeled and sliced
- 4 bacon strips, cooked and crumbled

1. Prepare quinoa according to package directions. Combine 3 Tbsp. olive oil, basil, 1 Tbsp. vinegar and lemon juice. Add to cooked quinoa; stir to combine.

2. Place 2-3 in. of water in a large skillet with high sides; add remaining vinegar. Bring to a boil; adjust heat to maintain a gentle simmer. Break 1 cold egg at a time into a small cup; holding cup close to surface of water, slip egg into water. Cook, uncovered, until whites are completely set and yolks begin to thicken but are not hard, 3-5 minutes. Using a slotted spoon, lift eggs out of water. Keep warm.

3. In a large skillet, heat remaining oil over medium heat. Cook tomatoes until they begin to release their juices, 8-10 minutes. Add arugula; cook and stir just until arugula is wilted, 1-2 minutes.

4. To serve, divide quinoa evenly among 4 bowls. Add cherry tomatoes, arugula, avocado slices and crumbled bacon. Top each with a poached egg.

Note: Look for quinoa in the cereal, rice or organic food aisle.

1 serving: 446 cal., 28g fat (5g sat. fat), 194mg chol., 228mg sod., 33g carb. (2g sugars, 6g fiber), 17g pro.

TEST KITCHEN TIP

Switch It Up

Use any grain you like in these hearty bowls. Many now come precooked in pouches, so it's an easy way to try one you have not prepared before.

FRENCH OMELET

This cheesy, full-of-flavor omelet is modeled after one I tasted and loved in a local restaurant. Mine is so hearty and rich-tasting that no one will guess it's lower in fat.
—*Bernice Morris, Marshfield, MO*

Takes: 20 min. • **Makes:** 2 servings

- 2 large eggs
- 4 large egg whites
- ¼ cup fat-free milk
- ⅛ tsp. salt
- ⅛ tsp. pepper
- ¼ cup cubed fully cooked ham
- 1 Tbsp. chopped onion
- 1 Tbsp. chopped green pepper
- ¼ cup shredded reduced-fat cheddar cheese

1. Whisk together first 5 ingredients.
2. Place a 10-in. skillet coated with cooking spray over medium heat. Pour in the egg mixture. Mixture should set immediately at edges. As the eggs set, push cooked portions toward the center, letting uncooked eggs flow underneath. When eggs are thickened and no liquid egg remains, top 1 half with remaining ingredients. Fold omelet in half. Cut in half to serve.
½ omelet: 186 cal., 9g fat (4g sat. fat), 207mg chol., 648mg sod., 4g carb. (3g sugars, 0 fiber), 22g pro. **Diabetic exchanges:** 3 lean meat, 1 fat.

HERB BREAKFAST FRITTATA

I came up with this recipe on a snowy day by using what I had in the fridge. Yukon Gold potatoes give this frittata a comforting bottom crust.

—*Katherine Hansen, Brunswick, ME*

- -

Takes: 30 min. • **Makes:** 4 servings

- ¼ cup thinly sliced red onion
- 1 Tbsp. olive oil
- 1 large Yukon Gold potato, peeled and thinly sliced
- 6 large eggs
- 1 tsp. minced fresh rosemary or ¼ tsp. dried rosemary, crushed
- 1 tsp. minced fresh thyme or ¼ tsp. dried thyme
- ¼ tsp. salt
- ⅛ tsp. crushed red pepper flakes
- ⅛ tsp. pepper
- 2 Tbsp. shredded cheddar cheese

1. In an 8-in. ovenproof skillet, saute onion in oil until tender. Using a slotted spoon, remove onion and keep warm. Arrange the potato slices in a single layer over bottom of pan. Preheat broiler.

2. In a small bowl, whisk the eggs, seasonings and onion; pour over potatoes. Cover and cook until nearly set, 4-6 minutes.

3. Uncover skillet. Broil 3-4 in. from the heat until eggs are completely set, 2-3 minutes. Sprinkle with cheese. Let stand for 5 minutes. Cut into wedges.

1 wedge: 204 cal., 12g fat (4g sat. fat), 321mg chol., 277mg sod., 13g carb. (2g sugars, 1g fiber), 11g pro. **Diabetic exchanges:** 1 starch, 1 medium-fat meat, 1 fat.

LEMON CHIA SEED PARFAITS

These bright and tangy parfaits start the day on a healthy note, but they're also sweet enough to double as dessert.
—*Crystal Schlueter, Babbitt, MN*

- -

Takes: 15 min. • **Makes:** 4 servings

- 2 **cups reduced-fat plain Greek yogurt**
- ¼ **cup agave nectar or honey**
- 2 **Tbsp. lemon juice**
- 2 **tsp. grated lemon zest**
- 2 **Tbsp. chia seeds or ground flaxseed**
- 1 **tsp. vanilla extract**
- 1 **cup fresh raspberries**
- 1 **cup fresh blueberries**

Combine the first 6 ingredients. Layer half of the yogurt mixture into 4 small parfait glasses or custard cups. Top with half of the berries. Repeat layers.

1 serving: 214 cal., 4g fat (2g sat. fat), 7mg chol., 48mg sod., 33g carb. (26g sugars, 5g fiber), 13g pro. **Diabetic exchanges:** 1½ starch, ½ fruit, ½ reduced-fat milk.

SLOW-COOKER HONEY NUT GRANOLA

I lightened up a friend's recipe and changed the add-ins to our tastes. It's now a family favorite! You can vary this recipe with different nuts, seeds or dried fruits.
—*Tari Ambler, Shorewood, IL*

Prep: 20 min. • **Cook:** 1½ hours
Makes: 8 cups

4½ cups old-fashioned oats
½ cup sunflower kernels
⅓ cup toasted wheat germ
¼ cup unsweetened shredded coconut
¼ cup sliced almonds
¼ cup chopped pecans
¼ cup chopped walnuts
¼ cup ground flaxseed
½ cup honey
⅓ cup water
3 Tbsp. canola oil
1 tsp. ground cinnamon
1 tsp. vanilla extract
½ tsp. ground nutmeg
Dash salt
¾ cup dried cranberries
¾ cup raisins
Yogurt, optional

1. In a 3- or 4-qt. slow cooker, combine the first 8 ingredients. In a small bowl, whisk honey, water, oil, cinnamon, vanilla, nutmeg and salt until blended; stir into oat mixture. Cook, covered, on high until crisp, 1½-2 hours, stirring well every 20 minutes.
2. Stir in cranberries and raisins. Spread evenly onto waxed paper or baking sheets; cool completely. Store in airtight containers. If desired, serve with yogurt.
Note: Look for unsweetened coconut in the baking or natural foods section.
½ cup: 267 cal., 12g fat (2g sat. fat), 0 chol., 43mg sod., 39g carb. (19g sugars, 5g fiber), 6g pro.

ITALIAN SAUSAGE BREAKFAST WRAPS

My husband leaves for work at 4 a.m., and I want him to have a healthy breakfast to start the day. I usually make half a dozen of these on Sunday and keep them in the fridge so he can grab one and go!

—*Dauna Harwood, Elkhart, IN*

Takes: 30 min. • **Makes:** 6 servings

¾ lb. Italian turkey sausage links, casings removed
1 small green pepper, finely chopped
1 small onion, finely chopped
1 medium tomato, chopped
4 large eggs
6 large egg whites
1 cup chopped fresh spinach
6 whole wheat tortillas (8 in.)
1 cup shredded reduced-fat cheddar cheese

1. In a large skillet, cook sausage, pepper, onion and tomato over medium heat until meat is no longer pink and vegetables are tender, breaking up sausage into crumbles; drain and return to pan.

2. In a small bowl, whisk eggs and egg whites until blended. Add egg mixture to sausage. Cook and stir until eggs are thickened and no liquid egg remains. Add spinach; cook and stir just until wilted.

3. Spoon ¾ cup egg mixture across center of each tortilla; top with about 2 Tbsp. cheese. Fold bottom and sides of tortilla over filling and roll up.

1 wrap: 327 cal., 14g fat (5g sat. fat), 175mg chol., 632mg sod., 26g carb. (4g sugars, 3g fiber), 23g pro. **Diabetic exchanges:** 3 lean meat, 1½ starch, 1 vegetable, 1 fat.

SPINACH POTATO PIE

When we have brunch with relatives, I like to make this crustless quiche with hash browns and spinach. We think it makes a fantastic midmorning meal with a side of fruit.
—*Deanna Phillips, Ferndale, WA*

Prep: 25 min. • **Bake:** 55 min.
Makes: 6 servings

- 5 large eggs, lightly beaten
- 4 cups frozen shredded hash brown potatoes
- 2 cups chopped fresh spinach
- ¾ cup chopped red onion
- ½ cup 2% cottage cheese
- 7 bacon strips, cooked and crumbled
- 3 green onions, chopped
- 4 garlic cloves, minced
- ½ tsp. salt
- ¼ tsp. pepper
- ⅛ tsp. hot pepper sauce
- 3 plum tomatoes, sliced
- ½ cup shredded Parmesan cheese

1. Preheat oven to 350°. In a large bowl, combine the first 11 ingredients. Pour into a greased 9-in. pie plate.
2. Bake 40 minutes. Arrange tomatoes over top; sprinkle with Parmesan cheese. Bake 15-20 minutes longer or until a knife inserted near the edge comes out clean. Let stand for 5 minutes before cutting.
1 piece: 204 cal., 10g fat (4g sat. fat), 192mg chol., 624mg sod., 15g carb. (3g sugars, 2g fiber), 15g pro. **Diabetic exchanges:** 2 medium-fat meat, 1 starch, ½ fat.

POWER BERRY SMOOTHIES

While you can't taste the spinach in these smoothies, you get all its nutrients with big berry flavor.
—*Christine Hair, Odessa, FL*

Takes: 10 min. • **Makes:** 3 servings

- ½ cup orange juice
- ½ cup pomegranate juice
- 1 container (6 oz.) mixed berry yogurt
- 1 cup frozen unsweetened strawberries
- 1 cup fresh baby spinach
- ½ medium ripe frozen banana, sliced
- ½ cup frozen unsweetened blueberries
- 2 Tbsp. ground flaxseed
  Sliced fresh strawberries, fresh blueberries, flax seeds and granola, optional

In a blender, combine first 8 ingredients; cover and process for 30 seconds or until smooth. Pour into chilled bowls; top as desired. Serve immediately.
1 cup: 172 cal., 3g fat (0 sat. fat), 3mg chol., 47mg sod., 35g carb. (28g sugars, 4g fiber), 5g pro.

HAM & EGG PITA POCKETS

I made these one day when the kids were running late for school and I needed a quick and healthy portable breakfast. The eggs cook quickly in the microwave, and the sandwiches are ready to eat in a snap.
—*Sue Olsen, Fremont, CA*

Takes: 10 min. • **Makes:** 1 serving

- 2 large egg whites
- 1 large egg
- ⅛ tsp. smoked or other paprika
- ⅛ tsp. freshly ground pepper
- 1 slice deli ham, chopped
- 1 green onion, sliced
- 2 Tbsp. shredded reduced-fat cheddar cheese
- 2 whole wheat pita pocket halves

In a microwave-safe bowl, whisk egg whites, egg, paprika and pepper until blended; stir in ham, green onion and cheese. Microwave, covered, on high for 1 minute. Stir; cook on high 30-60 seconds longer or until almost set. Serve in pitas.

2 filled pita halves: 323 cal., 10g fat (4g sat. fat), 231mg chol., 769mg sod., 34g carb. (3g sugars, 5g fiber), 27g pro. **Diabetic exchanges:** 3 lean meat, 2 starch.

SAUSAGE-SWEET POTATO HASH & EGGS

When I first began making this dish for breakfast, I served it with fried eggs on top. Now I sometimes make it for supper and serve it without eggs. It's great when I want a dish I can make quickly, with minimal cleanup.
—*Nancy Murphy, Mount Dora, FL*

Takes: 25 min. • **Makes:** 4 servings

- ½ **lb. Italian turkey sausage links, casings removed**
- 2 **medium sweet potatoes, peeled and cut into ¼-in. cubes**
- 2 **medium Granny Smith apples, chopped**
- ¼ **cup dried cranberries**
- ¼ **cup chopped pecans**
- ¼ **tsp. salt**
- 4 **green onions, sliced**
- 4 **large eggs**

1. In a large nonstick skillet coated with cooking spray, cook sausage and sweet potatoes over medium-high heat for 8-10 minutes or until sausage is no longer pink, breaking up sausage into crumbles.
2. Add apples, cranberries, pecans and salt; cook and stir 4-6 minutes longer or until potatoes are tender. Remove from pan; sprinkle with green onions. Keep warm.
3. Wipe skillet clean and coat with cooking spray; place skillet over medium-high heat. Break 1 egg at a time into pan. Reduce heat to low. Cook eggs to desired doneness, turning after whites are set, if desired. Serve with hash.
1 serving: 338 cal., 14g fat (3g sat. fat), 207mg chol., 465mg sod., 42g carb. (23g sugars, 6g fiber), 15g pro. **Diabetic exchanges:** 2 starch, 2 medium-fat meat, ½ fruit.

OVERNIGHT FLAX OATMEAL

Fans of the healthy benefits of flaxseed will enjoy this hearty oatmeal. It's full of yummy raisins and dried cranberries, too, but any combination of dried fruit will work. Feel free to get creative!
—*Susan Smith, Ocean View, NJ*

Prep: 10 min. • **Cook:** 7 hours
Makes: 4 servings

- 3 **cups water**
- 1 **cup old-fashioned oats**
- 1 **cup raisins**
- ½ **cup dried cranberries**
- ½ **cup ground flaxseed**
- ½ **cup 2% milk**
- 1 **tsp. vanilla extract**
- 1 **tsp. molasses**

In a 3-qt. slow cooker, combine all of the ingredients. Cover and cook on low for 7-8 hours or until liquid is absorbed and oatmeal is tender.
1 cup: 322 cal., 9g fat (1g sat. fat), 2mg chol., 28mg sod., 63g carb. (34g sugars, 8g fiber), 9g pro.

⑤ ◷

LEAN GREEN SMOOTHIE

Kids love the unusual color of this frosty and flavorful smoothie. It's fine-tuned to their liking with bananas, creamy yogurt and (*shh*) a bit of spinach.
—*Madison Mayberry, Ames, IA*

- -

Takes: 10 min. • **Makes:** 4 servings

¾	cup fat-free milk
1½	cups fat-free vanilla yogurt
1	cup ice cubes
1	cup fresh spinach
1	ripe medium banana
2	Tbsp. lemon juice

In a blender, combine all ingredients; cover and process for 30 seconds or until smooth. Pour into chilled glasses; serve immediately. **1 cup:** 99 cal., 0 fat (0 sat. fat), 4mg chol., 24mg sod., 19g carb. (12g sugars, 1g fiber), 5g pro. **Diabetic exchanges:** 1 fat-free milk, ½ fruit.

LOADED QUINOA BREAKFAST BOWL

After I was diagnosed with multiple sclerosis in 2001, I embarked on a journey to improve my diet and live a healthier lifestyle. I began developing recipes that were not only deliciously satisfying, but also anti-inflammatory and highly nutritious.
—*Chantale Michaud, Guelph, ON*

Prep: 15 min. + soaking • **Cook:** 15 min.
Makes: 1 serving

- ¾ cup water, divided
- ¼ cup tri-colored quinoa, rinsed
- 2 Tbsp. dried goji berries or dried cranberries
- 1 small banana
- ¼ cup unsweetened almond milk
- 1 Tbsp. maple syrup
- ⅛ tsp. ground cinnamon
- ⅛ tsp. vanilla extract
- ¼ cup fresh or frozen unsweetened blueberries
- 1 Tbsp. chopped walnuts
- 1 Tbsp. slivered almonds
- 1 Tbsp. fresh pumpkin seeds
  Additional unsweetened almond milk and maple syrup, optional

1. In a small saucepan, bring ½ cup water to a boil. Add quinoa. Reduce heat; simmer, covered, until the liquid is absorbed, 12-15 minutes. Meanwhile, soak the berries in remaining water for 10 minutes; drain. Halve banana crosswise. Slice 1 banana half; mash the other.

2. Remove quinoa from heat; fluff with a fork. Mix in mashed banana, almond milk, maple syrup, cinnamon and vanilla. Transfer to an individual bowl; add blueberries, walnuts, almonds, pumpkin seeds, banana slices and goji berries. If desired, serve with additional almond milk.

1 serving: 475 cal., 13g fat (1g sat. fat), 0 chol., 85mg sod., 83g carb. (35g sugars, 10g fiber), 13g pro.

SAVORY APPLE-CHICKEN SAUSAGE

These easy, healthy sausages taste incredible, and they are an excellent addition to any breakfast or brunch. The recipe is also very versatile—it can be doubled or tripled for a crowd, and the sausage freezes well whether cooked or raw.

—*Angela Buchanan, Longmont, CO*

- -

Takes: 25 min. • **Makes:** 8 patties

- 1   large tart apple, peeled and diced
- 2   tsp. poultry seasoning
- 1   tsp. salt
- ¼   tsp. pepper
- 1   lb. ground chicken

1. In a large bowl, combine the apple, poultry seasoning, salt and pepper. Crumble chicken over mixture and mix well. Shape into eight 3-in. patties.

2. In a large, greased cast-iron or other heavy skillet, cook patties over medium heat until no longer pink, 5-6 minutes on each side. Drain if necessary.

1 sausage patty: 92 cal., 5g fat (1g sat. fat), 38mg chol., 328mg sod., 4g carb. (3g sugars, 1g fiber), 9g pro. **Diabetic exchanges:** 1 medium-fat meat.

FIESTA TIME OMELET

I created this dish when I needed to use up some black olives and jalapenos. With the abundant filling, two of these large omelets can feed four people if served with sides.
—*Jennine Victory, Bee Branch, AR*

- -

Takes: 15 min. • **Makes:** 2 servings

 4 **large eggs**
 ¼ **cup fat-free milk**
 ¼ **tsp. salt**
 ¼ **cup queso fresco**
 ¼ **cup canned diced jalapeno peppers
       or chopped green chiles**
 2 **Tbsp. finely chopped
       sweet red pepper**
 2 **Tbsp. sliced ripe olives**
 2 **tsp. chopped fresh cilantro**
 ¼ **medium ripe avocado,
       peeled and sliced**

1. In a small bowl, whisk eggs, milk and salt until blended.
2. Place a lightly oiled 10-in. nonstick skillet over medium-high heat. Pour in egg mixture. Mixture should set immediately at edges. As the eggs set, push cooked portions toward the center, letting uncooked eggs flow underneath. When the eggs are thickened and no liquid egg remains, spoon cheese, peppers, olives and cilantro on one side. Fold omelet in half. Cut in half; slide onto 2 plates. Top with avocado.
½ omelet: 242 cal., 16g fat (5g sat. fat), 383mg chol., 601mg sod., 7g carb. (3g sugars, 2g fiber), 18g pro. **Diabetic exchanges:** 2 medium-fat meat, 1 fat, ½ starch.

CINNAMON BLUEBERRY FRENCH TOAST

I like to prep this breakfast in the afternoon, let it chill, then put it into the slow cooker before I go to bed. When we wake up in the morning, it's done just right.
—*Angela Lively, Conroe, TX*

- -

Prep: 15 min. + chilling • **Cook:** 3 hours
Makes: 6 servings

- 3 **large eggs**
- 2 **cups 2% milk**
- ¼ **cup sugar**
- 1 **tsp. ground cinnamon**
- 1 **tsp. vanilla extract**
- ¼ **tsp. salt**
- 9 **cups cubed French bread (about 9 oz.)**
- 1 **cup fresh or frozen blueberries, thawed**
  Maple syrup

1. Whisk together first 6 ingredients. Layer half of the bread in a greased 5-qt. slow cooker; top with ½ cup blueberries and half of milk mixture. Repeat layers. Refrigerate, covered, 4 hours or overnight.
2. Cook, covered, on low until a knife inserted in the center comes out clean, 3-4 hours. Serve warm with syrup.
1 cup: 265 cal., 6g fat (2g sat. fat), 100mg chol., 430mg sod., 42g carb. (18g sugars, 2g fiber), 11g pro.

> ### TEST KITCHEN TIP
> ### In Favor of Fiber
> Substitute whole wheat for white French bread to increase fiber. If you can't find it, cube 100% whole wheat buns.

BREAKFAST GRANOLA

This is one of my family's favorite breakfasts. It gives us the energy we need to get through the day's chores.
—*Wilma Beller, Hamilton, OH*

- -

Prep: 20 min. • **Bake:** 20 min. • **Makes:** 8 cups

- 4 **cups old-fashioned oats**
- ⅓ **cup honey or molasses**
- ¼ **cup canola oil**
- 1 **tsp. vanilla extract**
- 1 **cup chopped nuts**
- ¾ **cup uncooked oat bran cereal**
- 1 **cup sweetened shredded coconut**
- 1 **cup raisins**
- 1 **cup chopped dates**
  Yogurt and fresh fruit, optional

1. Spread the rolled oats on a 15x10x1-in. baking pan. Bake at 350° for 5 minutes. Stir; bake until toasted, about 5 minutes longer. Meanwhile, combine honey and oil in a small saucepan. Cook and stir over medium heat until heated through, 2-3 minutes. Remove from the heat; stir in extract. Remove oats from oven; toss with nuts, bran and coconut.
2. Pour the hot honey mixture over oat mixture; toss well. Return to oven and bake 20-25 minutes, stirring every 6 minutes. Remove from oven. Stir in raisins and dates. Cool. Store in an airtight container. Serve with yogurt and fresh fruit if desired.
Note: Look for oat bran cereal near the hot cereals or in the natural foods section.
½ cup: 275 cal., 12g fat (3g sat. fat), 0 chol., 18mg sod., 41g carb. (20g sugars, 4g fiber), 6g pro.

CHORIZO & GRITS BREAKFAST BOWLS

Growing up, I bonded with my dad over chorizo and eggs. My fresh approach combines them with grits and black beans. Add a spoonful of pico de gallo for an extra fun, flavorful kick.

—Jenn Tidwell, Fair Oaks, CA

- -

Takes: 30 min. • **Makes:** 6 servings

- 2 tsp. olive oil
- 1 pkg. (12 oz.) fully cooked chorizo chicken sausages or flavor of choice, sliced
- 1 large zucchini, chopped
- 3 cups water
- ¾ cup quick-cooking grits
- 1 can (15 oz.) black beans, rinsed and drained
- ½ cup shredded cheddar cheese
- 6 large eggs
  Pico de gallo and chopped fresh cilantro, optional

1. In a large nonstick skillet, heat oil over medium heat. Add sausage; cook and stir until lightly browned, 2-3 minutes. Add zucchini; cook and stir until tender, another 4-5 minutes. Remove from pan; keep warm.

2. Meanwhile, in a large saucepan, bring water to a boil. Slowly stir in grits. Reduce heat to medium-low; cook, covered, until thickened, about 5 minutes, stirring occasionally. Stir in beans and cheese until blended. Remove from heat.

3. Wipe skillet clean; coat with cooking spray and place over medium heat. In batches, break 1 egg at a time into pan. Immediately reduce heat to low; cook until whites are completely set and yolks begin to thicken but are not hard, about 5 minutes.

4. To serve, divide the grits mixture among 6 bowls. Top with chorizo mixture, eggs and, if desired, pico de gallo and cilantro.

1 serving: 344 cal., 14g fat (5g sat. fat), 239mg chol., 636mg sod., 30g carb. (4g sugars, 4g fiber), 24g pro. **Diabetic exchanges:** 3 medium-fat meat, 2 starch.

TEST KITCHEN TIP

Bring on the Beans!

Black beans can ramp up the iron, protein and fiber in a variety of dishes, from breakfast mains to soups, salads and entrees.

GINGER-KALE SMOOTHIES

Since I started drinking these smoothies for breakfast every day, I can honestly say I feel better! Substitute any fruit and juice to make this recipe your own healthy blend.
—*Linda Green, Kilauea, Kauai, HI*

- -

Takes: 15 min. • **Makes:** 2 servings

- 1¼ cups orange juice
- 1 tsp. lemon juice
- 2 cups torn fresh kale
- 1 medium apple, peeled and coarsely chopped
- 1 Tbsp. minced fresh gingerroot
- 4 ice cubes
- ⅛ tsp. ground cinnamon
- ⅛ tsp. ground turmeric or ¼-in. piece fresh turmeric, peeled and finely chopped
  Dash cayenne pepper

Place all ingredients in a blender; cover and process until blended. Serve immediately.
1 cup: 121 cal., 0 fat (0 sat. fat), 0 chol., 22mg sod., 29g carb. (21g sugars, 2g fiber), 1g pro.
Diabetic exchanges: 1½ fruit, 1 vegetable.

BREAKFAST PARFAITS

The combination of pineapples, raspberries and bananas in these yogurt treats makes a bright and cheerful morning breakfast.
—*Adell Meyer, Madison, WI*

Takes: 10 min. • **Makes:** 4 servings

2	**cups pineapple chunks**
1	**cup fresh or frozen raspberries**
1	**cup vanilla yogurt**
1	**cup sliced ripe banana**
½	**cup chopped dates or raisins**
¼	**cup sliced almonds**

In 4 parfait glasses or serving dishes, layer the pineapple, raspberries, yogurt, banana and dates. Sprinkle with almonds. Serve immediately.

1 parfait: 277 cal., 4g fat (1g sat. fat), 3mg chol., 52mg sod., 60g carb. (48g sugars, 6g fiber), 5g pro.

FRITTATA FLORENTINE

My family is all about brunchy meals like this gorgeous Italian omelet. Lucky for us, it's loaded with ingredients we tend to have at the ready.

—*Jenny Flake, Newport Beach, CA*

- -

Takes: 30 min. • **Makes:** 4 servings

- 6 **large egg whites**
- 3 **large eggs**
- ½ **tsp. dried oregano**
- ¼ **tsp. garlic powder**
- ¼ **tsp. salt**
- ¼ **tsp. pepper**
- 1 **Tbsp. olive oil**
- 1 **small onion, finely chopped**
- ¼ **cup finely chopped sweet red pepper**
- 2 **turkey bacon strips, chopped**
- 1 **cup fresh baby spinach**
- 3 **Tbsp. thinly sliced fresh basil leaves**
- ½ **cup shredded part-skim mozzarella cheese**

1. Preheat broiler. In a small bowl, whisk the first 6 ingredients.

2. In an 8-in. ovenproof skillet, heat oil over medium-high heat. Add onion, red pepper and bacon; cook and stir 4-5 minutes or until onion is tender. Reduce heat to medium-low; top with spinach.

3. Pour in egg mixture. As eggs set, push cooked portions toward the center, letting uncooked eggs flow underneath; cook until eggs are nearly thickened. Remove from heat; sprinkle with basil, then cheese.

4. Broil 3-4 in. from heat 2-3 minutes or until eggs are completely set. Let stand 5 minutes. Cut into wedges.

1 slice: 176 cal., 11g fat (4g sat. fat), 174mg chol., 451mg sod., 4g carb. (2g sugars, 1g fiber), 15g pro. **Diabetic exchanges:** 2 medium-fat meat, ½ fat.

TEST KITCHEN TIP

Cut Down on Cholesterol

To make this frittata even healthier, substitute 6 egg whites for the 3 whole eggs listed in the ingredients. This swap means you'll be using 12 egg whites in total to complete the recipe.

ARUGULA & MUSHROOM BREAKFAST PIZZA

Sometimes it's a challenge to get creative with breakfast every morning, but this recipe is a fun one the kids are sure to love. It's easy enough that they can even join in to help make it for breakfast. It's also convenient to make ahead and freeze for a weekday.
—*Melissa Pelkey Hass, Waleska, GA*

Prep: 20 min. • **Bake:** 15 min.
Makes: 6 servings

- 1 prebaked 12-in. thin whole wheat pizza crust
- ¾ cup reduced-fat ricotta cheese
- 1 tsp. garlic powder
- 1 tsp. paprika, divided
- 1 cup sliced baby portobello mushrooms
- ½ cup julienned soft sun-dried tomatoes (not packed in oil)
- 3 cups fresh arugula or baby spinach
- 2 Tbsp. balsamic vinegar
- 2 Tbsp. olive oil
- ¼ tsp. salt, divided
- ¼ tsp. pepper, divided
- 6 large eggs

1. Preheat oven to 450°. Place crust on a pizza pan. Spread with ricotta cheese; sprinkle with garlic powder and ½ tsp. paprika. Top with mushrooms and tomatoes.
2. With clean hands, massage arugula with vinegar, oil and ⅛ tsp. each salt and pepper until softened; arrange over pizza.
3. Using a spoon, make 6 indentations in arugula; carefully break an egg into each. Sprinkle with the remaining paprika, salt and pepper. Bake until egg whites are completely set and yolks begin to thicken but are not hard, 12-15 minutes.

Note: This recipe was tested with sun-dried tomatoes that can be used without soaking. When using other sun-dried tomatoes that are not oil-packed, cover with boiling water and let stand until soft. Drain before using.
1 slice: 299 cal., 13g fat (4g sat. fat), 194mg chol., 464mg sod., 31g carb. (8g sugars, 5g fiber), 15g pro. **Diabetic exchanges:** 2 medium-fat meat, 1½ starch, 1 vegetable, 1 fat.

SPICED BLUEBERRY QUINOA

I took up eating quinoa when I found out how much protein it has. For beginning quinoa fans, this is an easy dish to experiment with. My first version of the recipe was made with shredded apples instead of blueberries, but it's just as delicious either way!
—*Shannon Copley, Upper Arlington, OH*

- -

Prep: 10 min. • **Cook:** 30 min.
Makes: 2 servings

½ cup quinoa, rinsed and well drained
2 cups unsweetened almond milk
2 Tbsp. honey
½ tsp. ground cinnamon
¼ tsp. salt
1 cup fresh or frozen blueberries, thawed
¼ tsp. vanilla extract
2 Tbsp. chopped almonds, toasted

1. In a small saucepan, cook and stir the quinoa over medium heat until lightly toasted, 5-7 minutes. Stir in the almond milk, honey, cinnamon and salt; bring to a boil. Reduce heat; simmer, uncovered, until quinoa is tender and the liquid is almost absorbed, 20-25 minutes, stirring occasionally.
2. Remove from heat; stir in blueberries and vanilla. Sprinkle with almonds.
1 cup: 352 cal., 10g fat (1g sat. fat), 0 chol., 479mg sod., 59g carb. (25g sugars, 7g fiber), 9g pro.

TEST KITCHEN TIP

More Quinoa, Please!

Adding quinoa to your diet is a smart move. It's a good source of trace minerals—specifically manganese and copper—that help turn carbohydrates into energy. And it's one of the only plant foods that contains all 9 of the essential amino acids we need, making it an excellent source of protein.

GREEK VEGGIE OMELET

This cheesy, veggie-stuffed omelet is a family favorite in my house. It's quick and satisfying—not to mention yummy!
—Sharon Mannix, Windsor, NY

Takes: 20 min. • **Makes:** 2 servings

- 4   large eggs
- 2   Tbsp. fat-free milk
- ⅛   tsp. salt
- 3   tsp. olive oil, divided
- 2   cups sliced baby portobello mushrooms
- ¼   cup finely chopped onion
- 1   cup fresh baby spinach
- 3   Tbsp. crumbled feta cheese
- 2   Tbsp. sliced ripe olives
       Freshly ground pepper

1. Whisk together eggs, milk and salt. In a large nonstick skillet, heat 2 tsp. oil over medium-high heat; saute mushrooms and onion until golden brown, 5-6 minutes. Stir in spinach until wilted; remove from pan.
2. In same pan, heat the remaining oil over medium-low heat. Pour in egg mixture. As the eggs set, push cooked portions toward the center, letting uncooked eggs flow underneath. When eggs are thickened and no liquid egg remains, spoon vegetables on 1 side; sprinkle with cheese and olives. Fold to close; cut in half to serve. Sprinkle with ground pepper.
½ omelet: 271 cal., 19g fat (5g sat. fat), 378mg chol., 475mg sod., 7g carb. (3g sugars, 2g fiber), 18g pro. **Diabetic exchanges:** 2 medium-fat meat, 2 fat, 1 vegetable.

AVOCADO FRUIT SALAD

I'm glad a friend gave me this delicious recipe, which features four kinds of fruit as well as avocado. A light honey-lemon dressing enhances the already tasty flavor of the produce. My family loves this colorful mix, and so do I!
—Mildred Sherrer, Fort Worth, TX

Takes: 20 min. • **Makes:** 6 servings

- ½   cup plain yogurt
- 2   Tbsp. honey
- 1   tsp. grated lemon zest
- 1   tsp. plus 2 Tbsp. lemon juice, divided
- 3   medium ripe avocados, peeled and cubed
- 1   medium apple, chopped
- 1   cup halved seedless grapes
- 1   can (11 oz.) mandarin oranges, drained
- 1   medium firm banana, cut into ¼-in. slices

1. For dressing, mix yogurt, honey, lemon zest and 1 tsp. lemon juice. Toss avocados with remaining lemon juice.
2. In a large bowl, combine the remaining ingredients; gently stir in avocados. Serve with dressing.
¾ cup: 231 cal., 11g fat (2g sat. fat), 3mg chol., 22mg sod., 35g carb. (25g sugars, 6g fiber), 3g pro.

COOL SUMMERTIME OATMEAL

Start this breakfast the night before so you can catch a few extra zzz's in the morning! My husband sprinkles coconut in his bowl, and I add dried fruit to mine.

—*June Thomas, Chesterton, IN*

Prep: 10 min. + chilling • **Makes:** 4 servings

- 1⅓ **cups old-fashioned oats**
- ¾ **cup fat-free milk**
- ¾ **cup (6 oz.) reduced-fat plain yogurt**
- ¼ **cup honey**
- 1 **cup pitted fresh or frozen dark sweet cherries, thawed**
- 1 **cup fresh or frozen blueberries, thawed**
- ½ **cup chopped walnuts, toasted**

1. In a small bowl, combine oats, milk, yogurt and honey. Refrigerate, covered, overnight.
2. Top each serving with cherries, blueberries and walnuts.

To make individual servings: Stir together ⅓ cup oats, 3 Tbsp. each milk and yogurt and 1 Tbsp. honey in a resealable glass jar. Top with fruit and nuts; seal and refrigerate overnight.
1 serving: 350 cal., 12g fat (2g sat. fat), 4mg chol., 53mg sod., 55g carb. (31g sugars, 5g fiber), 10g pro.

SAUSAGE-EGG BURRITOS

My husband and I try to eat healthy, but finding new meals for breakfast is a challenge. By adding tomatoes, spinach and garlic to traditional eggs and egg whites, we can have a dish that is both light and satisfying.
—*Wendy Ball, Battle Creek, MI*

- -

Takes: 20 min. • **Makes:** 6 servings

- ½ lb. bulk lean turkey breakfast sausage
- 3 large eggs
- 4 large egg whites
- 1 Tbsp. olive oil
- 2 cups chopped fresh spinach
- 2 plum tomatoes, seeded and chopped
- 1 garlic clove, minced
- ¼ tsp. pepper
- 6 whole wheat tortillas (8 in.), warmed
  Salsa, optional

1. In a large nonstick skillet, cook sausage over medium heat until no longer pink, breaking into crumbles, 4-6 minutes. Remove from pan.
2. In a small bowl, whisk eggs and egg whites until blended. In same pan, add eggs; cook and stir over medium heat until eggs are thickened and no liquid egg remains. Remove from pan; wipe skillet clean if necessary.
3. In skillet, heat oil over medium-high heat. Add the spinach, tomatoes and garlic; cook and stir until spinach is wilted, 2-3 minutes. Stir in the sausage and eggs; heat through. Sprinkle with pepper.
4. To serve, spoon ⅔ cup filling across center of each tortilla. Fold bottom and sides of tortilla over filling and roll up. If desired, serve with salsa.
1 burrito: 258 cal., 10g fat (2g sat. fat), 134mg chol., 596mg sod., 24g carb. (1g sugars, 4g fiber), 20g pro. **Diabetic exchanges:** 2 medium-fat meat, 1½ starch, ½ fat.

AUTUMN PUMPKIN PORRIDGE

This rib-sticking porridge is made with oats and protein-rich quinoa. Adding pumpkin, maple syrup, walnuts and dried cranberries makes it a kid-friendly breakfast.
—*Jennifer Wickes, Pine Beach, NJ*

- -

Prep: 15 min. • **Cook:** 30 min.
Makes: 4 servings

- 3 cups water
- ¾ cup steel-cut oats
- ½ cup quinoa, rinsed
- ¼ tsp. salt
- ¾ cup canned pumpkin
- 1 tsp. pumpkin pie spice
- 3 Tbsp. agave nectar or maple syrup
- ½ cup dried cranberries
- ⅓ cup coarsely chopped walnuts, toasted
  Milk

1. In a large saucepan, combine the water, oats, quinoa and salt. Bring to a boil. Reduce heat; cover and simmer for 20 minutes.
2. Stir in the pumpkin, pie spice and agave nectar. Remove from the heat; cover and let stand for 5 minutes or until water is absorbed and grains are tender. Stir in cranberries and walnuts. Serve with milk if desired.
Note: Steel-cut oats are also known as Scotch oats or Irish oatmeal.
1 cup: 361 cal., 10g fat (1g sat. fat), 0 chol., 155mg sod., 65g carb. (24g sugars, 7g fiber), 9g pro.

MIXED FRUIT WITH LEMON-BASIL DRESSING

A slightly savory dressing complements the sweet fruit in this fresh medley. I also use the dressing on salad greens.
—Dixie Terry, Goreville, IL

Takes: 15 min. • **Makes:** 8 servings

 2 Tbsp. lemon juice
 ½ tsp. sugar
 ¼ tsp. salt
 ¼ tsp. ground mustard
 ⅛ tsp. onion powder
    Dash pepper
 6 Tbsp. olive oil
 4½ tsp. minced fresh basil
 1 cup cubed fresh pineapple
 1 cup sliced fresh strawberries
 1 cup sliced peeled kiwifruit
 1 cup seedless watermelon balls
 1 cup fresh blueberries
 1 cup fresh raspberries

1. Place the first 6 ingredients in a blender; cover and process for 5 seconds. While processing, gradually add the oil in a steady stream. Stir in basil.
2. In a large bowl, combine the fruit. Drizzle with dressing and toss to coat. Refrigerate until serving.
¾ cup: 145 cal., 11g fat (1g sat. fat), 0 chol., 76mg sod., 14g carb. (9g sugars, 3g fiber), 1g pro. **Diabetic exchanges:** 2 fat, 1 fruit.

GREEK BREAKFAST CASSEROLE

Here's a wonderful dish for a Sunday brunch, or you can cut it into six pieces and freeze it so you have a quick and easy breakfast any day of the week. I also like to make it with broccoli, carrots, green onions, Canadian bacon and sharp cheddar cheese. The variations are endless!

—*Lauri Knox, Pine, CO*

- -

Prep: 35 min. • **Bake:** 45 min. + standing
Makes: 6 servings

- ½ **lb. Italian turkey sausage links, casings removed**
- ½ **cup chopped green pepper**
- 1 **shallot, chopped**
- 1 **cup water-packed artichoke hearts, rinsed, drained and chopped**
- 1 **cup chopped fresh broccoli**
- ⅓ **cup sun-dried tomatoes (not packed in oil), chopped**
- 6 **large eggs**
- 6 **large egg whites**
- 3 **Tbsp. fat-free milk**
- ½ **tsp. Italian seasoning**
- ¼ **tsp. garlic powder**
- ¼ **tsp. pepper**
- ⅓ **cup crumbled feta cheese**

1. Preheat oven to 350°. In a large skillet, cook sausage, green pepper and shallot over medium heat until sausage is no longer pink, breaking up sausage into crumbles, 8-10 minutes; drain. Transfer the mixture to an 8-in. square baking dish coated with cooking spray. Top with artichokes, broccoli and sun-dried tomatoes.

2. In a large bowl, whisk eggs, egg whites, milk and seasonings until blended; pour over top. Sprinkle with feta.

3. Bake, uncovered, until a knife inserted in the center comes out clean, 45-50 minutes. Let stand 10 minutes before serving.

Freeze option: Cool baked casserole; cover and freeze. To use, partially thaw in refrigerator overnight. Remove from the refrigerator 30 minutes before baking. Preheat oven to 325°. Bake casserole as directed until heated through and a thermometer inserted in the center reads 165°.

1 piece: 179 cal., 9g fat (3g sat. fat), 229mg chol., 435mg sod., 8g carb. (2g sugars, 1g fiber), 17g pro. **Diabetic exchanges:** 2 medium-fat meat, 1 vegetable.

GREEK VEGGIE TARTLETS,
PAGE 38

Mezze, Tapas & Small Plates

Whether you enjoy them during a casual night at home or use them to surprise friends at a potluck, these appetizers elevate your snacking game. See how the vibrant colors and refreshing flavors of the Mediterranean liven up any occasion.

GREEK VEGGIE TARTLETS

This recipe started out as a salad, which I re-created after a trip to Greece. When my husband suggested I serve the mixture in phyllo cups, it became my most requested appetizer of all time.
—*Radelle Knappenberger, Oviedo, FL*

Takes: 25 min. • **Makes:** 45 tartlets

- 3 pkg. (1.9 oz. each) frozen miniature phyllo tart shells
- ¾ cup finely chopped seeded peeled cucumber
- ¾ cup finely chopped red onion
- ¾ cup finely chopped seeded plum tomatoes
- ¾ cup finely chopped pitted Greek olives
- ½ cup Greek vinaigrette
- ¾ cup crumbled feta cheese

1. Preheat oven to 350°. Place shells on two 15x10x1-in. pans. Bake until lightly browned, 7-10 minutes. Cool completely.

2. Toss vegetables and olives with vinaigrette. To serve, spoon about 1 Tbsp. mixture into each tart shell. Sprinkle with cheese.

1 tartlet: 43 cal., 3g fat (0 sat. fat), 1mg chol., 93mg sod., 3g carb. (0 sugars, 0 fiber), 1g pro.

GARLIC GARBANZO BEAN SPREAD

My friends and family always ask me to make this. I guarantee you'll be asked for the recipe. You can serve the hearty spread as a fast appetizer or a filling for sandwiches.
—*Lisa Moore, North Syracuse, NY*

Takes: 10 min. • **Makes:** 1½ cups

- 1 can (15 oz.) garbanzo beans or chickpeas, rinsed and drained
- ½ cup olive oil
- 2 Tbsp. minced fresh parsley
- 1 Tbsp. lemon juice
- 1 green onion, cut into three pieces
- 1 to 2 garlic cloves, peeled
- ¼ tsp. salt
  Assorted fresh vegetables and baked pita chips

In a food processor, combine the first 7 ingredients; cover and process until blended. Transfer to a bowl. Refrigerate until serving. Serve with vegetables and pita chips.

2 Tbsp.: 114 cal., 10g fat (1g sat. fat), 0 chol., 96mg sod., 6g carb. (1g sugars, 1g fiber), 1g pro. **Diabetic exchanges:** 2 fat, ½ starch.

WINE PAIRING

Colombard. This workhorse grape makes weighty, yet fresh and herbaceous, wines in hot climates like southwest France's Cotes de Gascogne region, Southern California and Israel.

GOAT CHEESE MUSHROOMS

Stuffed mushrooms are superstars in the hot appetizer category. I use baby portobello mushrooms and load them with creamy goat cheese and sweet red peppers.
—*Mike Bass, Alvin, TX*

Takes: 30 min. • **Makes:** 2 dozen

24 **baby portobello mushrooms (about 1 lb.), stems removed**
½ **cup crumbled goat cheese**
½ **cup chopped drained roasted sweet red peppers**
   Pepper to taste
4 **tsp. olive oil**
   Chopped fresh parsley

1. Preheat oven to 375°. Place mushroom caps in a greased 15x10x1-in. baking pan. Fill each cap with 1 tsp. cheese; top each cap with 1 tsp. red pepper. Sprinkle with pepper; drizzle with oil.
2. Bake 15-18 minutes or until mushrooms are tender. Sprinkle with parsley.
1 stuffed mushroom: 19 cal., 1g fat (0 sat. fat), 3mg chol., 31mg sod., 1g carb. (1g sugars, 0 fiber), 1g pro.

SLIM GREEK DEVILED EGGS

When you're in the mood for some good finger food, try this quick, delicious Greek variation on deviled eggs. They are a cinch to fill and make a popular contribution to a potluck or brunch.
—Taste of Home *Test Kitchen*

Takes: 20 min. • **Makes:** 1 dozen

6 hard-boiled large eggs
3 Tbsp. reduced-fat mayonnaise
2 Tbsp. crumbled feta cheese
1 tsp. dried oregano
½ tsp. grated lemon zest
½ tsp. lemon juice
⅛ tsp. salt
⅛ tsp. pepper
  Greek olives, optional

1. Cut eggs in half lengthwise. Remove yolks; set aside egg whites and 4 yolks (discard remaining yolks or save for another use).
2. In a large bowl, mash reserved yolks. Stir in mayonnaise, feta, oregano, lemon zest, lemon juice, salt and pepper. Stuff or pipe into egg whites. If desired, garnish with olives. Chill until serving.

1 stuffed egg half: 42 cal., 3g fat (1g sat. fat), 70mg chol., 96mg sod., 1g carb. (0 sugars, 0 fiber), 3g pro.

WATERMELON CUPS

This lovely appetizer is almost too pretty to eat! Adorable and sweet, these watermelon cubes hold a refreshing topping of cucumber, red onion and fresh herbs.
—Taste of Home *Test Kitchen*

Takes: 25 min. • **Makes:** 16 appetizers

- 16 seedless watermelon cubes (1 in.)
- ⅓ cup finely chopped cucumber
- 5 tsp. finely chopped red onion
- 2 tsp. minced fresh mint
- 2 tsp. minced fresh cilantro
- ½ to 1 tsp. lime juice

1. Using a small melon baller or measuring spoon, scoop out the center of each watermelon cube, leaving a ¼-in. shell (save pulp for another use).
2. In a small bowl, combine the remaining ingredients; spoon into watermelon cubes.
1 piece: 7 cal., 0 fat (0 sat. fat), 0 chol., 1mg sod., 2g carb. (2g sugars, 0 fiber), 0 pro.

READER RAVE

"How did I ever not think of this? It is so refreshing and just a delight—they are all gone each time I make them."
—BONITO15, TASTEOFHOME.COM

PICKLED SHRIMP WITH BASIL

Red wine vinegar plus the freshness of citrus and basil perk up marinated shrimp with hardly any prep. Serve over greens if you'd like a salad.

—*James Schend, Pleasant Prairie, WI*

Prep: 15 min. + marinating
Makes: 20 servings (½ cup each)

- ½ cup red wine vinegar
- ½ cup olive oil
- 2 tsp. seafood seasoning
- 2 tsp. stone-ground mustard
- 1 garlic clove, minced
- 2 lbs. peeled and deveined cooked shrimp (31-40 per lb.)
- 1 medium lemon, thinly sliced
- 1 medium lime, thinly sliced
- ½ medium red onion, thinly sliced
- ¼ cup thinly sliced fresh basil
- 2 Tbsp. capers, drained
- ¼ cup minced fresh basil
- ½ tsp. kosher salt
- ¼ tsp. coarsely ground pepper

1. In a large bowl, whisk first 5 ingredients. Add shrimp, lemon, lime, onion, sliced basil and capers; toss gently to coat. Refrigerate, covered, up to 8 hours, stirring occasionally.
2. Just before serving, stir minced basil, salt and pepper into shrimp mixture. Serve with a slotted spoon.

½ cup: 64 cal., 2g fat (0 sat. fat), 69mg chol., 111mg sod., 1g carb. (0 sugars, 0 fiber), 9g pro. **Diabetic exchanges:** 1 lean meat, ½ fat.

SPINACH DIP-STUFFED MUSHROOMS

I use a melon baller to hollow out the mushroom caps and make them easier to stuff. These apps fit neatly into muffin tins or a deviled egg tray for traveling.
—*Ashley Pierce, Brantford, ON*

Prep: 25 min. • **Bake:** 15 min.
Makes: 16 appetizers

- 16 **large fresh mushrooms (about 1½ lbs.)**
- 1 **Tbsp. olive oil**
- 2 **cups fresh baby spinach, coarsely chopped**
- 2 **garlic cloves, minced**
- ½ **cup reduced-fat sour cream**
- 3 **oz. reduced-fat cream cheese**
- ⅓ **cup shredded part-skim mozzarella cheese**
- 3 **Tbsp. grated Parmesan cheese**
- ¼ **tsp. salt**
- ¼ **tsp. cayenne pepper**
- ¼ **tsp. pepper**

1. Preheat oven to 400°. Remove stems from mushrooms and set caps aside; discard stems or save for another use. In a small skillet, heat oil over medium heat. Add spinach; saute until wilted. Add garlic; cook 1 minute longer.
2. Combine spinach mixture with remaining ingredients. Stuff into mushroom caps. Place the mushrooms in a 15x10x1-in. baking pan coated with cooking spray. Bake, uncovered, until mushrooms are tender, 12-15 minutes. Serve warm.
1 stuffed mushroom: 44 cal., 3g fat (2g sat. fat), 9mg chol., 100mg sod., 1g carb. (1g sugars, 0 fiber), 2g pro.

GARLICKY HERBED SHRIMP

I love shrimp, garlic and herbs. Cook 'em up in butter and what could be better?
—*Dave Levin, Van Nuys, CA*

- -

Takes: 25 min. • **Makes:** about 3 dozen

- 2 lbs. uncooked jumbo shrimp, peeled and deveined
- 5 garlic cloves, minced
- 2 green onions, chopped
- ½ tsp. garlic powder
- ½ tsp. ground mustard
- ¼ tsp. seasoned salt
- ¼ tsp. crushed red pepper flakes
- ⅛ tsp. pepper
- ½ cup butter, divided
- ¼ cup lemon juice
- 2 Tbsp. minced fresh parsley
- 1 Tbsp. minced fresh tarragon

1. In a large bowl, combine first 8 ingredients; toss to combine. In a large skillet, heat ¼ cup butter over medium-high heat. Add half of the shrimp mixture; cook and stir until shrimp turn pink, 4-5 minutes. Transfer mixture to a clean bowl.
2. Repeat with remaining butter and shrimp mixture. Return cooked shrimp to pan. Stir in lemon juice; heat through. Stir in herbs.
1 shrimp: 46 cal., 3g fat (2g sat. fat), 37mg chol., 61mg sod., 1g carb. (0 sugars, 0 fiber), 4g pro. **Diabetic exchanges:** ½ fat.

ROASTED RED PEPPER TAPENADE

When entertaining, I often rely on my pepper tapenade recipe because it doesn't take long to whip up and pop in the fridge. Feel free to use walnuts or pecans instead of almonds.
—*Donna Magliaro, Denville, NJ*

- -

Prep: 15 min. + chilling • **Makes:** 2 cups

- 3 garlic cloves, peeled
- 2 cups roasted sweet red peppers, drained
- ½ cup blanched almonds
- ⅓ cup tomato paste
- 2 Tbsp. olive oil
- ¼ tsp. salt
- ¼ tsp. pepper
     Minced fresh basil
     Toasted French bread baguette slices or water crackers

1. In a small saucepan, bring 2 cups water to a boil. Add garlic; cook, uncovered, just until tender, 6-8 minutes. Drain and pat dry. Place red peppers, blanched almonds, tomato paste, olive oil, garlic, salt and pepper in a small food processor; process until blended. Transfer to a small bowl. Refrigerate for at least 4 hours to allow flavors to blend.
2. Sprinkle with basil. Serve with toasted baguette slices or water crackers.
2 Tbsp. dip: 58 cal., 4g fat (0 sat. fat), 0 chol., 152mg sod., 3g carb. (2g sugars, 1g fiber), 1g pro. **Diabetic exchanges:** 1 fat.

LEMON-HERB OLIVES WITH GOAT CHEESE

Greek olives have a fruity flavor that comes into play when you mix them with lemon and fresh herbs. Spoon over goat cheese and slather on crackers.

—*Jeanne Ambrose, Milwaukee, WI*

Takes: 15 min. • **Makes:** 6 servings

- 3   Tbsp. olive oil
- 2   tsp. grated lemon zest
- 1   garlic clove, minced
- ½   tsp. minced fresh oregano or rosemary
- ¼   tsp. crushed red pepper flakes
- ½   cup assorted pitted Greek olives
- 1   pkg. (5.3 oz.) fresh goat cheese
- 1   Tbsp. minced fresh basil
     Assorted crackers

1. In a small skillet, combine the first 5 ingredients; heat over medium heat just until fragrant, 2-3 minutes, stirring occasionally. Stir in olives; heat through, allowing flavors to blend. Cool completely.

2. To serve, place cheese on a serving plate. Stir basil into olive mixture; spoon over cheese. Serve with crackers.

1 serving: 135 cal., 13g fat (3g sat. fat), 17mg chol., 285mg sod., 2g carb. (0 sugars, 0 fiber), 3g pro.

MARINATED ALMOND-STUFFED OLIVES

Marinated stuffed olives go over so well with company that I try to keep a batch of them in the fridge at all times.
—*Larissa Delk, Columbia, TN*

Prep: 15 min. + marinating • **Makes:** 8 cups

  1 cup blanched almonds, toasted
  3 cans (6 oz. each) pitted
     ripe olives, drained
  3 jars (7 oz. each) pimiento-
     stuffed olives, undrained
  ½ cup white balsamic vinegar
  ½ cup dry red wine
  ½ cup canola oil
  1 medium garlic clove, minced
  ½ tsp. sugar
  1 tsp. dried oregano
  1 tsp. pepper
  ½ tsp. dill weed
  ½ tsp. dried basil
  ½ tsp. dried parsley flakes

Insert an almond into each ripe olive; place in a large bowl. Add pimiento-stuffed olives with olive juice. In a small bowl, whisk vinegar, wine, oil, garlic, sugar and seasonings. Pour mixture over olives. Refrigerate, covered, 8 hours or overnight, stirring occasionally. Transfer to a serving bowl.
¼ cup: 78 cal., 7g fat (0 sat. fat), 0 chol., 455mg sod., 3g carb. (0 sugars, 1g fiber), 1g pro.

AROUND THE WORLD TAPENADE

This appetizer is truly a trip for the taste buds! Chopping the ingredients in a food processor keeps things quick and easy. You can even give it as a gift in a pretty jar.
—*Kim Rila, Leesburg, VA*

Takes: 10 min. • **Makes:** 16 appetizers

  ½ cup chopped roasted
     sweet red pepper
  ½ cup pitted Greek olives
  ¼ cup chopped poblano pepper
  2 Tbsp. lemon juice
  2 Tbsp. olive oil
  1 Tbsp. minced fresh parsley
  1 Tbsp. capers, drained
  2 garlic cloves, minced
  ¼ tsp. dried thyme
 16 slices French bread baguette
     (½ in. thick), toasted

In a food processor, combine the first 9 ingredients; cover and process until blended. Spoon 1 Tbsp. tapenade onto each toasted baguette slice.
Note: Wear disposable gloves when cutting hot peppers; the oils can burn skin. Avoid touching your face.
1 piece: 63 cal., 3g fat (0 sat. fat), 0 chol., 183mg sod., 7g carb. (0 sugars, 0 fiber), 1g pro. **Diabetic exchanges:** ½ starch, ½ fat.

LAYERED HUMMUS DIP

My love for Greece inspired this fast, easy Mediterranean dip. It's great for parties, and a delicious way to include garden-fresh veggies on your menu.

—*Cheryl Snavely, Hagerstown, MD*

- -

Takes: 15 min. • **Makes:** 12 servings

- 1 carton (10 oz.) hummus
- ¼ cup finely chopped red onion
- ½ cup Greek olives, chopped
- 2 medium tomatoes, seeded and chopped
- 1 large English cucumber, chopped
- 1 cup crumbled feta cheese
  Baked pita chips

Spread hummus into a shallow 10-in. round dish. Layer with onion, olives, tomatoes, cucumber and cheese. Refrigerate until serving. Serve with chips.

1 serving: 88 cal., 5g fat (2g sat. fat), 5mg chol., 275mg sod., 6g carb. (1g sugars, 2g fiber), 4g pro. **Diabetic exchanges:** 1 fat, ½ starch.

READER RAVE

"Quick, easy and tasty. I used roasted red pepper hummus for an extra layer of flavor."

—AELOVETERE, TASTEOFHOME.COM

SLOW-COOKER MARINATED MUSHROOMS

Here's a healthy addition to any buffet spread. Mushrooms and pearl onions seasoned with herbs, balsamic and red wine are terrific on their own or alongside a tenderloin roast.
—*Courtney Wilson, Fresno, CA*

Prep: 15 min. • **Cook:** 6 hours • **Makes:** 5 cups

- 2 lbs. medium fresh mushrooms
- 1 pkg. (14.4 oz.) frozen pearl onions, thawed
- 4 garlic cloves, minced
- 2 cups reduced-sodium beef broth
- ½ cup dry red wine
- 3 Tbsp. balsamic vinegar
- 3 Tbsp. olive oil
- 1 tsp. salt
- 1 tsp. dried basil
- ½ tsp. dried thyme
- ½ tsp. pepper
- ¼ tsp. crushed red pepper flakes

Place mushrooms, pearl onions and garlic in a 5- or 6-qt. slow cooker. In a small bowl, whisk remaining ingredients; pour over mushrooms. Cook, covered, on low until mushrooms are tender, 6-8 hours.

Freeze option: Freeze cooled mushrooms and juices in freezer containers. To use, partially thaw in refrigerator overnight. Microwave, covered, on high in a microwave-safe dish until heated through, stirring gently and adding a little broth or water if necessary.

¼ cup: 42 cal., 2g fat (0 sat. fat), 1mg chol., 165mg sod., 4g carb. (2g sugars, 0 fiber), 1g pro.

ZUCCHINI & CHEESE ROULADES

My husband enjoys this recipe so much that he even helps me roll up the roulades! You can change the filling if you like—I've used feta instead of Parmesan, or try sun-dried tomatoes in place of the olives.

—*April McKinney, Murfreesboro, TN*

Takes: 25 min. • **Makes:** 2 dozen

- 1 cup part-skim ricotta cheese
- ¼ cup grated Parmesan cheese
- 2 Tbsp. minced fresh basil or 2 tsp. dried basil
- 1 Tbsp. capers, drained
- 1 Tbsp. chopped Greek olives
- 1 tsp. grated lemon zest
- 1 Tbsp. lemon juice
- ⅛ tsp. salt
- ⅛ tsp. pepper
- 4 medium zucchini

1. In a small bowl, mix the first 9 ingredients.
2. Slice zucchini lengthwise into twenty-four ⅛-in.-thick slices. On a greased grill rack, cook zucchini in batches, covered, over medium heat. Grill until tender, 2-3 minutes each side.
3. Place 1 Tbsp. ricotta mixture on the end of each zucchini slice. Roll up and secure each with a toothpick.

1 appetizer: 24 cal., 1g fat (1g sat. fat), 4mg chol., 58mg sod., 2g carb. (1g sugars, 0 fiber), 2g pro.

9-LAYER GREEK DIP

Instead of bringing the same taco dip to every family event or potluck, try your hand at this light, cool and refreshing Greek dip. It looks and tastes healthy—and it is.
—*Shawn Barto, Winter Garden, FL*

Takes: 20 min. • **Makes:** 5½ cups

- 1 carton (10 oz.) hummus
- 1 cup refrigerated tzatziki sauce
- ½ cup chopped green pepper
- ½ cup chopped sweet red pepper
- ½ cup chopped peeled cucumber
- ½ cup chopped water-packed artichoke hearts, drained
- ½ cup chopped pitted Greek olives, optional
- ¼ cup chopped pepperoncini
- 1 cup crumbled feta cheese
  Baked pita chips

In a 9-in. deep-dish pie plate, layer first 6 ingredients; top with olives, if desired, and pepperoncini. Sprinkle with feta cheese. Refrigerate dip until serving. Serve dip with pita chips.

¼ cup: 60 cal., 4g fat (1g sat. fat), 5mg chol., 210mg sod., 4g carb. (1g sugars, 1g fiber), 3g pro. **Diabetic exchanges:** ½ starch, ½ fat.

TEST KITCHEN TIP

Do It Yourself

For that fresh-from-the-kitchen taste, make your own tzatziki sauce by combining ½ cup peeled, seeded and finely chopped cucumber with ½ cup plain Greek yogurt, 4 tsp. lemon juice, 1 Tbsp. chopped dill, 1 minced garlic clove, and salt and pepper to taste. Refrigerate until serving.

PEACH BRUSCHETTA

As a starter or light snack, this bruschetta is a wonderful way to savor the season with just a bite of fresh peach and a medley of flavors.
—*Nikiko Masumoto, Del Ray, CA*

Prep: 35 min. • **Cook:** 15 min.
Makes: 2 dozen

- ¼ cup chopped walnuts
- 1 garlic clove
- 1½ cups fresh arugula
- ¼ cup extra virgin olive oil
  Salt and pepper to taste

BRUSCHETTA

- 1 Tbsp. olive oil plus additional for brushing bread, divided
- 1 large red onion, thinly sliced (1½ cups)
- 1 tsp. minced fresh rosemary
- 24 slices French bread baguette (⅜ in. thick)
- 1 to 2 garlic cloves, halved
- 2 small ripe peaches, cut into ¼-in. slices
  Shaved Parmesan cheese
  Coarse salt

1. For pesto, place walnuts and garlic clove in a small food processor; pulse until finely chopped. Add arugula; process until blended. Continue processing while gradually adding oil in a steady stream. Season with salt and pepper to taste.

2. For the bruschetta, in a large skillet, heat 1 Tbsp. oil over medium heat. Add onion and rosemary; cook until onion is softened, 15-20 minutes, stirring occasionally.

3. Brush both sides of bread slices with additional oil. Grill, covered, over medium heat or broil 4 in. from heat until golden brown, 1-2 minutes on each side.

4. Rub garlic halves on both sides of toasts; discard garlic. Spread toasts with pesto. Top with onion mixture, peaches and cheese. If desired, sprinkle with coarse salt. Serve bruschetta immediately.

1 appetizer: 69 cal., 5g fat (1g sat. fat), 0 chol., 37mg sod., 5g carb. (1g sugars, 0 fiber), 0 pro.

CRUMB-TOPPED CLAMS

For us, it wouldn't be Christmas Eve without baked clams. But they make a special bite for any occasion, so enjoy them all year long!
—*Annmarie Lucente, Monroe, NY*

Prep: 35 min. • **Broil:** 10 min.
Makes: 2 dozen

- 2 lbs. kosher salt
- 2 dozen fresh littleneck clams
- ½ cup dry bread crumbs
- ¼ cup chicken broth
- 1 Tbsp. minced fresh parsley
- 2 Tbsp. olive oil
- 2 garlic cloves, minced
- ¼ tsp. dried oregano
  Dash pepper
- 1 Tbsp. panko (Japanese) bread crumbs
  Lemon wedges

1. Spread salt into an ovenproof metal serving platter or a 15x10x1-in. baking pan. Shuck clams, leaving clams and juices in bottom shells. Arrange in prepared platter; divide juices among shells.

2. In a small bowl, mix dry bread crumbs, chicken broth, parsley, oil, garlic, oregano and pepper; spoon over clams. Sprinkle with bread crumbs.

3. Broil 4-6 in. from heat 6-8 minutes or until clams are firm and crumb mixture is crisp and golden brown. Serve clams immediately with lemon wedges.

1 clam: 31 cal., 1g fat (0 sat. fat), 5mg chol., 35mg sod., 2g carb. (0 sugars, 0 fiber), 2g pro.

WINE PAIRING

Cava. Sparkling wine is great with crispy, crunchy foods like these golden crumb-topped clams. Cava, from Spain's Mediterranean coast, has a salty-air taste that's perfect with seafood.

SMOKED SALMON NEW POTATOES

Give twice-baked potatoes a rest this year and try these stuffed spuds. Smoked salmon and cream cheese blended with lemon juice and dill are piped into small red potatoes. Leftovers are even good with eggs for a quick breakfast.
—Taste of Home *Test Kitchen*

- -

Prep: 30 min. • **Cook:** 20 min.
Makes: 3 dozen

- 36 baby red potatoes (1½ in. wide, about 1½ lbs.)
- 1 pkg. (8 oz.) reduced-fat cream cheese, cubed
- 2 pkg. (3 oz. each) smoked salmon or lox
- 2 Tbsp. chopped green onion
- 2 Tbsp. snipped fresh dill or 2 tsp. dill weed
- 2 tsp. lemon juice
- ⅛ tsp. salt
- ⅛ tsp. pepper
- Fresh dill sprigs

1. Place potatoes in a large saucepan; add water to cover. Bring to a boil. Reduce heat; cook, covered, until tender, 15-20 minutes. Drain potatoes; immediately drop in ice water. Drain; pat dry.

2. Cut a thin slice off the bottom of each potato to allow them to lie flat. Using a melon baller, remove a small portion from the top of each potato.

3. For filling, place all remaining ingredients except dill sprigs in a food processor; process until smooth. To serve, pipe or spoon about 2 tsp. filling into each potato. Top with dill sprigs. Refrigerate leftovers.

1 appetizer: 35 cal., 2g fat (1g sat. fat), 6mg chol., 67mg sod., 4g carb. (0 sugars, 0 fiber), 2g pro.

HEALTHY GREEK BEAN DIP

This crowd-pleasing appetizer is healthy to boot! Folks will love to eat their veggies when they can dip them in this fresh and zesty alternative to hummus.
—Kelly Silvers, Edmond, OK

- -

Prep: 15 min. • **Cook:** 2 hours • **Makes:** 3 cups

- 2 cans (15 oz. each) cannellini beans, rinsed and drained
- ¼ cup water
- ¼ cup finely chopped roasted sweet red peppers
- 2 Tbsp. finely chopped red onion
- 2 Tbsp. olive oil
- 2 Tbsp. lemon juice
- 1 Tbsp. snipped fresh dill
- 2 garlic cloves, minced
- ¼ tsp. salt
- ¼ tsp. pepper
- 1 small cucumber, peeled, seeded and finely chopped
- ½ cup fat-free plain Greek yogurt
  Additional snipped fresh dill
  Baked pita chips or assorted fresh vegetables

Process beans and water in a food processor until smooth. Transfer to a greased 1½-qt. slow cooker. Add the next 8 ingredients. Cook, covered, on low until heated through, 2-3 hours. Stir in cucumber and yogurt; cool slightly. Sprinkle with additional dill. Serve warm or cold with baked pita chips or assorted fresh vegetables.

Freeze option: Omitting cucumber, yogurt and additional dill, freeze cooled dip in freezer containers. To use, thaw in the refrigerator overnight. To serve dip warm, heat through in a saucepan, stirring occasionally. Or serve cold. Stir cucumber and yogurt into finished dip; sprinkle with additional dill. Serve with chips or fresh vegetables.

¼ cup: 86 cal., 3g fat (0 sat. fat), 0 chol., 260mg sod., 11g carb. (1g sugars, 3g fiber), 4g pro. **Diabetic exchanges:** 1 starch, ½ fat.

CITRUS SPICED OLIVES

Lemon, lime and orange bring a burst of sunny citrus flavor to marinated olives. You can even blend the olives and spread the mixture onto baguette slices. Set them out for snacking at holiday buffets.
—*Ann Sheehy, Lawrence, MA*

- -

Prep: 20 min. + chilling • **Makes:** 4 cups

½ cup white wine
¼ cup canola oil
3 Tbsp. salt-free seasoning blend
4 garlic cloves, minced
½ tsp. crushed red pepper flakes
2 tsp. each grated orange,
   lemon and lime zest
3 Tbsp. each orange, lemon
   and lime juices
4 cups mixed pitted olives

In a large bowl, combine first 5 ingredients. Add the citrus zest and juices; whisk until blended. Add olives; toss to coat. Refrigerate, covered, at least 4 hours before serving.

¼ cup: 74 cal., 7g fat (1g sat. fat), 0 chol., 248mg sod., 3g carb. (1g sugars, 1g fiber), 0 pro.

CRAB PHYLLO CUPS

I always like a little extra chili sauce on top of these easy snacks. If you're out of crab, water-packed tuna works well, too.
—*Johnna Johnson, Scottsdale, AZ*

Takes: 20 min. • **Makes:** 2½ dozen

½   cup reduced-fat spreadable garden vegetable cream cheese
½   tsp. seafood seasoning
¾   cup lump crabmeat, drained
2   pkg. (1.9 oz. each) frozen miniature phyllo tart shells
5   Tbsp. chili sauce

In a small bowl, mix the cream cheese and seafood seasoning; gently stir in crab. Spoon 2 tsp. crab mixture into each tart shell; top with chili sauce.

1 filled phyllo cup: 34 cal., 2g fat (0 sat. fat), 5mg chol., 103mg sod., 3g carb. (1g sugars, 0 fiber), 1g pro.

ASPARAGUS WITH FRESH BASIL SAUCE

Add zip to your appetizer platter with the asparagus dip my husband and our friends absolutely love. If you have dip left over when the asparagus is gone, it makes a flavorful sandwich spread.

—*Janie Colle, Hutchinson, KS*

Takes: 15 min. • **Makes:** 12 servings

- ¾ cup reduced-fat mayonnaise
- 2 Tbsp. prepared pesto
- 1 Tbsp. grated Parmesan cheese
- 1 Tbsp. minced fresh basil
- 1 tsp. lemon juice
- 1 garlic clove, minced
- 1½ lbs. fresh asparagus, trimmed

1. In a small bowl, mix the first 6 ingredients until blended; refrigerate until serving.
2. In a Dutch oven, bring 12 cups water to a boil. Add asparagus in batches; cook, uncovered, until crisp-tender, 2-3 minutes. Remove and immediately drop into ice water. Drain and pat dry. Serve with sauce.
1 serving: 72 cal., 6g fat (1g sat. fat), 6mg chol., 149mg sod., 3g carb. (1g sugars, 1g fiber), 1g pro. **Diabetic exchanges:** 1½ fat.

PEA SOUP SHOOTERS

Appetizers really don't get any simpler than this. These shooters can be made ahead, they're colorful, and they won't weigh you down. Top with a dollop of plain yogurt for a little more tang.

—*Jacyn Siebert, San Francisco, CA*

Prep: 20 min. + chilling • **Makes:** 2 dozen

- 1 pkg. (16 oz.) frozen peas, thawed
- 1 cup reduced-sodium chicken broth
- ¼ cup minced fresh mint
- 1 Tbsp. lime juice
- 1 tsp. ground cumin
- ¼ tsp. salt
- 1½ cups plain yogurt
  Fresh mint leaves

1. Place the first 6 ingredients in a blender; cover and process until smooth. Add yogurt; process until blended. Transfer to a pitcher; refrigerate 1 hour to allow flavors to blend.

2. To serve, pour soup into shot glasses; top with mint leaves.

1 serving: 30 cal., 1g fat (0 sat. fat), 2mg chol., 92mg sod., 4g carb. (2g sugars, 1g fiber), 2g pro.

HONEY-MINT LAMB SKEWERS

These hearty lamb bites are delicious and convenient. Assemble them the day before, then pop them under the broiler when the party starts.
—*Trisha Kruse, Eagle, ID*

- -

Prep: 15 min. + marinating
Broil: 10 min./batch
Makes: 3 dozen (2 cups dip)

½	cup olive oil
5	Tbsp. lemon juice
¼	cup minced fresh mint
2	Tbsp. honey
5	garlic cloves, minced
	Dash salt
	Dash pepper
3	lbs. lamb stew meat

LEMON FETA DIP

1	cup sour cream
2	Tbsp. lemon juice
2	cups crumbled feta cheese
2	pepperoncini, minced

1. Mix the first 7 ingredients in a shallow dish. Add lamb; turn to coat. Cover and refrigerate 4-6 hours.
2. Preheat broiler. For dip, place sour cream, lemon juice, feta cheese and pepperoncini in a blender; cover and process until smooth. Cover and refrigerate until serving.
3. Drain the lamb and discard marinade. Thread 2 pieces of lamb on each of 36 soaked wooden skewers; place in two 15x10-in. pans. Broil 6-8 in. from heat until lamb reaches desired doneness, 10-12 minutes, turning occasionally. Serve with dip.
1 skewer with 2½ tsp. dip: 105 cal., 7g fat (2g sat. fat), 29mg chol., 135mg sod., 2g carb. (1g sugars, 0 fiber), 9g pro.

SUMMER TEA SANDWICHES

These dainty finger sandwiches are perfect for casual picnics or luncheons with the gals. Tarragon-seasoned chicken complements cucumber and cantaloupe slices.
—Taste of Home *Test Kitchen*

- -

Prep: 45 min. • **Bake:** 20 min. + cooling
Makes: 12 servings

- ½ tsp. dried tarragon
- ½ tsp. salt, divided
- ¼ tsp. pepper
- 1 lb. boneless skinless chicken breasts
- ½ cup reduced-fat mayonnaise
- 1 Tbsp. finely chopped red onion
- 1 tsp. dill weed
- ½ tsp. lemon juice
- 24 slices soft multigrain bread, crusts removed
- 1 medium cucumber, thinly sliced
- ¼ medium cantaloupe, cut into 12 thin slices

1. Preheat oven to 350°. Combine the tarragon, ¼ tsp. salt and pepper; rub over chicken. Place on a baking sheet coated with cooking spray.

2. Bake 20-25 minutes or until a thermometer inserted in chicken reads 170°. Cool chicken to room temperature; thinly slice.

3. In a small bowl, combine the mayonnaise, onion, dill, lemon juice and remaining salt; spread over 12 bread slices. Top with cucumber, chicken, cantaloupe and remaining bread. Cut sandwiches in half diagonally. Serve immediately.

2 sandwich halves: 212 cal., 6g fat (1g sat. fat), 24mg chol., 450mg sod., 27g carb. (5g sugars, 4g fiber), 13g pro.

CAPRESE SALAD KABOBS

Trade in the usual veggie party platter for these fun kabobs. I often make them for my family to snack on, and it's a great recipe for the kids to help with.
—*Christine Mitchell, Glendora, CA*

- -

Takes: 10 min. • **Makes:** 12 kabobs

- 24 grape tomatoes
- 12 cherry-size fresh mozzarella cheese balls
- 24 fresh basil leaves
- 2 Tbsp. olive oil
- 2 tsp. balsamic vinegar

On each of 12 appetizer skewers, alternately thread 2 tomatoes, 1 cheese ball and 2 basil leaves. To serve, whisk together olive oil and vinegar; drizzle over kabobs.

1 kabob: 44 cal., 4g fat (1g sat. fat), 5mg chol., 10mg sod., 2g carb. (1g sugars, 0 fiber), 1g pro. **Diabetic exchanges:** 1 fat.

WINE PAIRING

Lambrusco. This Italian wine is a little tart and a little sweet, just like a good balsamic vinegar. It has a fun kiss of bubbles to boot. The Italians call such lightly sparkling wines *frizzante.*

SMOKED TROUT PATÉ

This tasty spread is easy to make in a food processor, and it's a guaranteed winner at any party. The recipe is versatile, so feel free to substitute other favorite smoked fish.

—*Judy Walle, Toledo, OH*

Prep: 15 min. + chilling • **Makes:** 2⅔ cups

- 1 lb. flaked smoked trout
- 3 oz. reduced-fat cream cheese
- ½ cup half-and-half cream
- 1 Tbsp. horseradish sauce
- 1 Tbsp. lemon juice
- ⅛ tsp. pepper
- 2 tsp. minced fresh parsley
  Cucumber slices
  Assorted crackers

Pulse first 7 ingredients in a food processor until blended. Refrigerate, covered, until serving. Serve with cucumber slices and assorted crackers.

2 Tbsp.: 55 cal., 3g fat (1g sat. fat), 16mg chol., 174mg sod., 1g carb. (1g sugars, 0 fiber), 5g pro.

CRISP CUCUMBER SALSA

Here's a fantastic way to use cucumbers. You'll love the creamy and crunchy texture and super fresh flavors.

—*Charlene Skjerven, Hoople, ND*

Takes: 20 min. • **Makes:** 2½ cups

- 2 cups finely chopped cucumber, peeled and seeded
- ½ cup finely chopped seeded tomato
- ¼ cup chopped red onion
- 2 Tbsp. minced fresh parsley
- 1 jalapeno pepper, seeded and chopped
- 4½ tsp. minced fresh cilantro
- 1 garlic clove, minced
- ¼ cup reduced-fat sour cream
- 1½ tsp. lemon juice
- 1½ tsp. lime juice
- ¼ tsp. ground cumin
- ¼ tsp. seasoned salt
  Baked tortilla chip scoops

In a small bowl, combine first 7 ingredients. In another bowl, combine the sour cream, lemon juice, lime juice, cumin and seasoned salt. Pour over cucumber mixture and toss gently to coat. Serve immediately with chips.
Note: Wear disposable gloves when cutting hot peppers; the oils can burn skin. Avoid touching your face.
¼ cup: 16 cal., 1g fat (0 sat. fat), 2mg chol., 44mg sod., 2g carb. (1g sugars, 0 fiber), 1g pro. **Diabetic exchanges:** 1 free food.

TEST KITCHEN TIP

Keep It Crunchy

Don't skip seeding the cucumber. If you do, you may end up with a watery salad. To make seeding a breeze, halve cucumbers lengthwise and use a spoon to scoop out the pulpy centers. This crisp cucumber salsa is a stellar topping for simple grilled salmon.

TWO-BEAN HUMMUS

My children love this easy hummus and even like to help me make it! Hummus is a great way to sneak some beans and important soluble fiber into their diets. I also serve this hummus in a bread bowl with my vegetable platter for our Thanksgiving dinner.

—*Kelly Andreas, Eau Claire, WI*

Takes: 15 min. • **Makes:** 2 cups

- 1 can (15 oz.) garbanzo beans or chickpeas, rinsed and drained
- 1 can (15 oz.) cannellini beans, rinsed and drained
- ¼ cup olive oil
- 2 Tbsp. lemon juice
- 2 garlic cloves, minced
- ¼ tsp. salt
  Assorted fresh vegetables

Process first 6 ingredients in a food processor until smooth. Transfer to a serving bowl; serve with vegetables.
¼ cup: 152 cal., 8g fat (1g sat. fat), 0 chol., 209mg sod., 16g carb. (1g sugars, 4g fiber), 4g pro. **Diabetic exchanges:** 1½ fat, 1 starch.

MARINATED SHRIMP & OLIVES

This is my favorite appetizer to serve party guests. The flavors in this colorful dish blend beautifully, and the marinated shrimp are tender and delicious.

—Carol Gawronski, Lake Wales, FL

- -

Prep: 10 min. • **Cook:** 5 min. + chilling
Makes: 20 servings

1½ lbs. peeled and deveined cooked
    shrimp (31-40 per lb.)
1 can (6 oz.) pitted ripe olives, drained
1 jar (5¾ oz.) pimiento-stuffed
    olives, drained
2 Tbsp. olive oil
1½ tsp. curry powder
½ tsp. ground ginger
¼ tsp. salt
¼ tsp. pepper
2 Tbsp. lemon juice
1 Tbsp. minced fresh parsley or
    1 tsp. dried parsley flakes

1. Combine shrimp and olives; set aside.
2. In a small saucepan, heat oil over medium heat. In a small bowl, combine curry, ginger, salt and pepper; whisk into hot oil. Cook and stir 1 minute. Remove from heat; stir in lemon juice and parsley. Immediately drizzle over shrimp mixture; toss gently to coat.
3. Refrigerate, covered, up to 6 hours, stirring occasionally. Serve with toothpicks.
⅓ cup: 71 cal., 4g fat (0 sat. fat), 52mg chol., 292mg sod., 2g carb. (0 sugars, 0 fiber), 7g pro. **Diabetic exchanges:** 1 lean meat, 1 fat.

CREAMY FETA-SPINACH DIP

Garlic and feta make a powerfully tasty pair in this addictive dip. I first tried it at a party and had to drag myself away from the bowl!
—*Elissa Armbruster, Medford, NJ*

Prep: 15 min. + chilling • **Makes:** 2 cups

- 1 cup fat-free plain yogurt
- ¾ cup crumbled feta cheese
- 2 oz. reduced-fat cream cheese, cubed
- ¼ cup reduced-fat sour cream
- 1 garlic clove, minced
- 1½ cups finely chopped fresh spinach
- 1 tsp. dill weed
- ⅛ tsp. pepper
- Fresh vegetables and/or sliced bread

1. Line a strainer with 4 layers of cheesecloth or 1 coffee filter; place over a bowl. Place yogurt in prepared strainer; cover yogurt with edges of cheesecloth. Refrigerate for 2 hours or until yogurt has thickened to the consistency of whipped cream.

2. Transfer yogurt to a food processor (discard liquid from bowl). Add the feta cheese, cream cheese, sour cream and garlic; cover and process until smooth.

3. Transfer to a small bowl. Stir in the spinach, dill and pepper. Cover and refrigerate until chilled. Serve with vegetables and/or bread.

¼ cup: 68 cal., 4g fat (3g sat. fat), 14mg chol., 158mg sod., 4g carb. (2g sugars, 1g fiber), 5g pro. **Diabetic exchanges:** ½ starch, ½ fat.

ROAST BEEF AIOLI BUNDLES

Everyone will want to try these delicious, dainty bundles. And while they look impressive, they're actually quite easy!
—Taste of Home *Test Kitchen*

Takes: 30 min. • **Makes:** 16 appetizers

- 16 fresh asparagus spears, trimmed
- ⅓ cup mayonnaise
- 1 garlic clove, minced
- 1 tsp. Dijon mustard
- 1 tsp. lemon juice
- ⅛ tsp. ground cumin
- 8 thin slices deli roast beef, cut in half lengthwise
- 1 medium sweet yellow pepper, thinly sliced
- 1 medium sweet orange pepper, thinly sliced
- 1 medium sweet red pepper, thinly sliced
- 16 whole chives

1. In a large skillet, bring 1 in. of water to a boil. Add asparagus; cover and cook for 3 minutes. Drain and immediately place in ice water. Drain and pat dry.

2. In a small bowl, combine mayonnaise, garlic, mustard, lemon juice and cumin. Place the roast beef slices on a work surface; spread each slice with 1 tsp. aioli. Top each slice with an asparagus spear and pepper strips. Roll up tightly; tie bundles with chives. Serve immediately.

1 appetizer: 52 cal., 4g fat (1g sat. fat), 6mg chol., 74mg sod., 2g carb. (1g sugars, 1g fiber), 2g pro. **Diabetic exchanges:** 1 fat.

SHRIMP SALAD APPETIZERS

This refreshing hors d'oeuvre has gained a big following since a friend shared her family recipe with me. My 7-year-old son says it best: The celery and shrimp are so good together.
—Solie Kimble, Kanata, ON

Takes: 15 min. • **Makes:** 2 dozen

- 1 lb. peeled and deveined cooked shrimp, chopped
- 1 can (6 oz.) lump crabmeat, drained
- 2 celery ribs, finely chopped
- ¼ cup Dijon-mayonnaise blend
- 24 Belgian endive leaves (3-4 heads) or small butterhead lettuce leaves Chopped fresh parsley, optional

In a large bowl, combine shrimp, crab and celery. Add mayonnaise blend; toss to coat. To serve, top each leaf with about 2 Tbsp. shrimp mixture. If desired, top with chopped fresh parsley.

1 appetizer: 31 cal., 0 fat (0 sat. fat), 35mg chol., 115mg sod., 1g carb. (0 sugars, 0 fiber), 5g pro.

5i **L**

ROSEMARY BEET PHYLLO BITES

The sweet-and-sour flavor of pickled beets is a match made in heaven with rich and tangy goat cheese. These pretty tartlets will make a splash on the buffet table.
—Taste of Home *Test Kitchen*

- -

Takes: 25 min. • **Makes:** 6 dozen

1	jar (16 oz.) pickled whole beets, drained and chopped
1	Tbsp. olive oil
2	tsp. minced fresh rosemary
1	tsp. grated orange zest
2	cups fresh arugula, torn
72	frozen miniature phyllo tart shells
¾	cup crumbled feta cheese

1. Pat beets dry with paper towels; place in a small bowl. Add the olive oil, rosemary and orange zest; toss to combine.

2. Divide arugula among tart shells; top with beet mixture. Sprinkle with feta cheese.

1 appetizer: 31 cal., 1g fat (0 sat. fat), 1mg chol., 33mg sod., 3g carb. (1g sugars, 0 fiber), 1g pro.

HOT CRAB PINWHEELS

I got the recipe for these crabmeat bites from a friend. What amazed me most is that my husband, who hates seafood, couldn't stop eating them.

—Kitti Boesel, Woodbridge, VA

Prep: 15 min. + chilling • **Bake:** 10 min.
Makes: 3 dozen

- 1 pkg. (8 oz.) reduced-fat cream cheese
- 1 can (6 oz.) crabmeat, drained, flaked and cartilage removed
- ¾ cup diced sweet red pepper
- ½ cup shredded reduced-fat cheddar cheese
- 2 green onions, thinly sliced
- 3 Tbsp. minced fresh parsley
- ¼ to ½ tsp. cayenne pepper
- 6 flour tortillas (6 in.)

1. Beat cream cheese until smooth; stir in crab, red pepper, cheese, green onions, parsley and cayenne. Spread ⅓ cup filling over each tortilla; roll up tightly. Wrap in plastic, twisting ends to seal; refrigerate at least 2 hours.

2. To serve, preheat oven to 350°. Unwrap rolls; trim ends and cut each into 6 slices. Place on baking sheets coated with cooking spray. Bake until bubbly, about 10 minutes. Serve warm.

1 pinwheel: 44 cal., 2g fat (1g sat. fat), 10mg chol., 98mg sod., 3g carb. (0 sugars, 0 fiber), 2g pro.

HERB-ROASTED OLIVES & TOMATOES

Eat these roasted veggies with a crunchy baguette or a couple of cheeses. You can also double or triple the amounts and have leftovers to toss with spaghetti the next day.
—*Anndrea Bailey, Huntington Beach, CA*

- -

Takes: 20 min. • **Makes:** 4 cups

2	cups cherry tomatoes
1	cup garlic-stuffed olives
1	cup Greek olives
1	cup pitted ripe olives
8	garlic cloves, peeled
3	Tbsp. olive oil
1	Tbsp. herbes de Provence
¼	tsp. pepper

Preheat oven to 425°. Combine the first 5 ingredients on a greased 15x10x1-in. baking pan. Add oil and seasonings; toss to coat. Roast until the tomatoes are softened, 15-20 minutes, stirring occasionally.
Note: Look for herbes de Provence in the spice aisle.
¼ cup: 71 cal., 7g fat (1g sat. fat), 0 chol., 380mg sod., 3g carb. (1g sugars, 1g fiber), 0 pro.

WINE PAIRING

Rosé. Grab a dry one from Provence on southern France's Mediterranean coast to go perfectly with this nosh. It'll play up the tomatoes, salty olives and herbs.

PARMESAN BAKED COD,
PAGE 72

Fish & Seafood

Get ready to reel in compliments when you serve any of these Mediterranean-inspired fish and seafood entrees. Quick, easy, delicious and full of heart-healthy omega-3s, these catch-of-the-day selections will have you hooked.

PARMESAN BAKED COD

Here's a goof-proof way to make oven-baked cod moist and flavorful. My mom shared this recipe with me years ago, and I've been loving it ever since.
—*Mary Jo Hoppe, Pewaukee, WI*

- -

Takes: 25 min. • **Makes:** 4 servings

- 4 cod fillets (4 oz. each)
- ⅔ cup mayonnaise
- 4 green onions, chopped
- ¼ cup grated Parmesan cheese
- 1 tsp. Worcestershire sauce

1. Preheat oven to 400°. Place cod in an 8-in. square baking dish coated with cooking spray. Mix remaining ingredients; spread over fillets.
2. Bake, uncovered, until fish just begins to flake easily with a fork, 15-20 minutes.
1 fillet: 247 cal., 15g fat (2g sat. fat), 57mg chol., 500mg sod., 7g carb. (2g sugars, 0 fiber), 20g pro. **Diabetic exchanges:** 3 lean meat, 3 fat.

READER RAVE

"Wow! Amazingly good, given the simplicity of ingredients. I had a request to use this recipe every time I make cod."
—JUSTMBETH, TASTEOFHOME.COM

BLACKENED TILAPIA WITH ZUCCHINI NOODLES

Quick and bright meals like this one-skillet wonder are winners every time. I usually make an easy homemade pico de gallo the night before, but you can use your favorite store-bought version, too.
—*Tammy Brownlow, Dallas, TX*

- -

Takes: 30 min. • **Makes:** 4 servings

- 2 large zucchini (about 1½ lbs.)
- 1½ tsp. ground cumin
- ¾ tsp. salt, divided
- ½ tsp. smoked paprika
- ½ tsp. pepper
- ¼ tsp garlic powder
- 4 tilapia fillets (6 oz. each)
- 2 tsp. olive oil
- 2 garlic cloves, minced
- 1 cup pico de gallo

1. Trim ends of zucchini. Using a spiralizer, cut zucchini into thin strands.
2. Mix cumin, ½ tsp. salt, smoked paprika, pepper and garlic powder; sprinkle the seasonings generously onto both sides of tilapia. In a large nonstick skillet, heat oil over medium-high heat. In batches, cook tilapia until fish just begins to flake easily with a fork, 2-3 minutes per side. Remove from the pan; keep warm.
3. In same pan, cook zucchini with minced garlic over medium-high heat until slightly softened, 1-2 minutes, tossing constantly with tongs (do not overcook). Sprinkle with remaining salt. Serve with tilapia and pico de gallo.
Note: If a spiralizer is not available, cut zucchini into ribbons using a vegetable peeler. Saute as directed, increasing time as necessary.
1 serving: 203 cal., 4g fat (1g sat. fat), 83mg chol., 522mg sod., 8g carb. (5g sugars, 2g fiber), 34g pro. **Diabetic exchanges:** 5 lean meat, 1 vegetable, ½ fat.

SHRIMP PICCATA

I often serve this succulent pasta with French bread and asparagus. Cook it the next time you're hosting dinner, and get ready for the recipe requests.
—*Holly Bauer, West Bend, WI*

- -

Takes: 25 min. • **Makes:** 4 servings

- ½ lb. uncooked angel hair pasta
- 2 shallots, finely chopped
- 2 garlic cloves, minced
- 2 Tbsp. olive oil
- 1 lb. uncooked large shrimp, peeled and deveined
- 1 tsp. dried oregano
- ⅛ tsp. salt
- 1 cup chicken broth
- 1 cup white wine or additional chicken broth
- 4 tsp. cornstarch
- ⅓ cup lemon juice
- ¼ cup capers, drained
- 3 Tbsp. minced fresh parsley

1. Cook pasta according to the package directions.
2. Meanwhile, in a large skillet, saute shallots and garlic in oil for 1 minute. Add the shrimp, oregano and salt; cook and stir until shrimp turn pink. In small bowl, combine the broth, wine and cornstarch; gradually stir into pan. Bring to a boil; cook and stir for 2 minutes or until thickened. Remove from the heat.
3. Drain pasta. Add the pasta, lemon juice, capers and parsley to the skillet; toss to coat.
1½ cups: 295 cal., 9g fat (1g sat. fat), 139mg chol., 715mg sod., 27g carb. (2g sugars, 2g fiber), 22g pro. **Diabetic exchanges:** 3 lean meat, 1½ starch, 1 fat.

TUNA & WHITE BEAN LETTUCE WRAPS

Here's a great way to dress up ordinary tuna salad. My recipe makes a light dinner or a workday lunch, and it's good for you, too.
—*Heather Senger, Madison, WI*

Takes: 20 min. • **Makes:** 4 servings

1 can (12 oz.) light tuna in water, drained and flaked
1 can (15 oz.) cannellini beans, rinsed and drained
¼ cup chopped red onion
2 Tbsp. olive oil
1 Tbsp. minced fresh parsley
⅛ tsp. salt
⅛ tsp. pepper
12 Bibb or Boston lettuce leaves (about 1 medium head)
1 medium ripe avocado, peeled and sliced

In a small bowl, combine first 7 ingredients; toss lightly to combine. Serve in lettuce leaves; top with avocado.

3 wraps: 279 cal., 13g fat (2g sat. fat), 31mg chol., 421mg sod., 19g carb. (1g sugars, 7g fiber), 22g pro. **Diabetic exchanges:** 3 lean meat, 2 fat, 1 starch.

WINE PAIRING

Muscadet. This racy and bone-dry white wine from France's west coast actually tastes like salt! It'll cut through the richness of these wraps and really liven things up.

SHRIMP WITH TOMATOES & FETA

Any recipe that is special enough for guests but easy enough for a weeknight family meal is a favorite in my book. All you need to round it out is a salad and crusty French bread to soak up the delicious tomato and wine juices.
—*Susan Seymour, Valatie, NY*

Takes: 30 min. • **Makes:** 6 servings

- 3 **Tbsp. olive oil**
- 2 **shallots, finely chopped**
- 2 **garlic cloves, minced**
- 6 **plum tomatoes, chopped**
- ½ **cup white wine or chicken broth**
- 1 **Tbsp. dried oregano**
- ½ **tsp. salt**
- ½ **tsp. crushed red pepper flakes**
- ¼ **tsp. sweet paprika**
- 2 **lbs. uncooked large shrimp, peeled and deveined**
- ⅔ **cup crumbled feta cheese**
- 2 **tsp. minced fresh mint**
   Hot cooked rice

1. In a large skillet, heat oil over medium-high heat. Add shallots and garlic; cook and stir until tender. Add tomatoes, wine, oregano, salt, pepper flakes and paprika; bring to a boil. Reduce heat; simmer, uncovered, 5 minutes.
2. Stir in the shrimp and cheese; cook until shrimp turn pink, 5-6 minutes. Stir in mint. Serve with rice.
1 cup: 261 cal., 11g fat (3g sat. fat), 191mg chol., 502mg sod., 8g carb. (2g sugars, 2g fiber), 28g pro. **Diabetic exchanges:** 4 lean meat, 1 vegetable, 1 fat.

CRUNCHY SALMON CAKES

Whether you use fresh or leftover salmon, you can serve these cakes as a main dish or an appetizer. They're delicious atop a green salad, too.

—Cindy Fan, San Gabriel, CA

Prep: 30 min. + chilling • **Bake:** 15 min.
Makes: 4 servings

- 1¼ lbs. salmon fillet
- ⅛ tsp. plus ¼ tsp. pepper, divided
- 1 tsp. olive oil
- 1 small onion, finely chopped
- 2 Tbsp. minced fresh parsley
- 1½ cups panko (Japanese) bread crumbs, divided
- ½ cup reduced-fat mayonnaise
- 1 Tbsp. lemon juice
- ¼ tsp. salt
- 1 tsp. hot pepper sauce, optional
- 2 egg whites, lightly beaten
  Cooking spray

SAUCE
- ¼ cup reduced-fat plain Greek yogurt
- 1 tsp. snipped fresh dill
- ¾ tsp. lemon juice
- ¼ tsp. capers, drained and chopped

1. Place salmon on a baking sheet coated with cooking spray; sprinkle with ⅛ tsp. pepper. Bake, uncovered, at 350° until fish flakes easily with a fork, 14-17 minutes. Cool slightly; remove skin, if necessary. Transfer salmon to a shallow dish; refrigerate, covered, until chilled, about 2 hours.

2. In a large skillet, heat oil over medium-high heat. Add onion; cook and stir until tender. Stir in parsley.

3. In a large bowl, combine ½ cup bread crumbs, mayonnaise, lemon juice, salt, remaining pepper and the onion mixture; if desired, add pepper sauce. Flake salmon; add to bread crumb mixture, mixing lightly. Shape into eight 2½-in. patties.

4. Place egg whites and remaining bread crumbs in separate shallow bowls. Dip salmon patties in egg whites, then roll in crumbs to coat. Place on a baking sheet coated with cooking spray. Spritz tops with cooking spray. Bake, uncovered, at 425° until golden brown, 14-17 minutes.

5. In a small bowl, mix sauce ingredients; serve with salmon cakes.

2 salmon cakes with 1 Tbsp. sauce: 422 cal., 25g fat (4g sat. fat), 82mg chol., 541mg sod., 17g carb. (3g sugars, 1g fiber), 29g pro.

READER RAVE

"The salmon cakes and sauce are both amazing. I got tons of compliments when I cooked them for friends. Also, very easy to make."
—SMH372, TASTEOFHOME.COM

GRILLED TILAPIA PICCATA

We aren't big fish eaters, but a friend made this for us, and now we can't get enough. I also make it for company because it's simple and looks and tastes like something from an upscale restaurant.
—*Beth Cooper, Columbus, OH*

Takes: 25 min. • **Makes:** 4 servings

½	tsp. grated lemon zest
3	Tbsp. lemon juice
2	Tbsp. olive oil
2	garlic cloves, minced
2	tsp. capers, drained
3	Tbsp. minced fresh basil, divided
4	tilapia fillets (6 oz. each)
½	tsp. salt
¼	tsp. pepper

1. In a small bowl, whisk lemon zest, lemon juice, oil and garlic until blended; stir in capers and 2 Tbsp. basil. Reserve 2 Tbsp. mixture for drizzling over cooked fish. Brush remaining mixture onto both sides of tilapia; sprinkle with salt and pepper.

2. Grill tilapia, covered, on a lightly oiled rack over medium heat or broil 4 in. from heat until fish just begins to flake easily with a fork, 3-4 minutes on each side. Drizzle with the reserved lemon mixture; sprinkle with remaining basil.

1 fillet: 206 cal., 8g fat (2g sat. fat), 83mg chol., 398mg sod., 2g carb. (0 sugars, 0 fiber), 32g pro. **Diabetic exchanges:** 5 lean meat, 1½ fat.

COD & ASPARAGUS BAKE

The lemon pulls this flavorful and healthy dish together. If asparagus isn't in season, fresh green beans make a tasty substitute and cook in about the same amount of time. You can also use grated Parmesan cheese instead of Romano if you like.

—*Thomas Faglon, Somerset, NJ*

- -

Takes: 30 min. • **Makes:** 4 servings

  4   cod fillets (4 oz. each)
  1   lb. fresh thin asparagus, trimmed
  1   pint cherry tomatoes, halved
  2   Tbsp. lemon juice
1½ tsp. grated lemon zest
 ¼ cup grated Romano cheese

1. Preheat oven to 375°. Place the cod and asparagus in a 15x10x1-in. baking pan brushed with oil. Add tomatoes, cut sides down. Brush fish with lemon juice; sprinkle with lemon zest. Sprinkle the fish and vegetables with Romano cheese. Bake until fish just begins to flake easily with a fork, about 12 minutes.
2. Remove pan from oven; preheat broiler. Broil cod mixture 3-4 in. from heat until vegetables are lightly browned, 2-3 minutes.
1 serving: 141 cal., 3g fat (2g sat. fat), 45mg chol., 184mg sod., 6g carb. (3g sugars, 2g fiber), 23g pro. **Diabetic exchanges:** 3 lean meat, 1 vegetable.

TEST KITCHEN TIP

We tested this recipe with cod fillets that were about ¾ in. thick. You'll need to adjust the bake time up or down if your fillets are thicker or thinner.

MEDITERRANEAN COD IN PARCHMENT

My friends and I agree this is one of the best things we have ever eaten. We each take a bundle and eat it right out of the parchment paper. Cleanup is so easy!

—*Melissa Chilton, Harlowton, MT*

- -

Prep: 25 min. • **Bake:** 15 min.
Makes: 4 servings

  4   cups shredded cabbage
  1   large sweet onion, thinly sliced
  4   garlic cloves, minced
  4   cod fillets (6 oz. each)
 ¼ cup pitted Greek olives, chopped
 ½ cup crumbled feta cheese
 ¼ tsp. salt
 ¼ tsp. pepper
  4   tsp. olive oil

1. Cut parchment paper or heavy-duty foil into four 18x12-in. pieces; place 1 cup cabbage on each piece. Top with onion, garlic, cod, olives, cheese, salt and pepper; drizzle with oil.
2. Fold parchment paper over fish. Bring edges of paper together on all sides and crimp to seal, forming a packet. Repeat with remaining packets. Place on baking sheets.
3. Bake at 450° for 12-15 minutes or until fish flakes easily with a fork. Open packets carefully to allow steam to escape.
1 packet: 270 cal., 10g fat (3g sat. fat), 72mg chol., 532mg sod., 12g carb. (4g sugars, 3g fiber), 31g pro. **Diabetic exchanges:** 5 lean meat, 2 vegetable, 2 fat.

TILAPIA & VEGGIES WITH RED PEPPER SAUCE

The impressive look and taste of this dish are delectably deceiving. Only the cook needs to know how quickly the saucy fish and sauteed veggies come together.

—*Helen Conwell, Portland, OR*

Takes: 30 min. • **Makes:** 6 servings

- ½ cup dry white wine or chicken broth
- ¼ cup water
- 1 Tbsp. lemon juice
- 1 tsp. salt, divided
- 6 tilapia fillets (4 oz. each)
- 2 small yellow summer squash, cut into ¼-in. slices
- 1 medium zucchini, cut into ¼-in. slices
- 1 medium onion, halved and sliced
- 1 Tbsp. olive oil
- 1 garlic clove, minced
- ¼ tsp. pepper
- ⅓ cup roasted sweet red peppers, drained
- 1 Tbsp. white balsamic vinegar

1. In a large skillet, bring wine, water, lemon juice and ½ tsp. salt to a boil. Reduce heat; add tilapia. Poach, uncovered, until fish flakes easily with a fork, 5-10 minutes, turning once. Remove and keep warm.

2. Bring poaching liquid to a boil; cook until reduced to about ½ cup. Meanwhile, in another skillet, saute the yellow squash, zucchini and onion in oil until tender. Add garlic; cook 1 minute longer. Sprinkle with pepper and remaining salt.

3. In a blender, combine the reduced liquid, roasted peppers and vinegar; cover and process until smooth. Serve sauce with fish and vegetables.

1 serving: 163 cal., 3g fat (1g sat. fat), 55mg chol., 490mg sod., 7g carb. (5g sugars, 2g fiber), 23g pro. **Diabetic exchanges:** 3 lean meat, 1 vegetable, ½ fat.

ORANGE TILAPIA IN PARCHMENT

Sweet orange juice and spicy cayenne pepper give this no-fuss dish fabulous flavor. These fillets bake in parchment paper, so cleanup is a breeze!

—*Tiffany Diebold, Nashville, TN*

Takes: 30 min. • **Makes:** 4 servings

- ¼ cup orange juice
- 4 tsp. grated orange zest
- ¼ tsp. salt
- ¼ tsp. cayenne pepper
- ¼ tsp. pepper
- 4 tilapia fillets (6 oz. each)
- ½ cup julienned carrot
- ½ cup julienned zucchini

1. Preheat oven to 450°. In a small bowl, combine first 5 ingredients; set aside. Cut parchment or heavy-duty foil into four 18x12-in. lengths; place a fish fillet on each. Top with carrot and zucchini; drizzle with orange juice mixture.

2. Fold parchment over fish. Working from bottom inside corner, fold up about ¾ in. of the paper and crimp both layers to seal. Repeat, folding edges up and crimping, until a half-moon-shaped packet is formed. Repeat for remaining packets. Place packets on baking sheets.

3. Bake until fish flakes easily with a fork, 12-15 minutes. Open packets carefully to allow steam to escape.

1 packet: 158 cal., 2g fat (1g sat. fat), 83mg chol., 220mg sod., 4g carb. (2g sugars, 1g fiber), 32g pro. **Diabetic exchanges:** 5 lean meat.

SHRIMP ORZO WITH FETA

Tender, healthy and flavorful, this recipe is one of my favorites. Garlic and a splash of lemon add to the fresh taste.
—*Sarah Hummel, Moon Township, PA*

- -

Takes: 25 min. • **Makes:** 4 servings

- 1¼ **cups uncooked whole wheat orzo pasta**
- 2 **Tbsp. olive oil**
- 2 **garlic cloves, minced**
- 2 **medium tomatoes, chopped**
- 2 **Tbsp. lemon juice**
- 1¼ **lbs. uncooked shrimp (26-30 per lb.), peeled and deveined**
- 2 **Tbsp. minced fresh cilantro**
- ¼ **tsp. pepper**
- ½ **cup crumbled feta cheese**

1. Cook orzo according to the package directions. Meanwhile, in a large skillet, heat oil over medium heat. Add garlic; cook and stir 1 minute. Add tomatoes and lemon juice. Bring to a boil. Stir in shrimp. Reduce heat; simmer, uncovered, 4-5 minutes or until shrimp turn pink.
2. Drain orzo. Add orzo, cilantro and pepper to shrimp mixture; heat through. Sprinkle with feta cheese.

1 cup: 406 cal., 12g fat (3g sat. fat), 180mg chol., 307mg sod., 40g carb. (2g sugars, 9g fiber), 33g pro. **Diabetic exchanges:** 4 lean meat, 2 starch, 1 fat.

LEMONY SHRIMP & TOMATOES

My family loves grilled shrimp, so creating the recipe for these skewers was easy. I love it because it's quick, delicious and healthy.
—*Lisa Speer, Palm Beach, FL*

Prep: 20 min. + marinating • **Grill:** 5 min.
Makes: 4 kabobs (½ cup sauce)

- ⅓ cup lemon juice
- 2 Tbsp. olive oil
- 2 garlic cloves, minced
- ½ tsp. grated lemon zest
- 1 lb. uncooked jumbo shrimp, peeled and deveined
- ⅔ cup fresh arugula
- 2 green onions, sliced
- ¼ cup plain yogurt
- 2 tsp. 2% milk
- 1 tsp. cider vinegar
- 1 tsp. Dijon mustard
- ½ tsp. sugar
- ½ tsp. salt, divided
- 12 cherry tomatoes
- ¼ tsp. pepper

1. In a large bowl, whisk lemon juice, oil, garlic and lemon zest until blended. Add the shrimp; toss to coat. Let stand 10 minutes.

2. Place arugula, green onions, yogurt, milk, vinegar, mustard, sugar and ¼ tsp. salt in a food processor; process until smooth.

3. On 4 metal or soaked wooden skewers, alternately thread shrimp and tomatoes. Sprinkle with pepper and remaining salt.

4. Grill, covered, over medium-high heat or broil 3-4 in. from heat 2-3 minutes on each side or until shrimp are no longer pink. Serve with sauce.

1 kabob with 2 Tbsp. sauce: 147 cal., 5g fat (1g sat. fat), 140mg chol., 475mg sod., 6g carb. (3g sugars, 1g fiber), 20g pro. **Diabetic exchanges:** 3 lean meat, ½ starch, ½ fat.

5i ⬤

STUFFED-OLIVE COD

Take advantage of your supermarket's olive bar to put a new twist on cod. This high-protein, low-fat dish is a weeknight lifesaver.
—*Tria Olsen, Queen Creek, AZ*

- -

Takes: 25 min. • **Makes:** 4 servings

4	cod fillets (6 oz. each)
1	tsp. dried oregano
¼	tsp. salt
1	medium lemon, thinly sliced
1	shallot, thinly sliced
⅓	cup garlic-stuffed olives, halved
2	Tbsp. water
2	Tbsp. olive juice

1. Place fillets in a large nonstick skillet coated with cooking spray. Sprinkle with oregano and salt; top with lemon and shallot.
2. Scatter olives around fish; add water and olive juice. Bring to a boil. Reduce heat to low; gently cook, covered, 8-10 minutes or until fish just begins to flake easily with a fork.
1 fillet: 163 cal., 3g fat (0 sat. fat), 65mg chol., 598mg sod., 4g carb. (1g sugars, 0 fiber), 27g pro. **Diabetic exchanges:** 4 lean meat.

TEST KITCHEN TIP

Olives are a good source of fiber, iron and copper. However, it is best to consume them in moderation; they have a high salt content because of the brine in which they are preserved.

SWEET-CHILI SALMON WITH BLACKBERRIES

Most of the inspiration for my cooking comes from one beloved place: my garden. I have a large berry patch, so I enjoy using just-picked berries to add natural sweetness and pop to savory dishes like this one.
—*Roxanne Chan, Albany, CA*

- -

Takes: 25 min. • **Makes:** 4 servings

- 1   cup fresh or frozen blackberries, thawed
- 1   cup finely chopped English cucumber
- 1   green onion, finely chopped
- 2   Tbsp. sweet chili sauce, divided
- 4   salmon fillets (6 oz. each)
- ½   tsp. salt
- ½   tsp. pepper

1. In a small bowl, combine blackberries, cucumber, green onion and 1 Tbsp. chili sauce; toss to coat.

2. Sprinkle salmon with salt and pepper. Place fillets on greased grill rack, skin side down. Grill, covered, over medium-high heat or broil 4 in. from heat until fish flakes easily with a fork, 10-12 minutes. Brush with remaining chili sauce during the last 2-3 minutes of cooking. Serve salmon with blackberry mixture.

1 fillet with ½ cup berry mixture: 303 cal., 16g fat (3g sat. fat), 85mg chol., 510mg sod., 9g carb. (6g sugars, 2g fiber), 30g pro.
Diabetic exchanges: 5 lean meat, ½ starch.

SPICY SHRIMP & WATERMELON KABOBS

My three sons can polish off a watermelon in one sitting. Before they dig in, I set aside a few slices to make these zesty shrimp kabobs.
—*Jennifer Fisher, Austin, TX*

- -

Takes: 30 min. • **Makes:** 4 servings

- 1 Tbsp. reduced-sodium soy sauce
- 1 Tbsp. Sriracha chili sauce
- 1 Tbsp. honey
- 1 garlic clove, minced
- 4 cups cubed seedless watermelon (1 in.), divided
- 1 lb. uncooked shrimp (16-20 per lb.), peeled and deveined
- 1 medium red onion, cut into 1-in. pieces
- ½ tsp. sea salt
- ¼ tsp. coarsely ground pepper
  Minced fresh cilantro, optional

1. For glaze, place soy sauce, chili sauce, honey, garlic and 2 cups watermelon in a blender; cover and process until pureed. Transfer to a small saucepan; bring to a boil. Cook, uncovered, over medium-high heat until the mixture is reduced by half, about 10 minutes. Reserve ¼ cup glaze for serving.
2. On 4 metal or soaked wooden skewers, alternately thread the shrimp, onion and remaining watermelon. Sprinkle ingredients with salt and pepper.
3. Place kabobs on an oiled grill rack over medium heat. Grill, covered, 3-4 minutes on each side or until shrimp turn pink, brushing with the remaining glaze during the last 2 minutes. If desired, sprinkle with cilantro. Serve with reserved glaze.
1 kabob with 1 Tbsp. glaze: 172 cal., 2g fat (0 sat. fat), 138mg chol., 644mg sod., 23g carb. (19g sugars, 2g fiber), 20g pro. **Diabetic exchanges:** 3 lean meat, 1 fruit, ½ starch.

WINE PAIRING

White Zinfandel. Its sweetness will play up the charred melon and honey-Sriracha sauce without being overwhelmed. Or try this dish with moscato or a sweet German riesling.

LINGUINE SHRIMP

This simple dish has lots of Mediterranean flavor and a little kick of heat from red pepper flakes. To save time, most of the chopping and prep work can be done ahead of time.
—*Megan Hidalgo, Quarryville, PA*

Prep: 20 min. • **Cook:** 20 min.
Makes: 8 servings

- 1 pkg. (16 oz.) linguine
- 2 lbs. uncooked medium shrimp, peeled and deveined
- 1 medium onion, chopped
- 6 Tbsp. olive oil
- 4 garlic cloves, minced
- 1 cup chopped roasted sweet red peppers
- 2 cans (2¼ oz. each) sliced ripe olives, drained
- ½ cup minced fresh parsley
- ½ cup white wine or chicken broth
- ½ tsp. crushed red pepper flakes
- ½ tsp. kosher salt
- ½ tsp. dried oregano
- ½ tsp. pepper
- ¾ cup crumbled feta cheese
- 2 Tbsp. lemon juice

1. Cook the linguine according to the package directions.
2. Meanwhile, in a large skillet, saute shrimp and onion in oil until shrimp turn pink. Add garlic; cook 1 minute longer. Stir in the red peppers, olives, parsley, wine, pepper flakes, salt, oregano and pepper. Reduce the heat.
3. Drain linguine, reserving ½ cup cooking water. Add linguine and reserved water to the skillet. Stir in cheese and lemon juice; cook and stir until cheese is melted.
1⅓ cups: 462 cal., 16g fat (3g sat. fat), 144mg chol., 610mg sod., 48g carb. (4g sugars, 3g fiber), 28g pro.

TOMATO-POACHED HALIBUT

My simple halibut with a burst of lemon comes together in one pan. Try it with polenta, angel hair pasta or crusty bread.
—*Danna Rogers, Westport, CT*

Takes: 30 min. • **Makes:** 4 servings

- 1 Tbsp. olive oil
- 2 poblano peppers, finely chopped
- 1 small onion, finely chopped
- 1 can (14½ oz.) fire-roasted diced tomatoes, undrained
- 1 can (14½ oz.) no-salt-added diced tomatoes, undrained
- ¼ cup chopped pitted green olives
- 3 garlic cloves, minced
- ¼ tsp. pepper
- ⅛ tsp. salt
- 4 halibut fillets (4 oz. each)
- ⅓ cup chopped fresh cilantro
- 4 lemon wedges
  Crusty whole grain bread, optional

1. In a large nonstick skillet, heat the oil over medium-high heat. Add poblano peppers and onion; cook and stir for 4-6 minutes or until vegetables are tender.
2. Stir in tomatoes, olives, garlic, pepper and salt. Bring to a boil. Adjust heat to maintain a gentle simmer. Add fillets. Cook, covered, 8-10 minutes or until fish just begins to flake easily with a fork. Sprinkle with cilantro. Serve with lemon wedges and, if desired, bread.
1 fillet with 1 cup sauce: 224 cal., 7g fat (1g sat. fat), 56mg chol., 651mg sod., 17g carb. (8g sugars, 4g fiber), 24g pro. **Diabetic exchanges:** 3 lean meat, 1 starch, ½ fat.

TOMATO-HERB GRILLED TILAPIA

My tilapia with ginger and lemon takes dinner over the top with minimal prep. Grilling the fish in foil is about as easy as it gets.

—Trisha Kruse, Eagle, ID

- -

Takes: 30 min. • **Makes:** 4 servings

- 1 cup fresh cilantro leaves
- 1 cup fresh parsley leaves
- 2 Tbsp. olive oil
- 2 tsp. grated lemon zest
- 2 Tbsp. lemon juice
- 1 Tbsp. coarsely chopped fresh gingerroot
- ¾ tsp. sea salt or kosher salt, divided
- 2 cups grape tomatoes, halved lengthwise
- 1½ cups fresh or frozen corn (about 8 oz.), thawed
- 4 tilapia fillets (6 oz. each)

1. Place the first 6 ingredients in a food processor; add ½ tsp. salt. Pulse until the mixture is finely chopped.

2. In a bowl, combine tomatoes and corn; stir in 1 Tbsp. herb mixture and remaining salt.

3. Place each fillet on a piece of heavy-duty foil (about 12 in. square). Top with herb mixture; spoon tomato mixture alongside fish. Fold foil around fish and vegetables, sealing tightly.

4. Grill, covered, over medium-high heat 6-8 minutes or until fish just begins to flake easily with a fork. Open foil carefully to allow steam to escape.

1 serving: 270 cal., 9g fat (2g sat. fat), 83mg chol., 443mg sod., 15g carb. (6g sugars, 3g fiber), 35g pro. **Diabetic exchanges:** 5 lean meat, 1½ fat, 1 vegetable, ½ starch.

PESTO GRILLED SALMON

Buttery, colorful and flaky, this rich and impressive salmon will be your new family favorite. If you have leftovers, add them to tomorrow night's pasta dish.
—*Sonya Labbe, West Hollywood, CA*

Takes: 30 min. • **Makes:** 12 servings

- 1 salmon fillet (3 lbs.)
- ½ cup prepared pesto
- 2 green onions, finely chopped
- ¼ cup lemon juice
- 2 garlic cloves, minced

1. Place salmon skin side down on a lightly oiled grill rack. Grill, covered, over medium heat or broil 4 in. from heat for 5 minutes.
2. In a small bowl, combine the pesto, onions, lemon juice and garlic. Carefully spoon some of the pesto mixture over salmon. Grill until fish flakes easily with a fork, 15-20 minutes longer, basting occasionally with remaining pesto mixture.

3 oz. cooked salmon: 262 cal., 17g fat (4g sat. fat), 70mg chol., 147mg sod., 1g carb. (0 sugars, 0 fiber), 25g pro. **Diabetic exchanges:** 3 lean meat, 3 fat.

Glazed Asian Salmon: Replace the basting ingredients with ½ cup reduced-sodium soy sauce; ¼ cup brown sugar; ½ tsp. each crushed red pepper flakes and ground ginger; and ¼ tsp. sesame oil. Grill and baste the salmon as directed.

Herbed Salmon: Place salmon on double thickness of heavy-duty foil. Mix ½ cup softened butter with ¼ cup each minced fresh chives, tarragon and thyme; spread over salmon. Top with ⅓ cup finely chopped red onion; ¼ tsp. each salt and pepper; and 1 thinly sliced lemon. Seal foil and grill 20-25 minutes. Open carefully to allow steam to escape.

SAVORY TOMATO-BRAISED TILAPIA

I shared this recipe with my bunco group, and now one of my friends makes it all the time. Try it yourself, and you'll agree it's a winner!
—*Nancy Shively, Shorewood, IL*

Takes: 30 min. • **Makes:** 4 servings

- 4 tilapia fillets (6 oz. each)
- ¼ tsp. seasoned salt
- 1 Tbsp. lemon juice
- 2 Tbsp. olive oil
- 1 small red onion, chopped
- 1 can (10 oz.) diced tomatoes and green chiles, undrained
- ¾ cup chopped roasted sweet red peppers
- ½ cup chicken broth
- ¼ cup tomato paste
- 1 tsp. garlic powder
- 1 tsp. dried oregano
  Hot cooked pasta, optional

1. Sprinkle fillets with seasoned salt; drizzle with lemon juice. In a large skillet, heat oil over medium-high heat. Add onion; cook and stir until tender. Add tomatoes, peppers, broth, tomato paste, garlic powder and oregano; cook and stir 2-3 minutes longer.
2. Place fillets over tomato mixture; cook, covered, 6-8 minutes or until fish flakes easily with a fork. If desired, serve with pasta.

1 fillet with ½ cup sauce: 254 cal., 8g fat (2g sat. fat), 83mg chol., 740mg sod., 10g carb. (4g sugars, 2g fiber), 34g pro. **Diabetic exchanges:** 5 lean meat, 1½ fat, 1 vegetable.

CITRUS SCALLOPS

My husband and I like to eat seafood at least once a week. Oranges and lemon juice give scallops a refreshing burst of flavor.
—*Cheri Hawthorne, North Canton, OH*

Takes: 15 min. • **Makes:** 4 servings

- 1 medium green or sweet red pepper, julienned
- 4 green onions, chopped
- 1 garlic clove, minced
- 2 Tbsp. olive oil
- 1 lb. sea scallops
- ½ tsp. salt
- ¼ tsp. crushed red pepper flakes
- 2 Tbsp. lime juice
- ½ tsp. grated lime zest
- 4 medium navel oranges, peeled and sectioned
- 2 tsp. minced fresh cilantro
  Hot cooked rice or pasta

In a large skillet, saute the pepper, onions and garlic in oil for 1 minute. Add scallops, salt and pepper flakes; cook for 4 minutes. Add lime juice and zest; cook for 1 minute. Reduce heat. Add orange sections and cilantro; cook 2 minutes longer or until scallops are opaque. Serve with rice or pasta.

1 serving: 240 cal., 8g fat (1g sat. fat), 37mg chol., 482mg sod., 23g carb. (14g sugars, 4g fiber), 21g pro. **Diabetic exchanges:** 3 lean meat, 1½ fat, 1 fruit.

TUNA TERIYAKI KABOBS

I love to grill out, but don't always have room for a big, heavy dinner like steaks or burgers. These tuna skewers are for perfect warmer weather, and you'll have enough room for a sweet dessert!

—Holly Battiste, Barrington, NJ

- -

Prep: 25 min. + marinating • **Grill:** 15 min.
Makes: 8 kabobs

- 1½ lbs. tuna steaks, cut into 1½-in. chunks
- 2 medium sweet red peppers, cut into 1-in. pieces
- 1 large sweet onion, cut into 1-in. pieces

MARINADE/DRESSING
- ¼ cup minced fresh cilantro
- ¼ cup sesame oil
- 3 Tbsp. lime juice
- 2 Tbsp. soy sauce
- 2 Tbsp. extra virgin olive oil
- 1 Tbsp. minced fresh gingerroot
- 2 garlic cloves, minced

SALAD
- 1 pkg. (5 oz.) fresh baby spinach
- 1 medium sweet yellow pepper, cut into 1-in. pieces
- 8 cherry tomatoes, halved

1. Thread tuna chunks onto 4 metal or soaked wooden skewers. Thread pepper and onion pieces onto 4 more skewers. Place skewers in a 13x9-in. baking dish.

2. Whisk together marinade ingredients. Reserve half of mixture for salad dressing. Pour remaining marinade over skewers; refrigerate, covered, 30 minutes.

3. Grill kabobs, covered, on a greased grill rack over medium heat, turning occasionally, until tuna is slightly pink in center for medium-rare (2-3 minutes per side) and vegetables are crisp-tender (10-12 minutes). Remove tuna kabobs from direct heat and keep warm while vegetables finish grilling.

4. For salad, toss spinach, yellow pepper and cherry tomatoes with reserved dressing. For each portion, serve a tuna kabob and vegetable kabob over salad.

2 kabobs: 389 cal., 16g fat (2g sat. fat), 66mg chol., 444mg sod., 15g carb. (9g sugars, 4g fiber), 45g pro. **Diabetic exchanges:** 5 lean meat, 2 vegetable, 2 fat.

BAYOU GULF SHRIMP GUMBO

This recipe skips the traditional hard-to-find spices but still delivers the true seafood flavor beloved in the Louisiana bayou and beyond.
—*Wolfgang Hanau, West Palm Beach, FL*

Prep: 35 min. • **Cook:** 5 hours
Makes: 6 servings

- ½ lb. bacon strips, chopped
- 3 celery ribs, chopped
- 1 medium onion, chopped
- 1 medium green pepper, chopped
- 2 garlic cloves, minced
- 2 bottles (8 oz. each) clam juice
- 1 can (14½ oz.) diced tomatoes, undrained
- 2 Tbsp. Worcestershire sauce
- 1 tsp. dried marjoram
- 2 lbs. uncooked large shrimp, peeled and deveined
- 2½ cups frozen sliced okra, thawed
  Hot cooked brown rice, optional

1. In a large skillet, cook bacon over medium heat until crisp. Remove to paper towels with a slotted spoon; drain, reserving 2 Tbsp. drippings. Saute the celery, onion, green pepper and garlic in drippings until tender.

2. Transfer to a 4-qt. slow cooker. Stir in the bacon, clam juice, tomatoes, Worcestershire sauce and marjoram. Cover and cook on low for 4 hours.

3. Stir in shrimp and okra. Cover and cook 1 hour longer or until shrimp turn pink and okra is heated through. Serve gumbo with hot cooked rice if desired.

1½ cups: 287 cal., 12g fat (4g sat. fat), 204mg chol., 792mg sod., 13g carb. (5g sugars, 3g fiber), 31g pro. **Diabetic exchanges:** 4 lean meat, 2 vegetable, 2 fat.

LEMON PARSLEY SWORDFISH

This dish looks impressive and it's easy to prepare, making it a winner in my book. I like that it comes together fast enough for a family weeknight meal, but it's special enough to serve guests for Sunday dinner.
—*Nathan Leopold, Mechanicsburg, PA*

Takes: 25 min. • **Makes:** 4 servings

- 4 swordfish steaks (7 oz. each)
- ½ tsp. salt
- ½ cup minced fresh parsley, divided
- ⅓ cup olive oil
- 1 Tbsp. lemon juice
- 2 tsp. minced garlic
- ¼ tsp. crushed red pepper flakes

1. Preheat oven to 425°. Place fish in a greased 13x9-in. baking dish; sprinkle with salt. In a small bowl, combine ¼ cup parsley, oil, lemon juice, garlic and pepper flakes; spoon over fish.

2. Bake, uncovered, until fish flakes easily with a fork, 15-20 minutes, basting occasionally. Sprinkle with remaining parsley.
1 swordfish steak: 390 cal., 26g fat (5g sat. fat), 72mg chol., 171mg sod., 1g carb. (0 sugars, 0 fiber), 37g pro.
Artichoke-Tomato Swordfish: Omit the last 6 ingredients. Place fish in prepared dish. Mix 2 jars (7½ oz. each) chopped, drained artichoke hearts; ½ cup chopped, drained, oil-packed sun-dried tomatoes; and 4 chopped shallots. Spread over fish. Drizzle with 2 Tbsp. melted butter and 1 tsp. lemon juice. Bake, covered, for 15 minutes. Uncover; bake another 6-8 minutes.

CRAB-STUFFED FLOUNDER WITH HERBED AIOLI

If you're a seafood lover, look no further. The light and creamy aioli tops off the flounder with fresh tones of chives and garlic.
—*Beverly O'Ferrall, Linkwood, MD*

Prep: 20 min. • **Bake:** 20 min.
Makes: 6 servings

- ¼ cup egg substitute
- 2 Tbsp. fat-free milk
- 1 Tbsp. minced chives
- 1 Tbsp. reduced-fat mayonnaise
- 1 Tbsp. Dijon mustard
  Dash hot pepper sauce
- 1 lb. lump crabmeat
- 6 flounder fillets (6 oz. each)
  Paprika

AIOLI
- ⅓ cup reduced-fat mayonnaise
- 2 tsp. minced chives
- 2 tsp. minced fresh parsley
- 2 tsp. lemon juice
- 1 garlic clove, minced

1. In a small bowl, combine first 6 ingredients; gently fold in the crabmeat. Cut the fillets in half widthwise; place 6 halves in a 15x10x1-in. baking pan coated with cooking spray. Spoon crab mixture over fillets; top with remaining fish. Sprinkle with paprika.

2. Bake at 400° for 20-24 minutes or until fish flakes easily with a fork. Meanwhile, combine the aioli ingredients. Serve with fish.

1 stuffed fillet with 2½ tsp. aioli: 276 cal., 8g fat (1g sat. fat), 153mg chol., 585mg sod., 3g carb. (1g sugars, 0 fiber), 45g pro. **Diabetic exchanges:** 5 lean meat, 1 fat.

HALIBUT STEAKS WITH PAPAYA MINT SALSA

The combination of zesty fruit salsa and tender halibut makes this dish the catch of the day!

—*Sonya Labbe, West Hollywood, CA*

- -

Takes: 20 min. • **Makes:** 4 servings

- 1   **medium papaya, peeled, seeded and chopped**
- ¼   **cup chopped red onion**
- ¼   **cup fresh mint leaves**
- 1   **tsp. finely chopped chipotle pepper in adobo sauce**
- 2   **Tbsp. olive oil, divided**
- 1   **Tbsp. honey**
- 4   **halibut steaks (6 oz. each)**

1. In a small bowl, combine the papaya, onion, mint, chipotle pepper, 1 Tbsp. oil and honey. Cover and refrigerate until serving.

2. In a large skillet, cook halibut in remaining oil for 4-6 minutes on each side or until fish flakes easily with a fork. Serve with salsa.

1 halibut steak with ½ cup salsa: 300 cal., 11g fat (2g sat. fat), 54mg chol., 105mg sod., 13g carb. (9g sugars, 2g fiber), 36g pro.
Diabetic exchanges: 5 lean meat, 1 starch, 1 fat.

WINE PAIRING

Riesling. Aromatic and minerally, it's a natural with spicy foods (like the kiss of chipotle in this salsa). Australian rieslings often taste like tropical fruits—another bonus.

TUSCAN-STYLE GRILLED TROUT

My husband is an avid fisherman, so I have the joy of creating delicious recipes that make the most of his catch. The Tuscan accents shine through here, making this grilled fish one of our favorites.

—Roxanne Chan, Albany, CA

Prep: 25 min. • **Grill:** 15 min.
Makes: 4 servings (3 cups relish)

- 4 pan-dressed trout (about 8 oz. each)
- 1 Tbsp. olive oil
- ½ cup shredded zucchini
- ¼ cup chopped roasted sweet red peppers
- 2 Tbsp. tapenade or ripe olive bruschetta topping
- 1 Tbsp. minced fresh parsley
- 1 garlic clove, minced
- 1 tsp. balsamic vinegar

RELISH

- 2 large tomatoes, chopped
- ½ cup chopped fennel bulb
- 1 green onion, thinly sliced
- 2 Tbsp. pine nuts, toasted
- 2 Tbsp. minced fresh basil
- 1 tsp. lemon juice
- ½ tsp. lemon-pepper seasoning

1. Rub trout with oil. In a small bowl, combine the zucchini, red peppers, tapenade, parsley, garlic and vinegar; spoon into fish cavities.
2. Place fish in a well-greased grill basket. Grill, covered, over medium heat until fish is browned on the bottom, 8-10 minutes. Turn; grill until fish flakes easily with a fork, 5-7 minutes longer.
3. In a small bowl, combine relish ingredients; serve with trout.
1 grilled trout with ¾ cup relish: 369 cal., 18g fat (4g sat. fat), 120mg chol., 291mg sod., 7g carb. (4g sugars, 2g fiber), 42g pro. **Diabetic exchanges:** 6 lean meat, 1½ fat, 1 vegetable.

MEDITERRANEAN TILAPIA

I recently became a fan of tilapia. The mild flavor makes it easy to top with our favorite ingredients. And it's low in calories and fat. What's not to love?

—Robin Brenneman, Hilliard, OH

Takes: 20 min. • **Makes:** 6 servings

- 6 tilapia fillets (6 oz. each)
- 1 cup canned Italian diced tomatoes
- ½ cup water-packed artichoke hearts, chopped
- ½ cup sliced ripe olives
- ½ cup crumbled feta cheese

Preheat oven to 400°. Place fillets in a 15x10x1-in. baking pan coated with cooking spray. Top with tomatoes, artichoke hearts, olives and cheese. Bake, uncovered, until fish flakes easily with a fork, 15-20 minutes.
1 fillet: 197 cal., 4g fat (2g sat. fat), 88mg chol., 446mg sod., 5g carb. (2g sugars, 1g fiber), 34g pro. **Diabetic exchanges:** 5 lean meat, ½ fat.
Italian Tilapia: Follow method as directed, but top the fillets with 1 cup canned diced tomatoes with roasted garlic; ½ cup each julienned roasted sweet red pepper, sliced fresh mushrooms and diced fresh mozzarella cheese; and ½ tsp. dried basil.
Southwest Tilapia: Follow the recipe method as directed, but top the tilapia fillets with 1 cup canned diced tomatoes with mild green chiles; ½ cup each cubed avocado, frozen corn (thawed) and cubed cheddar cheese; and ½ tsp. dried cilantro.

RED PEPPER & PARMESAN TILAPIA

My husband and I are always looking for light fish recipes to add to our healthy diets. This one's a hit with us both. We serve it at dinner parties, too. It's one for the keeper file!
—*Michelle Martin, Durham, NC*

Takes: 20 min. • **Makes:** 4 servings

- ¼ cup egg substitute
- ½ cup grated Parmesan cheese
- 1 tsp. Italian seasoning
- ½ to 1 tsp. crushed red pepper flakes
- ½ tsp. pepper
- 4 tilapia fillets (6 oz. each)

1. Place egg substitute in a shallow bowl. In another shallow bowl, combine Parmesan cheese, Italian seasoning, pepper flakes and pepper. Dip fillets in egg substitute, then cheese mixture.

2. Place in a 15x10x1-in. baking pan coated with cooking spray. Bake at 425° until fish flakes easily with a fork, 10-15 minutes.

1 fillet: 179 cal., 4g fat (2g sat. fat), 89mg chol., 191mg sod., 1g carb. (trace sugars, 0 fiber), 35g pro. **Diabetic exchanges:** 5 lean meat.

SHRIMP MARINARA

Let the sauce simmer in the slow cooker for a few hours before dinner, then toss in the shrimp right before mealtime. Serve over hot pasta for a simple dish that feels dressed.up.
—*Sue Mackey, Jackson, WI*

Prep: 30 min. • **Cook:** 3¼ hours
Makes: 6 servings

1   can (14½ oz.) Italian diced tomatoes, undrained
1   can (6 oz.) tomato paste
½ to 1 cup water
2   garlic cloves, minced
2   Tbsp. minced fresh parsley
½ tsp. salt
1   tsp. dried oregano
½ tsp. dried basil
¼ tsp. pepper
1   lb. uncooked shrimp (26-30 per lb.), peeled and deveined
¾ lb. spaghetti, cooked and drained
    Shredded Parmesan cheese, optional

1. In a 3-qt. slow cooker, combine the first 9 ingredients. Cover and cook on low for 3-4 hours.
2. Stir in shrimp. Cover and cook on high 15-25 minutes or just until shrimp turn pink. Serve with spaghetti. Sprinkle with cheese if desired.
1 serving: 328 cal., 2g fat (0 sat. fat), 92mg chol., 527mg sod., 55g carb. (9g sugars, 3g fiber), 22g pro.

CRUNCHY OVEN-BAKED TILAPIA

This baked tilapia is perfectly crunchy. Dip it in the fresh lime mayo for a bright burst of citrus flavor.

—*Leslie Palmer, Swampscott, MA*

Takes: 25 min. • **Makes:** 4 servings

- 4   tilapia fillets (6 oz. each)
- 1   Tbsp. reduced-fat mayonnaise
- 1   Tbsp. lime juice
- ¼   tsp. grated lime zest
- ½   tsp. salt
- ¼   tsp. onion powder
- ¼   tsp. pepper
- ½   cup panko (Japanese) bread crumbs
      Cooking spray
- 2   Tbsp. minced fresh cilantro or parsley

1. Preheat oven to 425°. Place fillets on a baking sheet coated with cooking spray. In a small bowl, mix the mayonnaise, lime juice and zest, salt, onion powder and pepper. Spread mayonnaise mixture over fish. Sprinkle with bread crumbs; spritz with cooking spray.

2. Bake until fish just begins to flake easily with a fork, 15-20 minutes. Sprinkle fish with cilantro.

1 fillet: 186 cal., 3g fat (1g sat. fat), 84mg chol., 401mg sod., 6g carb. (0 sugars, 0 fiber), 33g pro. **Diabetic exchanges:** 5 lean meat, ½ starch.

SHRIMP ARTICHOKE PASTA

This healthy dish looks as if it came from an Italian restaurant. When I'm in a rush, I use jarred tomato sauce and omit the tomatoes and seasonings. You can also fix this ahead and reheat on a busy night.

—Nancy Deans, Acton, ME

- -

Takes: 30 min. • **Makes:** 6 servings

- 9   oz. uncooked linguine
- 2   Tbsp. olive oil
- 1   cup sliced fresh mushrooms
- 1   lb. uncooked medium shrimp, peeled and deveined
- 3   medium tomatoes, chopped
- 1   can (14 oz.) water-packed artichoke hearts, rinsed, drained and halved
- 1   can (6 oz.) pitted ripe olives, drained and halved
- 2   garlic cloves, minced
- 1   tsp. dried oregano
- ½   tsp. salt
- ½   tsp. dried basil
- ⅛   tsp. pepper

1. Cook linguine according to the package directions. Meanwhile, in a large skillet, heat oil over medium-high heat. Add mushrooms; cook and stir 4 minutes. Add the remaining ingredients; cook and stir 5 minutes or until shrimp turn pink.

2. Drain linguine; serve with shrimp mixture.

1 serving: 328 cal., 9g fat (1g sat. fat), 112mg chol., 748mg sod., 41g carb. (4g sugars, 3g fiber), 21g pro. **Diabetic exchanges:** 2 starch, 2 lean meat, 1½ fat, 1 vegetable.

LEMON-LIME SALMON WITH VEGGIE SAUTE

Whether you serve my salmon recipe for a healthy weeknight meal or on the weekend when hosting company, everyone who tries it will be in awe. The assortment of veggies adds a splash of color and awesome flavor to this entree.

—*Brian Hill, West Hollywood, CA*

- -

Takes: 30 min. • **Makes:** 6 servings

6	salmon fillets (4 oz. each)
½	cup lemon juice
½	cup lime juice
1	tsp. seafood seasoning
¼	tsp. salt
2	medium sweet red peppers, sliced
2	medium sweet yellow peppers, sliced
1	large red onion, halved and sliced
2	tsp. olive oil
1	pkg. (10 oz.) frozen corn, thawed
2	cups baby portobello mushrooms, halved
2	cups cut fresh asparagus (1-in. pieces)
2	Tbsp. minced fresh tarragon or 2 tsp. dried tarragon

1. Place salmon in a 13x9-in. baking dish; add lemon and lime juices. Sprinkle with seafood seasoning and salt. Bake, uncovered, at 425° for 10-15 minutes or until fish flakes easily with a fork.

2. Meanwhile, in a large skillet coated with cooking spray, saute peppers and onion in oil for 3 minutes. Add the corn, mushrooms and asparagus; cook and stir just until vegetables reach desired doneness, 3-4 minutes longer. Stir in tarragon. Serve with salmon.

1 fillet with 1¼ cups vegetables: 329 cal., 15g fat (3g sat. fat), 67mg chol., 283mg sod., 25g carb. (7g sugars, 4g fiber), 27g pro. **Diabetic exchanges:** 3 lean meat, 1½ starch, 1½ fat.

TUNA WITH TUSCAN WHITE BEAN SALAD

My homemade bean medley is a savory complement to flavorful grilled tuna. Once the tuna hits the grill, do not move it around, or the tuna may tear. This recipe cooks to medium-rare, but increase grilling time if you like it well-done.
—Vance Werner Jr., Franklin, WI

Takes: 30 min. • **Makes:** 4 servings

- 1 can (15 oz.) cannellini beans, rinsed and drained
- 3 celery ribs, finely chopped
- 1 medium sweet red pepper, finely chopped
- 1 plum tomato, seeded and finely chopped
- ½ cup fresh basil leaves, thinly sliced
- ¼ cup finely chopped red onion
- 3 Tbsp. olive oil
- 2 Tbsp. red wine vinegar
- 1 Tbsp. lemon juice
- ¼ tsp. salt
- ¼ tsp. pepper

TUNA
- 4 tuna steaks (6 oz. each)
- 1 Tbsp. olive oil
- ¼ tsp. salt
- ¼ tsp. pepper

1. In a large bowl, combine first 6 ingredients. In a small bowl, whisk the olive oil, red wine vinegar, lemon juice, salt and pepper. Pour over bean mixture; toss to coat. Refrigerate until serving.
2. Brush tuna with oil. Sprinkle with salt and pepper; place on greased grill rack. Cook, covered, over high heat or broil 3-4 in. from the heat until slightly pink in the center for medium-rare, 3-4 minutes on each side. Serve with salad.

1 tuna steak with 1 cup salad: 409 cal., 16g fat (2g sat. fat), 77mg chol., 517mg sod., 20g carb. (3g sugars, 6g fiber), 45g pro. **Diabetic exchanges:** 5 lean meat, 3 fat, 1 starch, 1 vegetable.

GRILLED PISTACHIO-LEMON PESTO SHRIMP

Not your ordinary pesto, this one is made with arugula and pistachios. It's excellent on more than shrimp, too. Try spreading it on crostini or tossing it with pasta.
—Amy Dale, Long Beach, CA

Prep: 15 min. + chilling • **Grill:** 5 min.
Makes: 8 servings

- ¾ cup fresh arugula
- ½ cup minced fresh parsley
- ⅓ cup shelled pistachios
- 2 Tbsp. lemon juice
- 1 garlic clove, peeled
- ¼ tsp. grated lemon zest
- ½ cup olive oil
- ¼ cup shredded Parmesan cheese
- ¼ tsp. salt
- ⅛ tsp. pepper
- 1½ lbs. uncooked jumbo shrimp, peeled and deveined

1. Place the first 6 ingredients in a food processor; pulse until finely chopped. Continue processing while gradually adding oil in a steady stream. Add Parmesan cheese, salt and pepper; pulse just until combined. Transfer ⅓ cup pesto to a large bowl. Add shrimp; toss to coat. Refrigerate, covered, 30 minutes.
2. Thread shrimp onto 8 metal or soaked wooden skewers; place on greased grill rack. Cook, covered, over medium heat until shrimp turn pink, 5-6 minutes, turning once. Serve with remaining pesto.

1 skewer with about 1 Tbsp. pesto: 236 cal., 18g fat (3g sat. fat), 105mg chol., 241mg sod., 3g carb. (1g sugars, 1g fiber), 16g pro.

SALMON WITH HORSERADISH PISTACHIO CRUST

Impress everyone with this elegant but easy salmon. Feel free to switch up the ingredients to suit your tastes. Substitute scallions for the shallot or try almonds or pecans instead of pistachios. The nutty coating also goes well with chicken or pork.

—*Linda Press Wolfe, Cross River, NY*

- -

Takes: 30 min. • **Makes:** 6 servings

- 6 salmon fillets (4 oz. each)
- ⅓ cup sour cream
- ⅔ cup dry bread crumbs
- ⅔ cup chopped pistachios
- ½ cup minced shallots
- 2 Tbsp. olive oil
- 1 to 2 Tbsp. prepared horseradish
- 1 Tbsp. snipped fresh dill or 1 tsp. dill weed
- ½ tsp. grated lemon or orange zest
- ¼ tsp. crushed red pepper flakes
- 1 garlic clove, minced

Preheat oven to 350°. Place salmon, skin side down, in an ungreased 15x10x1-in. baking pan. Spread sour cream over each fillet. Combine remaining ingredients. Pat the crumb-nut mixture onto tops of salmon fillets, pressing to help coating adhere. Bake until fish just begins to flake easily with a fork, 12-15 minutes.

1 salmon fillet: 376 cal., 25g fat (5g sat. fat), 60mg chol., 219mg sod., 15g carb. (3g sugars, 2g fiber), 24g pro. **Diabetic exchanges:** 3 lean meat, 2 fat.

TEST KITCHEN TIP

For the best results, make sure to use plain horseradish, not horseradish sauce or creamed horseradish, when preparing this recipe. One tablespoon of horseradish adds a pleasant mild flavor, but feel free to increase the amount to 2 or 3 Tbsp. if you like a little more bite.

WINE PAIRING

Pinot Noir. The light-bodied red is a classic match for salmon. Try one from cool-climate Oregon. The flavor profile is lean and slightly spicy, with bright strawberry notes. It plays beautifully with the recipe's shallots, spices and herbs.

GREEK FISH BAKE

As a military spouse living overseas, I got the chance to try many styles of cooking. Here's a Mediterranean-inspired recipe that we both still enjoy today.
—*Stacey Boyd, Springfield, VA*

Takes: 30 min. • **Makes:** 4 servings

4	cod fillets (6 oz. each)
2	Tbsp. olive oil
¼	tsp. salt
⅛	tsp. pepper
1	small green pepper, cut into thin strips
½	small red onion, thinly sliced
¼	cup pitted Greek olives, sliced
1	can (8 oz.) tomato sauce
¼	cup crumbled feta cheese

1. Preheat oven to 400°. Place cod in a greased 13x9-in. baking dish. Brush with oil; sprinkle with salt and pepper. Top with green pepper, onion and olives.
2. Pour tomato sauce over top; sprinkle with cheese. Bake until fish just begins to flake easily with a fork, 15-20 minutes.
1 fillet with toppings: 246 cal., 12g fat (2g sat. fat), 68mg chol., 706mg sod., 6g carb. (2g sugars, 2g fiber), 29g pro. **Diabetic exchanges:** 4 lean meat, 1½ fat, 1 vegetable.

FETA SHRIMP SKILLET

My husband and I tasted a similar shrimp dish on our honeymoon in Greece. We liked it so much, I re-created the flavors when we got home. When I make it now, it brings back wonderful memories.

—Sonali Ruder, New York, NY

Takes: 30 min. • **Makes:** 4 servings

- 1 Tbsp. olive oil
- 1 medium onion, finely chopped
- 3 garlic cloves, minced
- 1 tsp. dried oregano
- ½ tsp. pepper
- ¼ tsp. salt
- 2 cans (14½ oz. each) diced tomatoes, undrained
- ¼ cup white wine, optional
- 1 lb. uncooked medium shrimp, peeled and deveined
- 2 Tbsp. minced fresh parsley
- ¾ cup crumbled feta cheese

1. In a large nonstick skillet, heat oil over medium-high heat. Add onion; cook and stir 4-6 minutes or until tender. Add garlic and seasonings; cook 1 minute longer. Stir in tomatoes and, if desired, wine. Bring to a boil. Reduce heat; simmer, uncovered, 5-7 minutes or until sauce is slightly thickened.

2. Add shrimp and parsley; cook 5-6 minutes or until shrimp turn pink, stirring occasionally. Remove from heat; sprinkle with cheese. Let stand, covered, until cheese is softened.

1¼ cups: 240 cal., 8g fat (3g sat. fat), 149mg chol., 748mg sod., 16g carb. (9g sugars, 5g fiber), 25g pro. **Diabetic exchanges:** 3 lean meat, 1 starch, 1 fat.

TEST KITCHEN TIP

For even more Mediterranean flavor, add ¼ cup chopped kalamata olives with the tomatoes. Like it spicy? Try adding a pinch of crushed red pepper with the other seasonings. Serve this saucy dish over hot cooked rice or pasta. Zucchini noodles and spaghetti squash also make delicious bases, and both are low-carb, too.

5i ⏱

TOMATO-BASIL BAKED FISH

Baked fish is delicious and healthy. I turn to this recipe often because it's so versatile and can be made with different kinds of fish depending on what I'm craving.
—*Annie Hicks, Zephyrhills, FL*

- -

Takes: 15 min. • **Makes:** 2 servings

1	Tbsp. lemon juice
1	tsp. olive oil
8	oz. red snapper, cod or haddock fillets
¼	tsp. dried basil
⅛	tsp. salt
⅛	tsp. pepper
2	plum tomatoes, thinly sliced
2	tsp. grated Parmesan cheese

1. In a shallow bowl, combine the lemon juice and oil. Add fish fillets; turn to coat. Place in a greased 9-in. pie plate. Sprinkle with half of the basil, salt and pepper. Arrange tomatoes over top; sprinkle with cheese and remaining seasonings.
2. Cover and bake at 400° for 10-12 minutes or until fish flakes easily with a fork.
1 serving: 121 cal., 4g fat (1g sat. fat), 24mg chol., 256mg sod., 4g carb. (2g sugars, 1g fiber), 18g pro. **Diabetic exchanges:** 3 lean meat, 1 vegetable, ½ fat.

PISTACHIO SALMON

This simple salmon gets its crunch from a coating of crushed pistachios, panko bread crumbs and Parmesan cheese. Add steamed veggies and rice and dinner's ready!

—Anthony Oraczewski, Port St. Lucie, FL

- -

Takes: 25 min. • **Makes:** 4 servings

- ⅓ **cup pistachios, finely chopped**
- ¼ **cup panko (Japanese) bread crumbs**
- ¼ **cup grated Parmesan cheese**
- 1 **salmon fillet (1 lb.)**
- ½ **tsp. salt**
- ¼ **tsp. pepper**

1. Preheat oven to 400°. In a shallow bowl, toss pistachios with bread crumbs and cheese.

2. Place salmon fillet on a greased foil-lined 15x10x1-in. pan, skin side down; sprinkle with with salt and pepper. Top with the pistachio mixture, pressing to adhere. Bake, uncovered, until fish just begins to flake easily with a fork, 15-20 minutes.

3 oz. cooked fish: 269 cal., 17g fat (3g sat. fat), 61mg chol., 497mg sod., 6g carb. (1g sugars, 1g fiber), 23g pro. **Diabetic exchanges:** 3 lean meat, 1 fat, ½ starch.

TEST KITCHEN TIP

Save any leftover pistachios for snacks. A serving (about 50 nuts) packs 6 grams of protein, 3 grams of fiber and over 10 percent of the B6, thiamine, copper and phosphorous we need daily.

SEA SCALLOPS & FETTUCCINE

When my husband and I decided to lose weight, we tried this recipe and loved it so much, we had it every Tuesday. It's so easy, he would fix it on nights I was running late.
—*Donna Thompson, Laramie, WY*

Takes: 30 min. • **Makes:** 2 servings

4	oz. uncooked fettuccine
1	Tbsp. olive oil
½	medium sweet red pepper, julienned
1	garlic clove, minced
½	tsp. grated lemon zest
¼	tsp. crushed red pepper flakes
½	cup reduced-sodium chicken broth
¼	cup white wine or additional broth
1	Tbsp. lemon juice
6	sea scallops (about ¾ lb.)
2	tsp. grated Parmesan cheese

1. Cook fettuccine according to package directions; drain.

2. Meanwhile, in a large skillet, heat oil over medium-high heat. Add red pepper, garlic, lemon zest and pepper flakes; cook and stir 2 minutes. Stir in broth, wine and lemon juice. Bring to a boil. Reduce the heat; simmer, uncovered, 5-6 minutes or until liquid is reduced by half.

3. Cut each scallop horizontally in half; add to skillet. Cook, covered, 4-5 minutes or until the scallops are firm and opaque, stirring occasionally. Serve with fettuccine. Sprinkle with cheese.

1 serving: 421 cal., 10g fat (2g sat. fat), 42mg chol., 861mg sod., 49g carb. (4g sugars, 3g fiber), 30g pro.

PRESSURE-COOKER RED CLAM SAUCE

This recipe tastes as if you've been working on it all day but comes together in minutes. What a classy way to jazz up pasta sauce!
—*JoAnn Brown, Latrobe, PA*

- -

Prep: 20 min. • **Cook:** 5 min. + releasing
Makes: 4 servings

1	Tbsp. canola oil
1	medium onion, chopped
2	garlic cloves, minced
2	cans (6½ oz. each) chopped clams, undrained
1	can (14½ oz.) diced tomatoes, undrained
1	can (6 oz.) tomato paste
¼	cup minced fresh parsley
1	bay leaf
1	tsp. sugar
1	tsp. dried basil
½	tsp. dried thyme
6	oz. linguine, cooked and drained

1. Select saute setting on a 6-qt. electric pressure cooker and adjust for medium heat. Add oil. When oil is hot, add onion; saute until tender. Add garlic; cook 1 minute longer. Press cancel.

2. Stir in the next 8 ingredients. Lock lid; close pressure-release vale. Adjust to pressure-cook on high for 3 minutes. Allow the pressure to naturally release for 5 minutes, then quick-release any remaining pressure. Discard bay leaf. Serve with linguine.

1 serving: 302 cal., 5g fat (0 sat. fat), 33mg chol., 667mg sod., 50g carb. (11g sugars, 5g fiber), 17g pro.

SHRIMP & SCALLOP COUSCOUS

Here's a quick and satisfying skillet dish that ranks as one of my favorites. It uses summer veggies in a sensational blend of flavors.
—*Marvin Meuser Jr., Princeton, IN*

- -

Takes: 30 min. • **Makes:** 4 servings

2	medium zucchini, julienned
1	medium green pepper, julienned
2	Tbsp. olive oil
3	plum tomatoes, chopped
4	green onions, chopped
1	Tbsp. minced fresh basil or 1 tsp. dried basil
3	tsp. chili powder
1	garlic clove, minced
½	tsp. dried oregano
½	lb. uncooked medium shrimp, peeled and deveined
½	lb. bay scallops
¼	tsp. salt
⅛	tsp. pepper
	Hot cooked couscous
	Thinly sliced fresh basil leaves, optional

1. In a large skillet, saute the zucchini and green pepper in oil until tender. Add the tomatoes, onions, basil, chili powder, garlic and oregano. Bring to a boil. Reduce heat; simmer, uncovered, for 5 minutes.

2. Stir in the shrimp, scallops, salt and pepper. Return to a boil. Reduce the heat; simmer, uncovered, for 5 minutes or until shrimp turn pink and scallops are opaque. Serve with couscous. Garnish with sliced basil if desired.

1 cup: 201 cal., 9g fat (1g sat. fat), 88mg chol., 342mg sod., 11g carb. (4g sugars, 3g fiber), 21g pro. **Diabetic exchanges:** 3 lean meat, 1½ fat, 1 vegetable.

SLOW-SIMMERED CHICKEN WITH
RAISINS, CAPERS & BASIL,
PAGE 114

Chicken & Turkey

Exotic spices, tangy glazes and more turn every meal into a memorable experience. Indulge in the flavors of classic Mediterranean ingredients such as figs, olives and feta when you enjoy these light and lively chicken and turkey entrees.

SLOW-SIMMERED CHICKEN WITH RAISINS, CAPERS & BASIL

Capers, golden raisins and fresh basil give this dish a sweetly savory flavor. And what is even better than that? The kids love it!

—*Nadine Mesch, Mount Healthy, OH*

Prep: 25 min. • **Cook:** 4 hours
Makes: 8 servings

- 2 Tbsp. olive oil, divided
- 8 boneless skinless chicken thighs (4 oz. each)
- 1 tsp. salt
- 1 tsp. pepper
- ½ cup Marsala wine
- 8 oz. sliced fresh mushrooms
- 1 medium sweet red pepper, thinly sliced
- 1 medium onion, thinly sliced
- 1 can (14½ oz.) diced tomatoes, undrained
- ½ cup golden raisins
- 2 Tbsp. capers, drained
- ¼ cup chopped fresh basil
  Hot cooked couscous

1. In a large skillet, heat 1 Tbsp. olive oil over medium-high heat. Sprinkle chicken with salt and pepper; brown chicken on both sides in batches, adding oil as needed. Transfer chicken to a 5- or 6-qt. slow cooker.
2. Add wine to the skillet, stirring to loosen browned bits; pour into slow cooker. Stir mushrooms, red pepper, onion, tomatoes, raisins and capers into slow cooker.
3. Cook, covered, until the chicken and vegetables are tender, 4-5 hours. Sprinkle with basil before serving. Serve with hot cooked couscous.
1 serving: 250 cal., 12g fat (3g sat. fat), 76mg chol., 494mg sod., 13g carb. (9g sugars, 2g fiber), 23g pro. **Diabetic exchanges:** 3 lean meat, 1 vegetable, 1 fat, ½ starch.

SIMPLE SAUSAGE PASTA TOSS

Need a little mealtime inspiration? Grab a skillet and stir up some turkey sausage with tomatoes, garlic and olives. Toss everything with spaghetti, and sprinkle with Parmesan.

—*Taste of Home Test Kitchen*

Takes: 25 min. • **Makes:** 5 servings

- 8 oz. uncooked multigrain spaghetti
- ¼ cup seasoned bread crumbs
- 1 tsp. olive oil
- ¾ lb. Italian turkey sausage links, cut into ½-in. slices
- 1 garlic clove, minced
- 2 cans (14½ oz. each) no-salt-added diced tomatoes, undrained
- 1 can (2¼ oz.) sliced ripe olives, drained

1. Cook spaghetti according to package directions; drain. Meanwhile, in a large skillet, toss the bread crumbs with oil; cook and stir over medium heat until toasted. Remove from pan.
2. Add sausage to same pan; cook and stir over medium heat until no longer pink. Add garlic; cook 30-60 seconds longer. Stir in tomatoes and olives; heat through. Add spaghetti and toss to combine. Sprinkle with toasted bread crumbs before serving.
1⅔ cups: 340 cal., 10g fat (2g sat. fat), 41mg chol., 689mg sod., 44g carb. (6g sugars, 6g fiber), 21g pro. **Diabetic exchanges:** 3 lean meat, 2 starch, 1 vegetable, ½ fat.

WINE PAIRING

Montepulciano. This grape makes food-friendly, easy-to-drink wine across central and southern Italy. It's great with pasta and meat sauce. The wines from Abruzzo, northeast of Rome, are especially famous.

5i ⏱

MOIST LEMON HERB CHICKEN

I wanted a healthy, flavorful chicken recipe that was fast, easy and a real crowd-pleaser. I got lucky and hit the jackpot with this one!
—*Kali Wraspir, Lacey, WA*

Takes: 25 min. • **Makes:** 4 servings

- 4 boneless skinless chicken breast halves (6 oz. each)
- ½ tsp. salt
- ¼ tsp. pepper
- 1 Tbsp. olive oil
- 1 Tbsp. herbes de Provence
- 2 tsp. grated lemon zest
- 3 Tbsp. lemon juice

1. Sprinkle chicken with salt and pepper. In a large ovenproof skillet coated with cooking spray, brown chicken in oil. Sprinkle herbes de Provence and lemon zest over chicken; add lemon juice to pan.

2. Bake, uncovered, at 375° for until a thermometer reads 170°, 12-15 minutes.

Note: Look for herbes de Provence in the spice aisle.

1 chicken breast half : 220 cal., 7g fat (2g sat. fat), 94mg chol., 378mg sod., 2g carb. (0 sugars, 1g fiber), 35g pro. **Diabetic exchanges:** 5 lean meat, ½ fat.

TAPENADE-STUFFED CHICKEN BREASTS

I created this recipe for my husband, who absolutely loves olives. I usually make a larger batch of the olive tapenade and serve it with bread or crackers as a snack or appetizer.

—*Jessica Levinson, Nyack, NY*

Takes: 30 min. • Makes: 4 servings

- 4 oil-packed sun-dried tomatoes
- 4 pitted Greek olives
- 4 pitted Spanish olives
- 4 pitted ripe olives
- ¼ cup roasted sweet red peppers, drained
- 4 garlic cloves, minced
- 1 Tbsp. olive oil
- 2 tsp. balsamic vinegar
- 4 boneless skinless chicken breast halves (6 oz. each)
  Grated Parmesan cheese

1. Place the first 8 ingredients in a food processor; pulse until tomatoes and olives are coarsely chopped. Cut a pocket horizontally in the thickest part of each chicken breast. Fill with olive mixture; secure with toothpicks.

2. Lightly coat grill rack with cooking oil. Grill chicken, covered, over medium heat or broil 4 in. from heat 8-10 minutes on each side or until a thermometer inserted into the stuffing reads 165°. Sprinkle with cheese. Discard toothpicks before serving.

1 stuffed chicken breast half: 264 cal., 11g fat (2g sat. fat), 94mg chol., 367mg sod., 5g carb. (1g sugars, 1g fiber), 35g pro. **Diabetic exchanges:** 5 lean meat, 1 fat.

SKILLET CHICKEN WITH OLIVES

While I was visiting my cousin Lilliana in Italy, she made this heavenly chicken for lunch. Now it's a family favorite stateside, too.
—*Rosemarie Pisano, Revere, MA*

Takes: 20 min. • **Makes:** 4 servings

- 4 boneless skinless chicken thighs (about 1 lb.)
- 1 tsp. dried rosemary, crushed
- ½ tsp. pepper
- ¼ tsp. salt
- 1 Tbsp. olive oil
- ½ cup pimiento-stuffed olives, coarsely chopped
- ¼ cup white wine or chicken broth
- 1 Tbsp. drained capers, optional

1. Sprinkle the chicken with rosemary, pepper and salt. In a large skillet, heat oil over medium-high heat. Brown the chicken on both sides.

2. Add olives, wine and, if desired, capers. Reduce heat; simmer, covered, 2-3 minutes or until a thermometer inserted reads 170°.

1 serving: 237 cal., 15g fat (3g sat. fat), 76mg chol., 571mg sod., 2g carb. (0 sugars, 0 fiber), 21g pro. **Diabetic exchanges:** 3 lean meat, 2 fat.

READER RAVE

"Excellent flavor, easy and fast. This is sure to be a regular at the table."
—BJSILVEO, TASTEOFHOME.COM

MUSHROOM-STUFFED TURKEY TENDERLOINS

I love this recipe because it looks beautiful, tastes delicious and is a healthy alternative to traditional turkey and dressing. Chicken broth may be substituted if turkey broth is not available.

—Joyce Conway, Westerville, OH

- -

Prep: 30 min. • **Bake:** 15 min.
Makes: 4 servings

- 1 pkg. (8 oz.) **frozen artichoke hearts, thawed and chopped**
- ½ lb. **baby portobello mushrooms, chopped**
- 2½ cups **reduced-sodium turkey broth, divided**
- 2 Tbsp. **lemon juice**
- ¼ cup **panko (Japanese) bread crumbs**
- 1 pkg. (20 oz.) **turkey breast tenderloins**
- ½ tsp. **salt**
- ¼ tsp. **pepper**
- 2 Tbsp. **all-purpose flour**
- 1 tsp. **grated lemon zest**

1. Preheat oven to 400°. Place artichoke hearts, mushrooms, ½ cup broth and lemon juice in a large saucepan; bring to a boil. Reduce heat; simmer, uncovered, until mushrooms are tender and liquid is evaporated, 7-9 minutes. Stir in bread crumbs; cool slightly.

2. Cut each tenderloin horizontally through the center to within ¼ in. of the opposite edge; open flat. Using a sharp knife, remove white tendons. Cover with plastic wrap; pound each with a meat mallet to an even thickness. Remove plastic; spread tops with artichoke mixture. Starting at a long side, roll up jelly-roll style; tie at 3-in. intervals with kitchen string.

3. Place 1 in. apart in a 13x9-in. baking pan, seam side down; pour 1 cup broth over top. Sprinkle turkey with salt and pepper. Bake, uncovered, until a thermometer reads 165°, 15-20 minutes.

4. Remove turkey from pan; tent with foil and let stand 5 minutes. Meanwhile, in a small saucepan, whisk flour and remaining broth until smooth; stir in pan juices. Bring to a boil; cook and stir until thickened, 2-3 minutes.

5. Remove string; cut tenderloins into slices. Serve with gravy; sprinkle with lemon zest.

1 serving: 228 cal., 3g fat (0 sat. fat), 56mg chol., 776mg sod., 14g carb. (3g sugars, 4g fiber), 41g pro. **Diabetic exchanges:** 4 lean meat, 1 vegetable, ½ starch.

LEMON CHICKEN SKEWERS

This is the one chicken dish my son doesn't put ketchup on, so it must be good. You can make them on smaller skewers, too.

—*Kathy Lewis-Martinez, Spring Valley, CA*

Takes: 30 min. • **Makes:** 4 servings

- ¾ cup reduced-fat plain yogurt
- 1 Tbsp. lemon juice
- 1 Tbsp. olive oil
- 1 tsp. poultry seasoning
- 1 tsp. dried oregano
- ½ tsp. salt
- ½ tsp. grated lemon zest
- ¼ tsp. onion powder
- ¼ tsp. pepper
- 1 lb. boneless skinless chicken breasts, cut into strips

1. In a large bowl, combine all ingredients, tossing lightly. Cover and refrigerate for 10 minutes or up to 8 hours.
2. Remove chicken from marinade; discard marinade. Thread chicken onto 8 metal or soaked wooden skewers.
3. Place chicken on greased grill rack. Grill, covered, over medium heat or broil 4 in. from the heat 5-7 minutes or until chicken is no longer pink, turning once.

1 chicken skewer: 134 cal., 3g fat (1g sat. fat), 63mg chol., 120mg sod., 1g carb. (1g sugars, 0 fiber), 23g pro. **Diabetic exchanges:** 3 lean meat.

TURKEY SAUSAGE PITAS

I nicknamed my sandwich "Thor's Pita" because it's robust and lightning-quick. The ingredient amounts don't really matter. Use more or less depending on what you have.
—*Teresa Aleksandrov, Ypsilanti, MI*

- -

Takes: 20 min. • **Makes:** 4 servings

- 4 whole wheat pita breads (6 in.)
- 1 cup plain yogurt
- 2 green onions, chopped
- 2 Tbsp. minced fresh parsley
- 1 tsp. lemon juice
- 1 garlic clove, minced
- ¾ lb. Italian turkey sausage links or other sausage links of your choice, casings removed
- 1 medium cucumber, seeded and chopped
- 1 medium tomato, chopped
   Additional minced fresh parsley

1. Preheat oven to 325°. Wrap pita breads in foil; warm in oven while preparing toppings.
2. In a small bowl, mix the yogurt, green onions, parsley, lemon juice and garlic. In a large skillet, cook sausage over medium heat 4-6 minutes or until no longer pink, breaking into crumbles.
3. To assemble, spoon sausage over pitas. Top with cucumber, tomato and yogurt mixture; sprinkle with additional parsley.

1 open-faced sandwich: 309 cal., 9g fat (3g sat. fat), 39mg chol., 667mg sod., 42g carb. (5g sugars, 6g fiber), 19g pro. **Diabetic exchanges:** 3 starch, 2 lean meat.

MARRAKESH CHICKEN & COUSCOUS

I love to make fast dinners with boxed grains. They already have a flavor packet, and the sky's the limit on their possibilities. Here, I transformed couscous into a one-pot delight that transports you to a faraway land of exotic flavor! My family loves this recipe.
—*Devon Delaney, Westport, CT*

- -

Takes: 30 min. • **Makes:** 6 servings

- 1 Tbsp. olive oil
- 1 lb. boneless skinless chicken thighs, cut into 1¼-in. pieces
- 1 can (14½ oz.) diced tomatoes, undrained
- 1 jar (7½ oz.) marinated quartered artichoke hearts, drained
- ¼ cup lemon juice
- 2 Tbsp. apricot preserves
- ½ tsp. salt
- ½ tsp. ground cumin
- ¼ tsp. crushed red pepper flakes
- ⅛ tsp. ground cinnamon
- 1 pkg. (5.8 oz.) roasted garlic and olive oil couscous
   Chopped smoked almonds, optional

1. In a 6-qt. stockpot, heat oil over medium-high heat. Brown chicken on both sides. Stir in tomatoes, artichoke hearts, lemon juice, preserves, salt, spices and seasoning packet from couscous; bring to a boil. Reduce heat; simmer, covered, 10 minutes to allow flavors to develop and for chicken to cook through.
2. Stir in couscous; remove from heat. Let stand, covered, 5 minutes. If desired, sprinkle with almonds.

1⅓ cups: 326 cal., 14g fat (3g sat. fat), 50mg chol., 751mg sod., 30g carb. (8g sugars, 2g fiber), 19g pro. **Diabetic exchanges:** 3 lean meat, 2 starch, ½ fat.

GREEK GODDESS PASTA BAKE

Here's a simple, healthy casserole made with easy-to-find ingredients. Take it to your next potluck or add a green salad and a crusty loaf of bread for a quick weeknight meal.
—*Anne Taglienti, Kennett Square, PA*

Prep: 20 min. • **Bake:** 25 min.
Makes: 8 servings

- 1 pkg. (13¼ oz.) whole wheat penne pasta
- 4 cups cubed cooked chicken breast
- 1 can (29 oz.) tomato sauce
- 1 can (14½ oz.) no-salt-added diced tomatoes, drained
- 1 pkg. (10 oz.) frozen chopped spinach, thawed and squeezed dry
- 2 cans (2¼ oz. each) sliced ripe olives, drained
- ¼ cup chopped red onion
- 2 Tbsp. chopped green pepper
- 1 tsp. dried basil
- 1 tsp. dried oregano
- ½ cup shredded part-skim mozzarella cheese
- ½ cup crumbled feta cheese

1. Preheat oven to 400°. Cook the pasta according to package directions; drain. In a large bowl, combine the pasta, chicken, tomato sauce, tomatoes, spinach, olives, onion, green pepper, basil and oregano.
2. Transfer to a 13x9-in. baking dish coated with cooking spray. Sprinkle with cheeses. Bake, uncovered, 25-30 minutes or until heated through and cheese is melted.
Freeze option: Cool unbaked casserole; cover and freeze. To use, partially thaw in refrigerator overnight. Remove from the refrigerator 30 minutes before baking. Preheat oven to 400°. Bake casserole as directed, increasing time as needed to heat through and for a thermometer inserted in center to read 165°.
1½ cups: 383 cal., 8g fat (2g sat. fat), 62mg chol., 776mg sod., 45g carb. (4g sugars, 9g fiber), 34g pro.

CHICKEN SAUSAGE & ORZO

Light, quick and tasty—that's my kind of recipe. If you like a milder dish, use less crushed red pepper. Or to really bring on the heat, add more.
—*Debra Paquette, Upton, MA*

Takes: 30 min. • **Makes:** 5 servings

- 1 cup uncooked orzo pasta
- 1 pkg. (12 oz.) fully cooked Italian chicken sausage links, cut into ¾-in. slices
- 3 tsp. olive oil, divided
- 1 cup chopped onion
- 3 garlic cloves, minced
- ¼ cup white wine or chicken broth
- 1 can (28 oz.) whole tomatoes, drained and chopped
- 2 Tbsp. minced fresh parsley
- 1 Tbsp. capers, drained
- ½ tsp. dried oregano
- ½ tsp. dried basil
- ¼ tsp. crushed red pepper flakes
- ¼ tsp. pepper
- ½ cup crumbled feta cheese

1. Cook the pasta according to package directions; drain.
2. Meanwhile, brown the sausages in 2 tsp. oil in a large skillet. Remove and keep warm. In the same pan, saute onion in remaining oil until tender. Add garlic and wine; cook 1 minute longer, stirring to loosen browned bits from pan.
3. Stir in the tomatoes, parsley, capers, oregano, basil, pepper flakes and pepper. Bring to a boil. Reduce heat; simmer, uncovered, for 5 minutes. Stir in orzo and sausage; heat through. Sprinkle with cheese.
1 cup: 363 cal., 11g fat (3g sat. fat), 58mg chol., 838mg sod., 42g carb. (7g sugars, 3g fiber), 21g pro. **Diabetic exchanges:** 2 starch, 2 lean meat, 2 vegetable, 1 fat.

TERRIFIC TURKEY MEAT LOAF

You'll love this moist, tender entree. Not only is it loaded with flavor, it's low in carbohydrates and saturated fat.
—*Wanda Bannister, New Bern, NC*

- -

Prep: 15 min. • **Bake:** 50 min.
Makes: 4 servings

1	large egg white, lightly beaten
½	cup oat bran
½	cup chopped green pepper
¼	cup finely chopped onion
3	Tbsp. ketchup
2	Tbsp. chopped ripe olives
1	Tbsp. Worcestershire sauce
1	garlic clove, minced
½	tsp. Dijon mustard
¼	tsp. celery salt
¼	tsp. dried marjoram
¼	tsp. rubbed sage
¼	tsp. pepper
1	lb. ground turkey

1. Preheat oven to 375°. In a large bowl, combine all ingredients except turkey. Add turkey; mix lightly but thoroughly. Pat into a loaf in an 11x7-in. baking dish coated with cooking spray.
2. Bake, uncovered, until a thermometer reads 165°, 50-60 minutes.

1 serving: 226 cal., 10g fat (2g sat. fat), 75mg chol., 381mg sod., 14g carb. (5g sugars, 3g fiber), 25g pro. **Diabetic exchanges:** 3 lean meat, ½ starch.

WINE PAIRING

Cabernet Franc. Juicy and light-bodied, herby and not very tannic, it'll make the savory herbs and vegetables pop without overwhelming the meat loaf's delicate flavors.

PARMESAN CHICKEN WITH ARTICHOKE HEARTS

I've liked the chicken and artichoke combo for a long time. Here's my own lemony twist. With all the praise it gets, this dinner is so much fun to serve.
—*Carly Giles, Hoquiam, WA*

- -

Prep: 20 min. • **Bake:** 20 min.
Makes: 4 servings

4	boneless skinless chicken breast halves (6 oz. each)
3	tsp. olive oil, divided
1	tsp. dried rosemary, crushed
½	tsp. dried thyme
½	tsp. pepper
2	cans (14 oz. each) water-packed artichoke hearts, drained and quartered
1	medium onion, coarsely chopped
½	cup white wine or reduced-sodium chicken broth
2	garlic cloves, chopped
¼	cup shredded Parmesan cheese
1	lemon, cut into 8 slices
2	green onions, thinly sliced

1. Preheat oven to 375°. Place chicken in a 15x10x1-in. baking pan coated with cooking spray; drizzle with 1½ tsp. oil. In a small bowl, mix rosemary, thyme and pepper; sprinkle half over chicken.

2. In a large bowl, combine artichoke hearts, onion, white wine, garlic, remaining oil and remaining herb mixture; toss to coat. Arrange around chicken. Sprinkle chicken with cheese; top with lemon slices.

3. Roast until a thermometer inserted in chicken reads 165°, 20-25 minutes. Sprinkle with green onions.

1 chicken breast half with ¾ cup artichoke mixture: 339 cal., 9g fat (3g sat. fat), 98mg chol., 667mg sod., 18g carb. (2g sugars, 1g fiber), 42g pro. **Diabetic exchanges:** 5 lean meat, 1 vegetable, 1 fat, ½ starch.

5i

CHICKEN PESTO ROLL-UPS

One night I looked in the refrigerator and thought, *What can I make with chicken, cheese, mushrooms and pesto?* This pretty dish was the result. Add Italian bread and fruit salad and you have a meal!
—Melissa Nordmann, Mobile, AL

- -

Prep: 15 min. • **Bake:** 30 min.
Makes: 4 servings

- 4 boneless skinless chicken breast halves (6 oz. each)
- ½ cup prepared pesto, divided
- 1 lb. medium fresh mushrooms, sliced
- 4 slices reduced-fat provolone cheese, halved

1. Preheat oven to 350°. Pound chicken breasts with a meat mallet to ¼-in. thickness. Spread ¼ cup pesto over chicken breasts.
2. Coarsely chop half the sliced mushrooms; scatter remaining sliced mushrooms in a 15x10x1-in. baking pan coated with cooking spray. Top each chicken breast with a fourth of the chopped mushrooms and a halved cheese slice. Roll up chicken from a short side; secure with toothpicks. Place seam side down on top of the sliced mushrooms.
3. Bake, covered, until chicken is no longer pink, 25-30 minutes. Preheat broiler; top chicken with remaining pesto and remaining halved cheese slices. Broil until cheese is melted and browned, 3-5 minutes longer. Discard toothpicks.

1 stuffed chicken breast half: 374 cal., 17g fat (5g sat. fat), 104mg chol., 582mg sod., 7g carb. (1g sugars, 1g fiber), 44g pro. **Diabetic exchanges:** 5 lean meat, 2 fat.

READER RAVE

"The pesto chicken roll-ups delivered a rather new taste sensation. It was a pleasant departure from many of what has become too common in the way of chicken dishes. I suggest giving this unique recipe a try."
—CATBIRD513, TASTEOFHOME.COM

ONE-POT CHICKEN PESTO PASTA

When my garden basil goes nuts, I make pesto and keep it frozen in small containers for the right opportunity, such as this saucy one-pot chicken with pasta.

—*Kimberly Fenwick, Hobart, IN*

- -

Takes: 30 min. • **Makes:** 4 servings

- 1 lb. boneless skinless chicken thighs, cut into 1-in. pieces
- 1 tsp. salt-free seasoning blend
- 2 tsp. olive oil
- 1 can (14½ oz.) reduced-sodium chicken broth
- 2 Tbsp. lemon juice
- 1 cup uncooked gemelli or spiral pasta
- 2 cups fresh broccoli florets
- 1 cup frozen peas
- ⅓ cup prepared pesto

1. Toss chicken with seasoning blend. In a large nonstick skillet, heat oil over medium-high heat. Add chicken and brown evenly; remove from pan.

2. In same pan, combine the broth and lemon juice; bring to a boil, stirring to loosen browned bits from pan. Stir in the pasta; return to a boil. Reduce heat; simmer, covered, 10 minutes.

3. Add broccoli; cook, covered, 5 minutes. Return chicken to pan; cook, covered, until pasta is tender and chicken is no longer pink, 2-3 minutes longer, stirring occasionally. Add peas; heat through. Stir in pesto.

1 cup: 404 cal., 18g fat (4g sat. fat), 76mg chol., 646mg sod., 29g carb. (4g sugars, 4g fiber), 30g pro. **Diabetic exchanges:** 3 lean meat, 2 starch, 2 fat.

RATATOUILLE CHICKEN

I loaded all the fresh produce I could find into this speedy chicken dinner. Serve it on its own or over pasta.
—*Judy Armstrong, Prairieville, LA*

- -

Prep: 25 min. • **Bake:** 1 hour
Makes: 6 servings

3	Japanese eggplants (about 1 lb.)
4	plum tomatoes
1	medium sweet yellow pepper
1	medium sweet red pepper
1	medium onion
1	can (14 oz.) water-packed artichoke hearts, drained and quartered
2	Tbsp. minced fresh thyme
2	Tbsp. capers, drained
2	Tbsp. olive oil
2	garlic cloves, minced
1	tsp. Creole seasoning, divided
1½	lbs. boneless skinless chicken breasts, cubed
1	cup white wine or chicken broth
¼	cup grated Asiago cheese
	Hot cooked pasta, optional

1. Preheat oven to 350°. Cut eggplants, tomatoes, peppers and onion into ¾-in. pieces; transfer to a large bowl. Stir in artichoke hearts, thyme, capers, oil, garlic and ½ tsp. Creole seasoning.

2. Sprinkle chicken with remaining Creole seasoning. Transfer chicken to a 13x9-in. baking dish coated with cooking spray; spoon vegetable mixture over chicken. Drizzle wine over vegetables.

3. Bake, covered, 30 minutes. Uncover; bake until chicken is no longer pink and vegetables are tender, 30-45 minutes longer. Sprinkle with cheese. If desired, serve with pasta.

1⅔ cups: 252 cal., 9g fat (2g sat. fat), 67mg chol., 468mg sod., 15g carb. (4g sugars, 4g fiber), 28g pro. **Diabetic exchanges:** 3 lean meat, 1 starch, 1 fat.

MEDITERRANEAN TURKEY POTPIES

Everyone will love these wonderful stick-to-the-ribs potpies with a tasty Mediterranean twist. I always use the leftovers from our big holiday turkey to prepare this recipe. I think my family enjoys the potpies more than the original feast!

—*Marie Rizzio, Interlochen, MI*

Prep: 30 min. • **Bake:** 20 min.
Makes: 6 servings

- 2   **medium onions, thinly sliced**
- 2   **tsp. olive oil**
- 3   **garlic cloves, minced**
- 3   **Tbsp. all-purpose flour**
- 1¼ **cups reduced-sodium chicken broth**
- 1   **can (14½ oz.) no-salt-added diced tomatoes, undrained**
- 2½ **cups cubed cooked turkey breast**
- 1   **can (14 oz.) water-packed artichoke hearts, rinsed, drained and sliced**
- ½   **cup pitted ripe olives, halved**
- ¼   **cup sliced pepperoncini**
- 1   **Tbsp. minced fresh oregano or 1 tsp. dried oregano**
- ¼   **tsp. pepper**

CRUST

- 1   **loaf (1 lb.) frozen pizza dough, thawed**
- 1   **large egg white**
- 1   **tsp. minced fresh oregano or ¼ tsp. dried oregano**

1. In a Dutch oven, saute onions in oil until tender. Add garlic; cook 2 minutes longer. In a small bowl, whisk flour and broth until smooth; gradually stir into onion mixture. Stir in tomatoes. Bring to a boil; cook and stir for 2 minutes or until thickened.

2. Remove from the heat. Add the turkey, artichokes, olives, pepperoncini, oregano and pepper; stir gently. Divide turkey mixture among six 10-oz. ramekins.

3. Roll out 2 oz. dough to fit each ramekin (reserve remaining dough for another use). Cut slits in dough; place over filling. Press to seal edges. Combine egg white and oregano; brush over dough.

4. Place ramekins on a baking sheet. Bake at 425° for 18-22 minutes or until crusts are golden brown.

1 potpie: 326 cal., 4g fat (1g sat. fat), 50mg chol., 699mg sod., 43g carb. (7g sugars, 3g fiber), 26g pro. **Diabetic exchanges:** 2 starch, 2 lean meat, 2 vegetable, ½ fat.

MEDITERRANEAN CHICKEN

As special as it is simple to prepare, this moist, flavorful chicken is dressed in tomatoes, olives and capers. It's always a knockout main dish at my house.

—*Mary Relyea, Canastota, NY*

- -

Takes: 25 min. • **Makes:** 4 servings

4	boneless skinless chicken breast halves (6 oz. each)
¼	tsp. salt
¼	tsp. pepper
3	Tbsp. olive oil
1	pint grape tomatoes
16	pitted Greek or ripe olives, sliced
3	Tbsp. capers, drained

1. Preheat oven to 475°. Sprinkle chicken with salt and pepper. In a large ovenproof skillet, cook chicken in oil over medium heat until golden brown, 2-3 minutes on each side. Add the tomatoes, olives and capers.

2. Bake, uncovered, until a thermometer reads 170°, 10-14 minutes.

1 serving: 336 cal., 18g fat (3g sat. fat), 94mg chol., 631mg sod., 6g carb. (3g sugars, 2g fiber), 36g pro. **Diabetic exchanges:** 5 lean meat, 3 fat, 1 vegetable.

TANDOORI-STYLE CHICKEN WITH CUCUMBER MELON RELISH

We all need a quick meal that's delicious yet healthy. I marinate the chicken before I leave for when work. When I get home, I grill the chicken and make the relish. My husband loves the spicy flavor. To amp up the heat, add more crushed red pepper flakes.

—*Naylet LaRochelle, Miami, FL*

Prep: 20 min. + marinating • **Grill:** 15 min.
Makes: 4 servings

1½ **cups reduced-fat plain yogurt**
2 **Tbsp. lemon juice, divided**
1½ **tsp. garam masala or curry powder**
½ **tsp. salt**
¼ **to ½ tsp. crushed red pepper flakes**
4 **boneless skinless chicken breast halves (6 oz. each)**
1½ **cups chopped cantaloupe**
½ **cup chopped seeded peeled cucumber**
2 **green onions, finely chopped**
2 **Tbsp. minced fresh cilantro**
1 **Tbsp. minced fresh mint**
¼ **cup toasted sliced almonds, optional**

1. In a small bowl, whisk yogurt, 1 Tbsp. lemon juice, garam masala, salt and pepper flakes until blended. Pour 1 cup marinade into a large bowl. Add chicken; turn to coat. Cover; refrigerate up to 6 hours. Cover and refrigerate remaining marinade.

2. For relish, in a small bowl, mix cantaloupe, cucumber, green onions, cilantro, mint and remaining lemon juice.

3. Drain chicken, discarding marinade. Grill chicken, covered, on a lightly oiled rack over medium heat or broil 4 in. from heat until a thermometer reads 165°, 6-8 minutes on each side. Serve with relish and reserved marinade. If desired, sprinkle with almonds.

Note: To toast nuts, bake in a shallow pan in a 350° oven for 5-10 minutes, or cook them in a skillet over low heat until lightly browned, stirring occasionally.

1 serving: 247 cal., 5g fat (2g sat. fat), 98mg chol., 332mg sod., 10g carb. (9g sugars, 1g fiber), 38g pro. **Diabetic exchanges:** 5 lean meat, ½ starch.

SPINACH-STUFFED CHICKEN BREASTS

After retiring to Tennessee, we missed the tastes of Chicago. Here's my version of a Greek entree we enjoyed.
—*Beverly Hemmerich, Fairfield Glade, TN*

- -

Prep: 25 min. • **Bake:** 55 min.
Makes: 6 servings

- 1 medium onion, chopped
- 1 garlic clove, minced
- ¼ tsp. crushed red pepper flakes
- 4 tsp. olive oil, divided
- 1 pkg. (10 oz.) frozen chopped spinach, thawed and squeezed dry
- 2 oz. crumbled feta cheese
- ¼ cup grated Parmesan cheese
- 6 bone-in chicken breast halves (9 oz. each)
- ¼ cup lemon juice
- 1 tsp. dried basil
- 1 tsp. dried oregano
- ½ tsp. salt
- ½ tsp. garlic powder
- ¼ tsp. pepper

1. In a nonstick skillet, saute the onion, garlic and pepper flakes in 2 tsp. oil until tender. Add spinach; cook and stir for 2 minutes or until heated through. Remove from the heat. Stir in cheeses.

2. Preheat oven to 400°. Cut a pocket in each chicken breast by slicing horizontally almost to the bone. Fill each pocket with ¼ cup spinach mixture. Place chicken in a 13x9-in. baking dish. In a small bowl, whisk the lemon juice, basil, oregano, salt, garlic powder, pepper and remaining oil; brush over chicken.

3. Cover and bake for 45 minutes. Uncover; bake 10-15 minutes longer or until a thermometer reads 170°. Remove skin before serving.

1 serving: 248 cal., 8g fat (3g sat. fat), 92mg chol., 490mg sod., 6g carb. (2g sugars, 2g fiber), 37g pro. **Diabetic exchanges:** 5 lean meat, 1 vegetable, 1 fat.

CHUNKY CHICKEN CACCIATORE

This recipe is so versatile! Look in your fridge for anything else you want to throw in, like red pepper, mushrooms, extra zucchini—you name it. And if you're a vegetarian, go ahead and leave out the chicken.
—*Stephanie Loaiza, Layton, UT*

- -

Prep: 10 min. • **Cook:** 4 hours
Makes: 6 servings

- 6 boneless skinless chicken thighs (about 1½ lbs.)
- 2 medium zucchini, cut into 1-in. slices
- 1 medium green pepper, cut into 1-in. pieces
- 1 large sweet onion, coarsely chopped
- ½ tsp. dried oregano
- 1 jar (24 oz.) garden-style spaghetti sauce
  Hot cooked spaghetti
  Sliced ripe olives and shredded Parmesan cheese, optional

1. Place chicken and vegetables in a 3-qt. slow cooker; sprinkle with oregano. Pour sauce over top. Cook, covered, on low 4-5 hours or until chicken is tender.

2. Remove chicken; break up slightly with 2 forks. Return to slow cooker. Serve with spaghetti. If desired, top with olives and Parmesan cheese.

Freeze option: Place the first 6 ingredients in a freezer container and freeze. To use, place container in refrigerator 48 hours or until contents are completely thawed. Cook and serve as directed.

1 serving: 285 cal., 11g fat (2g sat. fat), 76mg chol., 507mg sod., 21g carb. (14g sugars, 3g fiber), 24g pro. **Diabetic exchanges:** 3 lean meat, 1½ starch.

NORTH AFRICAN CHICKEN & RICE

I'm always looking to try recipes from different cultures and this one is a huge favorite. We love the spice combinations. This cooks equally well in a slow cooker or pressure cooker.

—*Courtney Stultz, Weir, KS*

Prep: 10 min. • **Cook:** 4 hours
Makes: 8 servings

- 1 **medium onion, diced**
- 1 **Tbsp. olive oil**
- 8 **boneless skinless chicken thighs (about 2 lbs.)**
- 1 **Tbsp. minced fresh cilantro**
- 1 **tsp. ground turmeric**
- 1 **tsp. paprika**
- 1 **tsp. sea salt**
- ½ **tsp. pepper**
- ½ **tsp. ground cinnamon**
- ½ **tsp. chili powder**
- 1 **cup golden raisins**
- ½ **to 1 cup chopped pitted green olives**
- 1 **medium lemon, sliced**
- 2 **garlic cloves, minced**
- ½ **cup chicken broth or water**
- 4 **cups hot cooked brown rice**

In a 3- or 4-qt. slow cooker, combine onion and oil. Place chicken thighs on top of onion; sprinkle with next 7 ingredients. Top with raisins, olives, lemon and garlic. Add broth. Cook, covered, on low until chicken is tender, 4-5 hours. Serve with hot cooked rice.
1 serving: 386 cal., 13g fat (3g sat. fat), 76mg chol., 556mg sod., 44g carb. (12g sugars, 3g fiber), 25g pro.

CHICKEN SAUSAGE & ZUCCHINI POCKETS

Chicken sausage comes in many flavors, so I try different ones when I make these pita pockets, inspired by the Greek gyro, with fresh basil and veggies.

—*Christina Price, Colorado Springs, CO*

Takes: 25 min. • **Makes:** 4 servings

- 6 **tsp. olive oil, divided**
- 1 **pkg. (12 oz.) fully cooked roasted garlic chicken sausage links or flavor of your choice, sliced**
- 1 **cup sliced fresh mushrooms**
- 1 **small onion, halved and sliced**
- 1 **medium zucchini, halved lengthwise and sliced**
- 1 **medium yellow summer squash, halved lengthwise and sliced**
- 3 **Tbsp. chopped fresh basil**
- 8 **whole wheat pita pocket halves, warmed**
  Sliced tomato and plain Greek yogurt, optional

1. In a large nonstick skillet, heat 2 tsp. oil over medium-high heat. Add sausage; cook and stir 4-6 minutes or until lightly browned. Remove from pan.

2. In same skillet, heat 2 tsp. oil over medium-high heat. Add mushrooms and onion; cook and stir 4-6 minutes or until tender. Remove from pan.

3. Add remaining oil to pan. Add zucchini and yellow squash; cook and stir 3-5 minutes or until tender. Stir in basil, sliced sausage and mushroom mixture; heat through. Serve in pitas. If desired, add tomato and yogurt.

2 filled pita halves: 376 cal., 16g fat (3g sat. fat), 70mg chol., 736mg sod., 39g carb. (5g sugars, 6g fiber), 22g pro. **Diabetic exchanges:** 3 lean meat, 2 starch, 1½ fat, 1 vegetable.

CHICKEN WITH PEACH-CUCUMBER SALSA

To keep our kitchen cool, we grill chicken outdoors and serve it with a minty peach salsa that can easily be made ahead.

—*Janie Colle, Hutchinson, KS*

Takes: 25 min. • **Makes:** 4 servings

- 1½ **cups chopped peeled fresh peaches (about 2 medium)**
- ¾ **cup chopped cucumber**
- 4 **Tbsp. peach preserves, divided**
- 3 **Tbsp. finely chopped red onion**
- 1 **tsp. minced fresh mint**
- ¾ **tsp. salt, divided**
- 4 **boneless skinless chicken breast halves (6 oz. each)**
- ¼ **tsp. pepper**

1. For salsa, in a small bowl, combine the peaches, cucumber, 2 Tbsp. peach preserves, onion, mint and ¼ tsp. salt.

2. Sprinkle chicken breasts with pepper and remaining salt. On a lightly greased grill rack, grill chicken, covered, over medium heat for 5 minutes. Turn; grill 7-9 minutes longer or until a thermometer reads 165°, brushing tops occasionally with remaining preserves. Serve with salsa.

1 chicken breast half with ½ cup salsa: 261 cal., 4g fat (1g sat. fat), 94mg chol., 525mg sod., 20g carb. (17g sugars, 1g fiber), 35g pro. **Diabetic exchanges:** 5 lean meat, ½ starch, ½ fruit.

WINE PAIRING

Moscato. Sweet, light and fun with its slightly spritzy *frizzante* texture, Moscato is packed with peachy flavor. The mint in the salsa will offset it nicely—as would a little fresh basil.

CHICKEN & BARLEY SAUTE

Barley is a chewier and more flavorful alternative to white rice. Try making the switch when you whip up this quick and colorful garden-fresh stir-fry.
—Taste of Home *Test Kitchen*

Takes: 30 min. • **Makes:** 4 servings

- 2 cups water
- 1 cup quick-cooking barley
- 1 lb. boneless skinless chicken breasts, cubed
- 3 tsp. olive oil, divided
- 1 medium onion, chopped
- 2 medium zucchini, chopped
- 2 garlic cloves, minced
- 1 tsp. dried oregano
- ½ tsp. dried basil
- ¼ tsp. salt
- ¼ tsp. pepper
  Dash crushed red pepper flakes
- 2 plum tomatoes, chopped
- ½ cup pitted Greek olives, chopped
- 1 Tbsp. minced fresh parsley

1. In a small saucepan, bring water to a boil. Stir in barley. Reduce heat; cover and simmer for 10-12 minutes or until barley is tender. Remove from heat; let stand for 5 minutes.
2. Meanwhile, in a large skillet or wok, stir-fry chicken in 2 tsp. olive oil until no longer pink. Remove and keep warm.
3. Stir-fry chopped onion in remaining oil for 3 minutes. Add the zucchini, garlic, oregano, basil, salt, pepper and pepper flakes; stir-fry 2-4 minutes longer or until vegetables are crisp-tender. Add the chicken, tomatoes, olives and parsley. Serve with barley.

1 cup chicken mixture with ¾ cup barley: 403 cal., 12g fat (2g sat. fat), 63mg chol., 498mg sod., 44g carb. (5g sugars, 11g fiber), 31g pro. **Diabetic exchanges:** 3 lean meat, 2 starch, 2 fat, 1 vegetable.

PELOPONNESIAN CHICKEN PASTA

We love a homemade meal at the end of the day. But the prep involved? Not so much. My Greek-inspired pasta is lemony, herby and, thankfully, easy.
—Roxanne Chan, Albany, CA

Prep: 30 min. • **Cook:** 10 min.
Makes: 4 servings

- 1 can (14½ oz.) reduced-sodium chicken broth
- 1 can (14½ oz.) no-salt-added diced tomatoes, undrained
- ¾ lb. boneless skinless chicken breasts, cut into 1-in. pieces
- ½ cup white wine or water
- 1 garlic clove, minced
- ½ tsp. dried oregano
- 4 oz. multigrain thin spaghetti
- 1 jar (7½ oz.) marinated quartered artichoke hearts, drained and coarsely chopped
- 2 cups fresh baby spinach
- ¼ cup roasted sweet red pepper strips
- ¼ cup sliced ripe olives
- 1 green onion, finely chopped
- 2 Tbsp. minced fresh parsley
- ½ tsp. grated lemon zest
- 2 Tbsp. lemon juice
- 1 Tbsp. olive oil
- ½ tsp. pepper
  Crumbled reduced-fat feta cheese, optional

1. In a large skillet, combine the first 6 ingredients; add spaghetti. Bring to a boil. Cook until chicken is no longer pink and spaghetti is tender, 5-7 minutes.
2. Stir in artichoke hearts, spinach, red pepper, olives, green onion, parsley, lemon zest, lemon juice, oil and pepper. Cook and stir until spinach is wilted, 2-3 minutes. If desired, sprinkle with cheese.

1½ cups: 373 cal., 15g fat (3g sat. fat), 47mg chol., 658mg sod., 30g carb. (8g sugars, 4g fiber), 25g pro. **Diabetic exchanges:** 2 starch, 2 lean meat, 2 fat, 1 vegetable.

SPANISH TURKEY TENDERLOINS

If you're hungry for warm-weather fare, try these tenderloins. The grilled turkey and the bright, sunny colors of the relish look and taste like summer.
—*Roxanne Chan, Albany, CA*

Prep: 20 min. • **Grill:** 15 min.
Makes: 6 servings

1 pkg. (20 oz.) turkey breast tenderloins
1 Tbsp. olive oil
½ tsp. salt
½ tsp. pepper
¼ tsp. paprika

RELISH

1 plum tomato, chopped
1 large navel orange, peeled, sectioned and chopped
¼ cup sliced pimiento-stuffed olives
1 green onion, finely chopped
2 Tbsp. minced fresh oregano or 2 tsp. dried oregano
2 Tbsp. sliced almonds
2 Tbsp. minced fresh parsley
1 large garlic clove, minced
1 Tbsp. capers, drained
1 tsp. lemon juice
½ tsp. grated lemon zest
¼ tsp. salt

1. Rub turkey with oil; sprinkle with salt, pepper and paprika.
2. Grill, covered, over medium heat or broil 4 in. from the heat, turning occasionally, 15-20 minutes or until a thermometer reads 170°. Let stand for 5 minutes before slicing.
3. Meanwhile, in a small bowl, combine the relish ingredients. Serve with turkey.
3 oz. cooked turkey with ¼ cup relish: 163 cal., 6g fat (1g sat. fat), 46mg chol., 510mg sod., 6g carb. (3g sugars, 1g fiber), 23g pro. **Diabetic exchanges:** 3 lean meat, ½ starch, ½ fat.

SLOW-COOKED GREEK CHICKEN DINNER

I got this recipe from my sister, and my family just loves how good it makes the kitchen smell. The amount of garlic might seem high, but you get every bit of the flavor without it overpowering the other ingredients.
—*Terri Christensen, Montague, MI*

Prep: 25 min. • **Cook:** 5 hours
Makes: 6 servings

6 medium Yukon Gold potatoes, quartered
1 broiler/fryer chicken (3½ lbs.), cut up and skin removed
2 large onions, quartered
1 whole garlic bulb, separated and peeled
3 tsp. dried oregano
1 tsp. salt
¾ tsp. pepper
½ cup plus 1 Tbsp. water, divided
1 Tbsp. olive oil
4 tsp. cornstarch

1. Place potatoes in a 5-qt. slow cooker. Add chicken, onions and garlic; sprinkle with seasonings. Pour ½ cup water over top. Drizzle with oil. Cook, covered, on low until chicken and vegetables are tender, 5-6 hours.
2. In a bowl, mix cornstarch and remaining water until smooth. Remove chicken and vegetables from slow cooker; keep warm. Strain cooking juices into a small saucepan; skim fat. Bring juices to a boil. Stir cornstarch mixture; stir into juices. Bring to a boil; cook and stir until thickened, 1-2 minutes. Serve with chicken and vegetables.
1 serving: 404 cal., 9g fat (2g sat. fat), 86mg chol., 482mg sod., 46g carb. (4g sugars, 6g fiber), 34g pro. **Diabetic exchanges:** 4 lean meat, 3 starch, ½ fat.

EASY CHICKEN & RICE

This quick-to-fix recipe was a perennial favorite with my friends during our college years, and it's still a favorite of mine now. I've also added olives and onions to the mix to give it a little something extra.
—*Caitlin Chaney, Tampa, FL*

- -

Takes: 30 min. • **Makes:** 4 servings

¾	lb. boneless skinless chicken breasts, cubed
1¼	tsp. Greek seasoning
1	Tbsp. olive oil
1	cup sliced fresh mushrooms
1	can (14½ oz.) no-salt-added diced tomatoes, undrained
1	can (14 oz.) water-packed quartered artichoke hearts, drained
2	cups cooked brown rice
¼	cup crumbled feta cheese

1. Toss chicken with Greek seasoning. In a large skillet, heat oil over medium-high heat. Add chicken; cook and stir until lightly browned. Add mushrooms; cook and stir 2 minutes longer.

2. Stir in tomatoes and artichoke hearts. Bring to a boil. Reduce heat; simmer, covered, for 8-12 minutes or until chicken is cooked through. Serve with rice. Top with cheese.

1 cup chicken mixture with ½ cup rice and 1 Tbsp. cheese: 309 cal., 7g fat (2g sat. fat), 51mg chol., 704mg sod., 34g carb. (4g sugars, 4g fiber), 25g pro. **Diabetic exchanges:** 3 lean meat, 2 vegetable, 1½ starch, 1 fat.

ARTICHOKE CHICKEN PASTA

Here's a colorful, delicious chicken dish that's easy enough for busy weeknights, yet special enough for guests. Oregano, garlic and a light wine sauce add lovely flavor.
—*Cathy Dick, Roanoke, VA*

Takes: 30 min. • **Makes:** 4 servings

- 6 oz. uncooked fettuccine
- 2 tsp. all-purpose flour
- ⅓ cup dry white wine or broth
- ¼ cup reduced-sodium chicken broth
- 3 tsp. olive oil, divided
- 1 lb. boneless skinless chicken breasts, cut into thin strips
- ½ cup fresh broccoli florets
- ½ cup sliced fresh mushrooms
- ½ cup cherry tomatoes, halved
- 2 garlic cloves, minced
- 1 can (14 oz.) water-packed artichoke hearts, drained and halved
- ½ tsp. salt
- ½ tsp. dried oregano
- 1 Tbsp. minced fresh parsley
- 1 Tbsp. shredded Parmesan cheese

1. Cook fettuccine according to package directions; drain.

2. Meanwhile, in a small bowl, mix flour, white wine and broth until smooth. In a large skillet coated with cooking spray, heat 2 tsp. olive oil over medium heat. Add chicken; cook and stir until no longer pink, 2-4 minutes. Remove from pan.

3. In same skillet, heat remaining oil over medium-high heat. Add broccoli; cook and stir 2 minutes. Add mushrooms, tomatoes and garlic; cook and stir 2 minutes longer. Stir in artichoke hearts, salt, oregano and flour mixture. Bring to a boil; cook and stir until thickened, 1-2 minutes.

4. Add fettuccine, chicken and parsley; heat through, tossing to combine. Sprinkle with Parmesan cheese.

2 cups: 378 cal., 8g fat (2g sat. fat), 64mg chol., 668mg sod., 41g carb. (2g sugars, 2g fiber), 33g pro. **Diabetic exchanges:** 3 lean meat, 2 starch, 2 vegetable, 1 fat.

TURKEY-STUFFED BANANA PEPPERS

If you're looking for a ground turkey recipe that delivers, this is the one! The filling is flavorful and the peppers add some nice heat. You can easily stuff them ahead of time and bake them up when you're ready.
—*Ola Snow, Powell, OH*

- -

Prep: 40 min. • **Bake:** 45 min.
Makes: 4 servings

- 8 **large banana peppers**
- ½ **tsp. olive oil**
- 1 **small onion, chopped**
- 2 **garlic cloves, minced**
- 3 **Tbsp. minced fresh basil or 1 Tbsp. dried basil**
- 8 **pitted Greek olives, sliced**
- ⅓ **cup crumbled feta cheese**
- ¼ **cup dry bread crumbs**
- ¼ **cup water**
- ¼ **cup egg substitute**
- ¼ **tsp. pepper**
- ¾ **lb. lean ground turkey**
- 2 **cans (8 oz. each) no-salt-added tomato sauce**

1. Preheat oven to 350°. Cut and discard tops from banana peppers; remove seeds. In a Dutch oven, cook peppers in boiling water 2 minutes. Drain; rinse in cold water; pat dry.
2. In a small skillet coated with cooking spray, heat oil over medium-high heat. Add onion; cook and stir until tender. Add garlic; cook 1 minute longer. Stir in basil; transfer to a large bowl. Stir in olives, feta cheese, bread crumbs, water, egg substitute and pepper. Add turkey; mix lightly but thoroughly.
3. Spoon mixture into banana peppers. Place in a 13x9-in. baking dish coated with cooking spray; top with tomato sauce. Bake, covered, 45-50 minutes or until a thermometer inserted in turkey mixture reads 165° and peppers are tender.
2 stuffed peppers: 298 cal., 12g fat (3g sat. fat), 72mg chol., 431mg sod., 24g carb. (11g sugars, 7g fiber), 22g pro. **Diabetic exchanges:** 2 lean meat, 1½ starch, 1 fat.

GRILLED CHICKEN CHOPPED SALAD

Layered desserts always grab my family's attention, but salads? Not so much. I wondered if presenting a healthy salad in an eye-catching way could get everyone on board. I'm happy to report that I was correct. Find tons more of my salads and other good stuff at *foodyschmoodyblog.com*.
—*Christine Hadden, Whitman, MA*

Takes: 30 min. • **Makes:** 4 servings

- 1 **lb. chicken tenderloins**
- 6 **Tbsp. zesty Italian salad dressing, divided**
- 2 **medium zucchini, quartered lengthwise**
- 1 **medium red onion, quartered**
- 2 **medium ears sweet corn, husks removed**
- 1 **bunch romaine, chopped**
- 1 **medium cucumber, chopped**
  Additional salad dressing, optional

1. In a bowl, toss chicken with 4 Tbsp. dressing. Brush zucchini and onion with remaining 2 Tbsp. dressing.

2. Place corn, zucchini and onion on a grill rack over medium heat; close lid. Grill the zucchini and red onion 2-3 minutes on each side or until tender. Grill corn 10-12 minutes or until tender, turning occasionally.

3. Drain chicken, discarding marinade. Grill chicken, covered, over medium heat 3-4 minutes on each side or until no longer pink.

4. Cut corn from cobs; cut zucchini, onion and chicken into bite-sized pieces. In a 3-qt. trifle bowl or other glass bowl, layer romaine, cucumber, grilled vegetables and chicken. If desired, serve with additional dressing.

3 cups: 239 cal., 5g fat (0 sat. fat), 56mg chol., 276mg sod., 21g carb. (9g sugars, 5g fiber), 32g pro. **Diabetic exchanges:** 3 lean meat, 2 vegetable, ½ starch, ½ fat.

CHICKEN ARTICHOKE SKILLET

My fast chicken entree featuring artichokes and olives has real Greek flair. Seasoned with lemon juice and oregano, the stovetop chicken turns out moist and tender.
—*Carol Latimore, Arvada, CO*

Takes: 25 min. • **Makes:** 4 servings

- 4 boneless skinless chicken breast halves (4 oz. each)
- ¼ tsp. salt
- ¼ tsp. pepper
- 2 tsp. olive oil
- 1 can (14 oz.) water-packed quartered artichoke hearts, rinsed and drained
- ⅔ cup reduced-sodium chicken broth
- ¼ cup halved pimiento-stuffed olives
- ¼ cup halved pitted Greek olives
- 2 Tbsp. minced fresh oregano or 2 tsp. dried oregano
- 1 Tbsp. lemon juice

1. Sprinkle chicken with salt and pepper. In a large skillet, heat oil over medium-high heat; brown chicken on both sides.

2. Add the remaining ingredients; bring to a boil. Reduce heat; simmer, covered, until a thermometer inserted in chicken reads 165°, 4-5 minutes.

1 serving: 225 cal., 9g fat (1g sat. fat), 63mg chol., 864mg sod., 9g carb. (0 sugars, 0 fiber), 26g pro. **Diabetic exchanges:** 3 lean meat, 1 vegetable.

WINE PAIRING

Sauvignon Blanc. It's acidic enough to dance with the dish's artichokes, olives and lemon. Get one from California: These generally have a broader, more savory taste than other sauv blancs.

FIG & WINE-SAUCED CHICKEN KABOBS

The well-balanced blend of flavors in these kabobs makes them extra special. Figs give the dish a wonderful fruity quality, and white wine, orange marmalade and lemon juice complement their honey-like sweetness.
—*Barbara Wheeler, Royal Oak, MI*

- -

Prep: 1 hour + marinating • **Grill:** 15 min.
Makes: 6 servings

5	small onions, divided
½	cup olive oil
2	garlic cloves, minced
1½	lbs. boneless skinless chicken breasts, cut into 1-in. cubes
1¼	lbs. dried figs
2½	cups sweet white wine
3	Tbsp. orange marmalade
2	Tbsp. fig preserves
2	Tbsp. lemon juice
½	tsp. salt
¼	tsp. white pepper
½	lb. small fresh portobello mushrooms Hot cooked rice Fresh mint leaves and lemon wedges, optional

1. Grate 2 onions; place in a large bowl. Add the oil, garlic and chicken; turn to coat. Cover and refrigerate 8 hours or overnight.

2. In a large saucepan, bring figs and wine to a boil. Reduce heat; simmer, uncovered, until figs are plumped and tender, 50-60 minutes. Remove figs; keep warm. Bring liquid to a boil; cook until reduced to ⅔ cup. Add marmalade, preserves, lemon juice, salt and pepper. Cook and stir until slightly thickened, 5-6 minutes.

3. Cut remaining onions into 1-in. pieces. Drain chicken; discard marinade. On 6 metal or soaked wooden skewers, alternately thread the chicken, onions and mushrooms.

4. Grill kabobs, covered, on an oiled rack over medium heat or broil 4 in. from heat until juices run clear, 10-15 minutes, turning occasionally.

5. Serve kabobs with rice and reserved figs; drizzle with sauce. Garnish with mint and lemon if desired.

1 kabob with 2 Tbsp. sauce: 529 cal., 9g fat (2g sat. fat), 63mg chol., 273mg sod., 80g carb. (59g sugars, 13g fiber), 28g pro.

MEDITERRANEAN ONE-DISH MEAL

I came up with this recipe one night while improvising with what I had on hand. I love to make simple, healthy one-dish dinners with lots of vegetables. Feta and Greek olives give this meal a depth of flavor that everyone seems to love!
—*Donna Jesser, Everett, WA*

- -

Prep: 15 min. • **Cook:** 25 min.
Makes: 4 servings

¾	lb. Italian turkey sausage links, cut into 1-in. pieces
1	medium onion, chopped
2	garlic cloves, minced
1	can (14½ oz.) no-salt-added diced tomatoes, undrained
¼	cup Greek olives
1	tsp. dried oregano
½	cup quinoa, rinsed
3	cups fresh baby spinach
½	cup crumbled feta cheese

1. In a large nonstick saucepan coated with cooking spray, cook sausage and onion over medium heat until sausage is browned and onion is tender. Add garlic; cook 1 minute longer. Stir in the tomatoes, olives and oregano; bring to a boil.

2. Stir in quinoa. Top with spinach. Reduce heat; cover and simmer for 12-15 minutes or until liquid is absorbed. Remove from the heat; fluff with a fork. Sprinkle with cheese.

Note: Look for quinoa in the cereal, rice or organic food aisle.

1 cup: 307 cal., 14g fat (3g sat. fat), 58mg chol., 845mg sod., 26g carb. (6g sugars, 5g fiber), 21g pro.

CHICKEN IN TOMATO-CAPER SAUCE

This is what I call an easy crowd-pleaser. I like to serve this entree with pasta and a nice salad. If you don't have capers, try using diced green olives instead.
—*Shemaine Rohrbach, Allentown, PA*

Prep: 20 min. • **Cook:** 15 min.
Makes: 4 servings

- 4 boneless skinless chicken breast halves (6 oz. each)
- ¼ tsp. pepper
- 2 Tbsp. olive oil, divided
- 1 medium onion, chopped
- 3 garlic cloves, minced
- 2 cans (14½ oz. each) no-salt-added diced tomatoes, undrained
- 1 pkg. (6 oz.) fresh baby spinach
- 2 Tbsp. drained capers
- 2 Tbsp. minced fresh basil or 2 tsp. dried basil
- ¼ tsp. cayenne pepper
- ½ cup shredded part-skim mozzarella cheese
- ½ cup grated Parmesan cheese

1. Pound chicken breasts with a meat mallet to ¼-in. thickness; sprinkle with pepper. In a large nonstick skillet, heat 1 Tbsp. oil over medium heat. Brown chicken on both sides; remove from pan.

2. In same skillet, heat remaining oil over medium-high heat. Add onion; cook and stir until tender. Add garlic; cook 1 minute longer. Stir in tomatoes, spinach, capers, basil and cayenne. Return chicken to pan. Cook, covered, 8-10 minutes or until chicken is no longer pink.

3. Sprinkle with cheeses. Remove from heat; let stand, covered, until cheese is melted.

1 serving: 392 cal., 16g fat (5g sat. fat), 111mg chol., 545mg sod., 17g carb. (10g sugars, 5g fiber), 45g pro. **Diabetic exchanges:** 6 lean meat, 1½ fat, 1 starch.

HEARTY CHICKEN GYROS

I love reinventing classic recipes to fit our taste and healthy living lifestyle. This recipe is quick to prepare and can be made ahead and served on the go. You can add Greek olives, omit the onion, or even use cubed pork tenderloin for a new taste.
—*Kayla Douthitt, Elizabethtown, KY*

Prep: 30 min. + marinating • **Cook:** 5 min.
Makes: 6 servings

- 1½ lbs. boneless skinless chicken breasts, cut into ½-in. cubes
- ½ cup salt-free lemon-pepper marinade
- 3 Tbsp. minced fresh mint

SAUCE
- ½ cup fat-free plain Greek yogurt
- 2 Tbsp. lemon juice
- 1 tsp. dill weed
- ½ tsp. garlic powder

ASSEMBLY
- 1 medium cucumber, seeded and chopped
- 1 medium tomato, chopped
- ¼ cup finely chopped onion
- 6 whole wheat pita pocket halves, warmed
- ⅓ cup crumbled feta cheese

1. Place chicken, marinade and mint in a shallow dish and turn to coat. Cover and refrigerate up to 6 hours.

2. Drain chicken, discarding marinade. Place a large nonstick skillet over medium-high heat. Add chicken; cook and stir 4-6 minutes or until no longer pink.

3. In a small bowl, mix sauce ingredients. In another bowl, combine cucumber, tomato and onion. Serve chicken in pita pockets with sauce, vegetable mixture and cheese.

1 gyro: 248 cal., 4g fat (2g sat. fat), 66mg chol., 251mg sod., 22g carb. (4g sugars, 3g fiber), 30g pro. **Diabetic exchanges:** 3 lean meat, 1½ starch, ½ fat.

GRECIAN CHICKEN

The caper, tomato and olive flavors whisk you away to the Greek isles in an easy skillet dish that's perfect for hectic weeknights.
—*Jan Marler, Murchison, TX*

- -

Takes: 30 min. • **Makes:** 4 servings

- 3 tsp. olive oil, divided
- 1 lb. chicken tenderloins
- 2 medium tomatoes, sliced
- 1 cup sliced fresh mushrooms
- ½ cup chopped onion
- 1 Tbsp. capers, drained
- 1 Tbsp. lemon-pepper seasoning
- 1 Tbsp. salt-free Greek seasoning
- 1 medium garlic clove, minced
- ½ cup water
- 2 Tbsp. chopped ripe olives
  Hot cooked orzo pasta, optional

1. In a large skillet, heat 2 tsp. olive oil over medium heat. Add chicken; saute until no longer pink, 7-9 minutes. Remove chicken and keep warm.

2. In same skillet, heat remaining oil; add the next 6 ingredients. Cook and stir until onion is translucent, 2-3 minutes. Stir in garlic; cook 1 minute more. Add water; bring to a boil. Reduce the heat; simmer, uncovered, until vegetables are tender, 3-4 minutes. Return chicken to skillet; add olives. Simmer, uncovered, until chicken is heated through, 2-3 minutes. If desired, serve with orzo.

1 serving: 172 cal., 5g fat (1g sat. fat), 56mg chol., 393mg sod., 6g carb. (3g sugars, 2g fiber), 28g pro. **Diabetic exchanges:** 3 lean meat, 1 vegetable, 1 fat.

LEMON-OLIVE CHICKEN WITH ORZO

This quick skillet recipe is a healthy all-in-one meal. I just add a tossed salad for a menu the entire family loves.

—Nancy Brown, Dahinda, IL

Takes: 30 min. • **Makes:** 4 servings

- 1 Tbsp. olive oil
- 4 boneless skinless chicken thighs (about 1 lb.)
- 1 can (14½ oz.) reduced-sodium chicken broth
- ⅔ cup uncooked whole wheat orzo pasta
- ½ medium lemon, cut into 4 wedges
- ½ cup pitted Greek olives, sliced
- 1 Tbsp. lemon juice
- 1 tsp. dried oregano
- ¼ tsp. pepper

1. In a large nonstick skillet, heat oil over medium heat. Brown chicken on both sides; remove from pan.

2. Add broth to skillet; increase heat to medium-high. Cook 1-2 minutes, stirring to loosen browned bits from pan. Stir in the remaining ingredients; bring to a boil. Reduce heat; simmer, uncovered, for 5 minutes, stirring occasionally.

3. Return chicken to pan. Cook, covered, 5-8 minutes or until pasta is tender and a thermometer inserted in chicken reads 170°.

1 serving: 345 cal., 17g fat (3g sat. fat), 76mg chol., 636mg sod., 22g carb. (1g sugars, 5g fiber), 26g pro. **Diabetic exchanges:** 3 lean meat, 2 fat, 1 starch.

TANDOORI SPICED CHICKEN PITA PIZZAS

My family and I are big picnickers, and I'm always looking for new, easy dishes to try in the great outdoors. The amazing flavors at our favorite Indian restaurant inspired these unique mini pizzas.

—*Angela Spengler, Niceville, FL*

Takes: 25 min. • **Makes:** 4 servings

- 1 cup plain Greek yogurt, divided
- 2 Tbsp. chopped fresh cilantro
- ½ tsp. ground coriander
- ½ tsp. ground cumin
- ½ tsp. ground ginger
- ½ tsp. ground turmeric
- ½ tsp. paprika
- ½ tsp. cayenne pepper
- ¾ lb. boneless skinless chicken breasts, cut into ½-in.-thick strips
- 4 whole wheat pita breads (6 in.)
- ⅔ cup crumbled feta cheese
- ⅓ cup chopped seeded tomato
- ⅓ cup chopped fresh Italian parsley

1. For sauce, mix ½ cup yogurt and cilantro. In a large bowl, mix spices and remaining yogurt; stir in chicken to coat.

2. Place chicken on an oiled grill rack over medium heat; grill, covered, until no longer pink, 2-3 minutes per side. Grill pita breads until warmed, about 1 minute per side.

3. Spread pitas with sauce. Top with chicken, cheese, tomato and parsley.

1 pizza: 380 cal., 12g fat (6g sat. fat), 72mg chol., 598mg sod., 41g carb. (5g sugars, 5g fiber), 29g pro. **Diabetic exchanges:** 3 lean meat, 2½ starch.

HEARTY PAELLA

I had paella for the first time in Spain, and it was so good that I've been on the quest to re-create the rich flavors of that dish ever since. We love the shrimp, chicken, veggie and olives in this easy homemade version.
—*Elizabeth Godecke, Chicago, IL*

- -

Prep: 25 min. • **Cook:** 30 min.
Makes: 6 servings

1¼ lbs. boneless skinless chicken
      breasts, cut into 1-in. cubes
1 Tbsp. olive oil
1 cup uncooked long grain rice
1 medium onion, chopped
2 garlic cloves, minced
2¼ cups reduced-sodium chicken broth
1 can (14½ oz.) diced
      tomatoes, undrained
1 tsp. dried oregano
½ tsp. paprika
¼ tsp. salt
¼ tsp. pepper
⅛ tsp. saffron threads
⅛ tsp. ground turmeric
1 lb. uncooked medium shrimp,
      peeled and deveined
¾ cup frozen peas
12 pimiento-stuffed olives
1 medium lemon, cut into 6 wedges

1. In a large skillet over medium heat, cook chicken in oil until no longer pink. Remove and keep warm. Add rice and onion to the pan; cook until rice is lightly browned and onion is tender, stirring frequently. Add garlic; cook 1 minute longer.

2. Stir in the broth, tomatoes, oregano, paprika, salt, pepper, saffron and turmeric. Bring to a boil. Reduce heat to low; cover and cook for 10 minutes.

3. Add the shrimp, peas and olives. Cover and cook until rice is tender, shrimp turn pink and liquid is absorbed, about 10 minutes longer. Add chicken; heat through. Serve with lemon wedges.

1⅓ cups: 367 cal., 8g fat (1g sat. fat), 144mg chol., 778mg sod., 36g carb. (5g sugars, 3g fiber), 37g pro. **Diabetic exchanges:** 5 lean meat, 2 starch, 1 vegetable, 1 fat.

WINE PAIRING

Rosé. Stay on point with one from Spain if you can find it; the country's hot climate makes these wines full-bodied and intense. But any dry rosé will do.

MARGHERITA CHICKEN

Basil gets all the respect in this super supper, which brings together the fresh ingredients of a margherita pizza on a chicken breast.
—*Judy Armstrong, Prairieville, LA*

Prep: 25 min. + marinating • **Grill:** 10 min.
Makes: 4 servings

- 4 boneless skinless chicken breast halves (6 oz. each)
- ½ cup reduced-fat balsamic vinaigrette
- 3 garlic cloves, minced
- ½ tsp. salt
- ¼ tsp. pepper
- ¼ cup marinara sauce
- 16 fresh basil leaves
- 2 plum tomatoes, thinly sliced lengthwise
- 1 cup frozen artichoke hearts, thawed and chopped
- 3 green onions, chopped
- ¼ cup shredded part-skim mozzarella cheese

1. Flatten chicken to ½-in. thickness. In a large bowl, combine vinaigrette and garlic. Add chicken; turn to coat. Cover; refrigerate for 30 minutes. Drain and discard marinade. Sprinkle chicken with salt and pepper.
2. On a lightly greased grill rack, grill chicken, covered, over medium heat or broil 4 in. from heat 5 minutes. Turn; top with marinara, basil, tomatoes, artichokes, onions and cheese. Cover and cook 5-6 minutes or until chicken is no longer pink and cheese is melted.

1 chicken breast: 273 cal., 8g fat (2g sat. fat), 98mg chol., 606mg sod., 10g carb. (4g sugars, 3g fiber), 38g pro. **Diabetic exchanges:** 5 lean meat, 1 vegetable, ½ fat.

ITALIAN CHICKEN CHARDONNAY

One day I needed to have dinner ready right when we walked in the door after work and school. So I altered a skillet dish that my family likes into this delicious slow-cooker meal. It's perfect for a weeknight meal but nice enough for company, too.

—Judy Armstrong, Prairieville, LA

Prep: 20 min. • **Cook:** 5 hours
Makes: 6 servings

- 2 tsp. paprika
- 1 tsp. salt
- 1 tsp. pepper
- ¼ tsp. cayenne pepper
- 3 lbs. bone-in chicken breast halves, skin removed
- ½ lb. baby portobello mushrooms, quartered
- 1 medium sweet red pepper, chopped
- 1 medium onion, chopped
- 1 can (14 oz.) water-packed artichoke hearts, rinsed and drained
- 1½ cups chardonnay
- 1 can (6 oz.) tomato paste
- 3 garlic cloves, minced
- 2 Tbsp. minced fresh thyme or 2 tsp. dried thyme
- ¼ cup minced fresh parsley
  Hot cooked pasta
  Grated Romano cheese

1. Combine the paprika, salt, pepper and cayenne; sprinkle over chicken. Place the chicken, mushrooms, red pepper, onion and artichokes in a 5-qt. slow cooker. In a small bowl, combine chardonnay, tomato paste, garlic and thyme; pour over vegetables.
2. Cook, covered, on low until chicken is tender, 5-6 hours. Serve with pasta; sprinkle with parsley and cheese.
1 serving: 282 cal., 5g fat (2g sat. fat), 103mg chol., 550mg sod., 16g carb. (6g sugars, 5g fiber), 43g pro. **Diabetic exchanges:** 5 lean meat, 1 starch.

GOLD MEDAL GARLIC CHICKEN

The lively flavors of the Greek isles come through in this chicken entree. I created it so my husband and I could have a nice dinner after a busy day out and about.

—Margee Berry, White Salmon, WA

Prep: 20 min. • **Cook:** 3½ hours
Makes: 6 servings

- ½ cup chopped onion
- 1 Tbsp. plus 1 tsp. olive oil, divided
- 3 Tbsp. minced garlic
- 2½ cups chicken broth, divided
- ¼ cup pitted Greek olives, chopped
- 3 Tbsp. chopped sun-dried tomatoes (not packed in oil)
- 1 Tbsp. quick-cooking tapioca
- 2 tsp. grated lemon zest
- 1 tsp. dried oregano
- 6 boneless skinless chicken breast halves (6 oz. each)
- 1¾ cups uncooked couscous
- ½ cup crumbled feta cheese

1. In a small skillet, saute the onion in 1 Tbsp. oil until crisp-tender. Add the garlic; cook 1 minute longer.
2. Transfer to a 5-qt. slow cooker. Stir in ¾ cup broth, olives, tomatoes, tapioca, lemon zest and oregano. Add chicken. Cover; cook on low for 3½-4 hours or until chicken is tender. If desired, cut chicken into pieces.
3. In a large saucepan, bring remaining olive oil and broth to a boil. Stir in couscous. Cover and remove from the heat; let stand until broth is absorbed, 5 minutes. Serve with chicken; sprinkle with feta cheese.
5 oz. cooked chicken with ¼ cup sauce and ¾ cup couscous: 475 cal., 11g fat (3g sat. fat), 101mg chol., 683mg sod., 48g carb. (3g sugars, 3g fiber), 44g pro.

**GRILLED GARDEN VEGGIE PIZZA,
PAGE 156**

Vegetarian
Mains

Whether you follow a strict vegetarian lifestyle
or just enjoy a meatless meal every now and
again, you'll love these bold and tantalizing
veggie-filled entrees.

GRILLED GARDEN VEGGIE PIZZA

Pile on the veggies! This colorful, healthy pizza with a crisp grilled crust looks as fresh as it tastes.
—Diane Halferty, Corpus Christi, TX

- -

Takes: 30 min. • **Makes:** 6 servings

- 1 medium red onion, cut crosswise into ½-in. slices
- 1 large sweet red pepper, halved, stemmed and seeded
- 1 small zucchini, cut lengthwise into ½-in. slices
- 1 yellow summer squash, cut lengthwise into ½-in. slices
- 2 Tbsp. olive oil
- ½ tsp. salt
- ¼ tsp. pepper
- 1 prebaked 12-in. thin whole wheat pizza crust
- 3 Tbsp. jarred roasted minced garlic
- 2 cups shredded part-skim mozzarella cheese, divided
- ⅓ cup torn fresh basil

1. Brush vegetables with oil; sprinkle with salt and pepper. Grill, covered, over medium heat until tender, 4-5 minutes per side for onion and pepper, 3-4 minutes per side for zucchini and squash.

2. Separate onion into rings; cut red pepper into strips. Spread pizza crust with minced garlic; sprinkle with 1 cup cheese. Top with grilled vegetables, then remaining cheese.

3. Grill pizza, covered, over medium heat until bottom is golden brown and cheese is melted, 5-7 minutes. Top with basil.

1 slice: 324 cal., 15g fat (6g sat. fat), 24mg chol., 704mg sod., 30g carb. (5g sugars, 5g fiber), 16g pro. **Diabetic exchanges:** 2 starch, 2 medium-fat meat, 1 fat.

SPICY LENTIL & CHICKPEA STEW

A friend gave me this slow-cooker recipe. I changed a few things until I had a version that my family loved. My husband farms, working outdoors for long hours at a time, and he finds it hearty enough to keep him warm and satisfied. My young son doesn't like things too spicy, so I make the stew milder for him.
—Melanie MacFarlane, Bedeque, PE

- -

Prep: 25 min. • **Cook:** 8 hours
Makes: 8 servings (2¾ qt.)

- 2 tsp. olive oil
- 1 medium onion, thinly sliced
- 1 tsp. dried oregano
- ½ tsp. crushed red pepper flakes
- 2 cans (15 oz. each) chickpeas or garbanzo beans, rinsed and drained
- 1 cup dried lentils, rinsed
- 1 can (2¼ oz.) sliced ripe olives, drained
- 3 tsp. smoked paprika
- 4 cups vegetable broth
- 4 cans (8 oz. each) no-salt-added tomato sauce
- 4 cups fresh baby spinach
- ¾ cup fat-free plain yogurt

1. In a small skillet, heat the olive oil over medium-high heat. Add onion, oregano and red pepper flakes; cook and stir until onion is tender, 8-10 minutes. Transfer to a 5- or 6-qt. slow cooker.

2. Add chickpeas, lentils, olives and paprika; stir in vegetable broth and tomato sauce. Cook, covered, on low 8-10 hours, until lentils are tender. Stir in baby spinach. Top servings with yogurt.

1⅓ cups: 266 cal., 4g fat (0 sat. fat), 0 chol., 712mg sod., 45g carb. (11g sugars, 10g fiber), 14g pro. **Diabetic exchanges:** 2 starch, 2 vegetable, 1 lean meat.

CALIFORNIA QUINOA

I'm always changing this salad up. Here I used tomato, zucchini and olives for a Greek-inspired take on it. Toss in a few more fresh veggies you know your family will love.
—Elizabeth Lubin, Huntington Beach, CA

Takes: 30 min. • **Makes:** 4 servings

1	Tbsp. olive oil
1	cup quinoa, rinsed and well drained
2	garlic cloves, minced
1	medium zucchini, chopped
2	cups water
¾	cup canned garbanzo beans or chickpeas, rinsed and drained
1	medium tomato, finely chopped
½	cup crumbled feta cheese
¼	cup finely chopped Greek olives
2	Tbsp. minced fresh basil
¼	tsp. pepper

In a large saucepan, heat oil over medium-high heat. Add quinoa and minced garlic; cook and stir 2-3 minutes or until quinoa is lightly browned. Stir in zucchini and water; bring to a boil. Reduce heat; simmer, covered, until liquid is absorbed, 12-15 minutes. Stir in the remaining ingredients; heat through.

1 cup: 310 cal., 11g fat (3g sat. fat), 8mg chol., 353mg sod., 42g carb. (3g sugars, 6g fiber), 11g pro. **Diabetic exchanges:** 2 starch, 1½ fat, 1 lean meat, 1 vegetable.

PUMPKIN LASAGNA

Even friends who aren't big fans of pumpkin are surprised by this delectable lasagna. It's a cinch to prepare.
—*Tamara Huron, New Market, AL*

Prep: 25 min. • **Bake:** 55 min. + standing
Makes: 6 servings

- ½ lb. sliced fresh mushrooms
- 1 small onion, chopped
- ½ tsp. salt, divided
- 2 tsp. olive oil
- 1 can (15 oz.) solid-pack pumpkin
- ½ cup half-and-half cream
- 1 tsp. dried sage leaves
  Dash pepper
- 9 no-cook lasagna noodles
- 1 cup reduced-fat ricotta cheese
- 1 cup shredded part-skim mozzarella cheese
- ¾ cup shredded Parmesan cheese

1. In a small skillet, saute the mushrooms, onion and ¼ tsp. salt in oil until tender; set aside. In a small bowl, combine the pumpkin, cream, sage, pepper and remaining salt.

2. Spread ½ cup pumpkin sauce in an 11x7-in. baking dish coated with cooking spray. Top with 3 noodles (noodles will overlap slightly). Spread ½ cup pumpkin sauce to edges of noodles. Top with half of mushroom mixture, ½ cup ricotta, ½ cup mozzarella and ¼ cup Parmesan cheese. Repeat layers. Top with remaining noodles and sauce.

3. Cover and bake at 375° for 45 minutes. Uncover; sprinkle with remaining Parmesan cheese. Bake 10-15 minutes longer or until cheese is melted. Let stand for 10 minutes before cutting.

Freeze option: Cover and freeze unbaked lasagna. To use, partially thaw in refrigerator overnight. Remove lasagna from refrigerator 30 minutes before baking. Preheat oven to 375°. Bake as directed, increasing the time as needed to heat through and for a thermometer inserted in center to read 165°.

1 piece: 310 cal., 12g fat (6g sat. fat), 36mg chol., 497mg sod., 32g carb. (7g sugars, 5g fiber), 17g pro. **Diabetic exchanges:** 2 starch, 2 fat, 1 lean meat.

WINE PAIRING

Chardonnay. Try a white Burgundy from France, or one from California (which will be more rounded and buttery). Prefer red wine? Then reach for a pinot noir.

CHOPPED GREEK SALAD

While living in San Diego during college, I had a favorite Greek restaurant. Now that I'm back in my hometown, I've re-created some dishes from the diner. This salad takes me right back.
—*Jenn Tidwell, Fair Oaks, CA*

Takes: 20 min. • **Makes:** 4 servings

- 4 cups chopped romaine
- 1 can (15 oz.) garbanzo beans or chickpeas, rinsed and drained
- 2 celery ribs, sliced
- 1 medium tomato, chopped
- ⅓ cup sliced Greek olives
- ⅓ cup crumbled feta cheese
- ¼ cup finely chopped pepperoncini

DRESSING

- 2 Tbsp. minced fresh basil
- 2 Tbsp. pepperoncini juice
- 2 Tbsp. extra virgin olive oil
- 1 Tbsp. lemon juice
- ¼ tsp. salt
- ¼ tsp. pepper

Place the first 7 ingredients in a large bowl. In a small bowl, whisk together dressing ingredients. Drizzle over salad; toss to combine. Serve immediately.

1½ cups: 235 cal., 14g fat (2g sat. fat), 5mg chol., 617mg sod., 22g carb. (4g sugars, 6g fiber), 7g pro. **Diabetic exchanges:** 2 fat, 1½ starch, 1 lean meat, 1 vegetable.

TEST KITCHEN TIP

Try kalamata olives in this recipe. Purple-black, almond-shaped olives native to Greece, they're usually packed in either olive oil or vinegar, giving them a stronger flavor than most other olives. Kalamatas can be found in larger supermarkets as well as smaller ethnic or specialty grocery stores.

CHICKPEA & RED ONION BURGERS

When the grill fills up with other goodies, I bake a batch of chickpea veggie burgers. Even die-hard meat eaters can't resist them.
—*Lily Julow, Lawrenceville, GA*

Takes: 30 min. • **Makes:** 6 servings

- 1 large red onion, thinly sliced
- ¼ cup fat-free red wine vinaigrette
- 2 cans (15 oz. each) chickpeas or garbanzo beans, rinsed and drained
- ⅓ cup chopped walnuts
- ¼ cup toasted wheat germ or dry bread crumbs
- ¼ cup packed fresh parsley sprigs
- 2 large eggs
- 1 tsp. curry powder
- ½ tsp. pepper
- ⅓ cup fat-free mayonnaise
- 2 tsp. Dijon mustard
- 6 sesame seed hamburger buns, split and toasted
- 6 lettuce leaves
- 3 Tbsp. thinly sliced fresh basil leaves

1. Preheat oven to 375°. In a small bowl, mix onion and vinaigrette. Place chickpeas, walnuts, wheat germ and parsley in a food processor; pulse until blended. Add eggs, curry and pepper; process until smooth.

2. Shape into 6 patties. Place on a baking sheet coated with cooking spray. Bake until a thermometer reads 160°, 10-15 minutes.

3. In a small bowl, mix the mayonnaise and mustard; spread over cut sides of buns. Serve patties on buns with lettuce, basil and onion mixture.

1 burger: 386 cal., 12g fat (2g sat. fat), 72mg chol., 732mg sod., 54g carb. (10g sugars, 9g fiber), 16g pro.

MUSHROOM & BROWN RICE HASH WITH POACHED EGGS

I made my mother's famous roast beef hash healthier by using cremini mushrooms instead of beef, and brown rice instead of potatoes. It's ideal for a light main dish.
—*Lily Julow, Lawrenceville, GA*

Takes: 30 min. • **Makes:** 4 servings

- 2 Tbsp. olive oil
- 1 lb. sliced baby portobello mushrooms
- ½ cup chopped sweet onion
- 1 pkg. (8.8 oz.) ready-to-serve brown rice
- 1 large carrot, grated
- 2 green onions, thinly sliced
- ½ tsp. salt
- ¼ tsp. pepper
- ¼ tsp. caraway seeds
- 4 large eggs

1. In a large skillet, heat oil over medium-high heat; saute portobello mushrooms until lightly browned, 5-7 minutes. Add sweet onion; cook 1 minute. Add rice and carrot; cook and stir until vegetables are tender, 4-5 minutes. Stir in the green onions, salt, pepper and caraway seeds; heat through.
2. Meanwhile, place 2-3 in. of water in a large saucepan or skillet with high sides. Bring to a boil; adjust heat to maintain a gentle simmer. Break cold eggs, one at a time, into a small bowl; holding bowl close to surface of water, slip egg into water.
3. Cook, uncovered, until egg whites are completely set and yolks begin to thicken but are not hard, 3-5 minutes. Using a slotted spoon, lift eggs out of water. Serve over the rice mixture.
1 serving: 282 cal., 13g fat (3g sat. fat), 186mg chol., 393mg sod., 26g carb. (4g sugars, 3g fiber), 13g pro. **Diabetic exchanges:** 1½ starch, 1½ fat, 1 medium-fat meat.

RICOTTA, TOMATO & CORN PASTA

I love to make healthy meals with produce from my latest farmers market trip. This pasta takes just 30 minutes from pantry to dinner table. You can easily make it a meat entree by adding cooked shredded chicken.
—*Jerilyn Korver, Bellflower, CA*

- -

Takes: 30 min. • **Makes:** 8 servings

- 3 **cups uncooked whole wheat elbow macaroni (about 12 oz.)**
- 1 **can (15 oz.) cannellini beans, rinsed and drained**
- 2 **cups cherry tomatoes, halved**
- 1 **cup fresh or frozen corn, thawed**
- ½ **cup finely chopped red onion**
- ½ **cup part-skim ricotta cheese**
- ¼ **cup grated Parmesan cheese**
- 2 **Tbsp. minced fresh basil or 2 tsp. dried basil**
- 1 **Tbsp. olive oil**
- 3 **garlic cloves, minced**
- 1 **tsp. salt**
- 1 **tsp. minced fresh rosemary or ½ tsp. dried rosemary, crushed**
- ½ **tsp. pepper**
- 3 **cups arugula or baby spinach Chopped fresh parsley, optional**

1. Cook the pasta according to package directions. Drain and rinse with cold water; drain well.

2. In a large bowl, combine beans, tomatoes, corn, onion, ricotta and Parmesan cheeses, basil, oil, garlic, salt, rosemary and pepper. Stir in pasta. Add arugula; toss gently to combine. If desired, sprinkle with parsley. Serve immediately.

1½ cups: 275 cal., 5g fat (1g sat. fat), 7mg chol., 429mg sod., 46g carb. (4g sugars, 8g fiber), 13g pro. **Diabetic exchanges:** 3 starch, 1 lean meat.

SPAGHETTI SQUASH WITH BALSAMIC VEGETABLES

The veggies for this dish can be prepped while the squash is cooking in the microwave. That means I can have a satisfying meal on the table in about half an hour.
—*Deanna McDonald, Muskegon, MI*

- -

Prep: 20 min. • **Cook:** 15 min.
Makes: 6 servings

- 1 **medium spaghetti squash (about 4 lbs.)**
- 1 **cup chopped carrots**
- 1 **small red onion, halved and sliced**
- 1 **Tbsp. olive oil**
- 4 **garlic cloves, minced**
- 1 **can (15½ oz.) great northern beans, rinsed and drained**
- 1 **can (14½ oz.) diced tomatoes, drained**
- 1 **can (14 oz.) water-packed artichoke hearts, rinsed, drained and halved**
- 1 **medium zucchini, chopped**
- 3 **Tbsp. balsamic vinegar**
- 2 **tsp. minced fresh thyme or ½ tsp. dried thyme**
- ¼ **tsp. salt**
- ¼ **tsp. pepper**
- ½ **cup pine nuts, toasted**

1. Cut squash in half lengthwise; discard seeds. Place the squash cut side down on a microwave-safe plate. Microwave, uncovered, on high until tender, 15-18 minutes.

2. Meanwhile, in a large nonstick skillet, saute carrots and onion in oil until tender. Add the garlic; cook 1 minute. Stir in beans, tomatoes, artichokes, zucchini, vinegar, thyme, salt and pepper. Cook and stir over medium heat until heated through, 8-10 minutes.

3. When squash is cool enough to handle, use a fork to separate strands. Serve with bean mixture. Sprinkle with nuts.

¾ cup bean mixture with ⅔ cup squash and 4 tsp. nuts: 275 cal., 10g fat (1g sat. fat), 0 chol., 510mg sod., 41g carb. (6g sugars, 10g fiber), 11g pro. **Diabetic exchanges:** 2½ starch, 1½ fat, 1 lean meat.

SKINNY EGGPLANT PARMESAN

You save a lot of calories when you bake the eggplant patties instead of frying them in oil. I add some strips of sweet red pepper while sauteing the mushrooms for a pop of color.

—Mary Bannister, Albion, NY

Prep: 45 min. • **Bake:** 30 min. + standing
Makes: 4 servings

- ½ cup fat-free milk
- 1 cup dry bread crumbs
- 2 tsp. Italian seasoning, divided
- 1 large eggplant, peeled and cut into ½-in. slices
- ½ lb. sliced fresh mushrooms
- 1 cup chopped sweet onion
- 2 tsp. olive oil
- 2 garlic cloves, minced
- 8 fresh basil leaves, thinly sliced
- 1 jar (24 oz.) marinara sauce
- ¼ cup dry red wine or vegetable broth
- ¾ cup shredded part-skim mozzarella cheese
- ¾ cup part-skim ricotta cheese
- ¼ cup shredded Parmesan cheese

1. Place milk in a shallow bowl. In another shallow bowl, combine bread crumbs and 1 tsp. Italian seasoning. Dip eggplant in milk, then bread crumb mixture. Place on a baking sheet coated with cooking spray. Bake at 350° until tender, 30-40 minutes.

2. Meanwhile, in a large skillet, saute mushrooms and onion in oil until tender. Add garlic; cook 1 minute longer. Remove from the heat. Stir in basil and remaining Italian seasoning.

3. Spread ½ cup marinara sauce into a 2-qt. baking dish coated with cooking spray. In a small bowl, combine wine and remaining marinara sauce. Layer with half of the eggplant, mushroom mixture, mozzarella cheese, ricotta cheese and ¾ cup sauce mixture. Repeat layers. Top with remaining sauce; sprinkle with Parmesan cheese.

4. Bake, uncovered, at 350° until ingredients are heated through and cheese is melted, 30-35 minutes. Let stand for 10 minutes before cutting.

1 serving: 342 cal., 11g fat (6g sat. fat), 31mg chol., 560mg sod., 42g carb. (21g sugars, 10g fiber), 20g pro. **Diabetic exchanges:** 2 lean meat, 2 vegetable, 1½ starch, ½ fat.

ARUGULA & BROWN RICE SALAD

When we have company, arugula with brown rice is always on the menu. It's my go-to pick for the potluck and party circuit, and I'm always sharing the recipe.
—*Mindy Oswalt, Winnetka, CA*

- -

Takes: 25 min. • **Makes:** 4 servings

- 1 pkg. (8.8 oz.) ready-to-serve brown rice
- 7 cups fresh arugula or baby spinach (about 5 oz.)
- 1 can (15 oz.) garbanzo beans or chickpeas, rinsed and drained
- 1 cup (4 oz.) crumbled feta cheese
- ¾ cup loosely packed basil leaves, torn
- ½ cup dried cherries or cranberries

DRESSING
- ¼ cup olive oil
- ¼ tsp. grated lemon zest
- 2 Tbsp. lemon juice
- ¼ tsp. salt
- ⅛ tsp. pepper

1. Heat rice according to package directions. Transfer to a large bowl; cool slightly.

2. Stir arugula, garbanzo beans, cheese, basil and cherries into rice. In a small bowl, whisk dressing ingredients. Drizzle over salad; toss to coat. Serve immediately.

2 cups: 473 cal., 22g fat (5g sat. fat), 15mg chol., 574mg sod., 53g carb. (17g sugars, 7g fiber), 13g pro.

5i

ROASTED CURRIED CHICKPEAS & CAULIFLOWER

Roast veggies and chickpeas for a comforting dinner. Add chicken or tofu if you like.
—Pam Correll, Brockport, PA

- -

Prep: 15 min. • **Bake:** 30 min.
Makes: 4 servings

- 2 lbs. potatoes (about 4 medium), peeled and cut into ½-in. cubes
- 1 small head cauliflower, broken into florets (about 3 cups)
- 1 can (15 oz.) chickpeas or garbanzo beans, rinsed and drained
- 3 Tbsp. olive oil
- 2 tsp. curry powder
- ¾ tsp. salt
- ¼ tsp. pepper
- 3 Tbsp. minced fresh cilantro or parsley

1. Preheat oven to 400°. Place the first 7 ingredients in a large bowl; toss to coat. Transfer to a 15x10x1-in. baking pan coated with cooking spray.
2. Roast until the vegetables are tender, 30-35 minutes, stirring occasionally. Sprinkle with cilantro.

1½ cups: 339 cal., 13g fat (2g sat. fat), 0 chol., 605mg sod., 51g carb. (6g sugars, 8g fiber), 8g pro.

WINE PAIRING

Cotes du Rhone. Earthy, spicy, powerful and still food-friendly, this blend from France's southern Rhone Valley is great with assertive flavors. Similar red blends from other parts of the world are labeled GSM, and they'd be good here, too. GSM is an acronym formed by the names of the prevalent grapes: grenache, syrah and mourvedre.

ZUCCHINI CRUST PIZZA

My mother-in-law shared this unique pizza recipe with me. It's just right for brunch, lunch or a light supper. Use a metal spatula to loosen the nutritious zucchini crust from the pizza pan.

—*Ruth Denomme, Englehart, ON*

Prep: 20 min. • **Bake:** 25 min.
Makes: 6 slices

- 2 cups shredded zucchini (1 to 1½ medium), squeezed dry
- ½ cup egg substitute or 2 large eggs, lightly beaten
- ¼ cup all-purpose flour
- ¼ tsp. salt
- 2 cups shredded part-skim mozzarella cheese, divided
- ½ cup grated Parmesan cheese, divided
- 2 small tomatoes, halved and sliced
- ½ cup chopped red onion
- ½ cup julienned bell pepper
- 1 tsp. dried oregano
- ½ tsp. dried basil
  Chopped fresh basil, optional

1. Preheat oven to 450°. In a large bowl, combine first 4 ingredients; stir in ½ cup mozzarella cheese and ¼ cup Parmesan cheese. Transfer to a 12-in. pizza pan coated generously with cooking spray; spread to an 11-in. circle.

2. Bake until golden brown, 13-16 minutes. Reduce the oven setting to 400°. Sprinkle with remaining mozzarella cheese; top with sliced tomatoes, onion, pepper, herbs and remaining Parmesan cheese. Bake until the crust edges are golden brown and cheese is melted, 10-15 minutes. Sprinkle with chopped fresh basil, if desired.

1 slice: 188 cal., 10g fat (5g sat. fat), 30mg chol., 514mg sod., 12g carb. (4g sugars, 1g fiber), 14g pro. **Diabetic exchanges:** 2 vegetable, 2 lean meat, ½ fat.

5I **L**

PERSONAL MARGHERITA PIZZAS

This family-friendly supper is simplicity at its finest. Delectable fresh mozzarella and a sprinkling of fresh basil give these little pies Italian flair.

—*Jerry Gulley, Pleasant Prairie, WI*

- -

Takes: 25 min. • **Makes:** 3 servings

- 1 pkg. (6½ oz.) pizza crust mix
- ½ tsp. dried oregano
- ¾ cup pizza sauce
- 6 oz. fresh mozzarella cheese, thinly sliced
- ¼ cup thinly sliced fresh basil leaves

1. Preheat oven to 425°. Prepare the pizza dough according to package directions, adding oregano before mixing. Divide into 3 portions.

2. Pat each portion of dough into an 8-in. circle on greased baking sheets. Bake until edges are lightly browned, 8-10 minutes.

3. Spread each crust with ¼ cup pizza sauce to within ½ in. of edge. Top with cheese. Bake until crust is golden and cheese is melted, 5-10 minutes longer. Sprinkle with basil.

1 pizza: 407 cal., 15g fat (8g sat. fat), 45mg chol., 675mg sod., 48g carb. (7g sugars, 3g fiber), 18g pro.

MEDITERRANEAN CHICKPEAS

Add this to your meatless Monday lineup.
It's great with feta cheese on top.
—*Elaine Ober, Brookline, MA*

- -

Takes: 25 min. • **Makes:** 4 servings

1	cup water
¾	cup uncooked whole wheat couscous
1	Tbsp. olive oil
1	medium onion, chopped
2	garlic cloves, minced
1	can (15 oz.) chickpeas or garbanzo beans, rinsed and drained
1	can (14½ oz.) no-salt-added stewed tomatoes, cut up
1	can (14 oz.) water-packed artichoke hearts, rinsed, drained and chopped
½	cup pitted Greek olives, coarsely chopped
1	Tbsp. lemon juice
½	tsp. dried oregano
	Dash pepper
	Dash cayenne pepper

1. In a small saucepan, bring water to a boil. Stir in couscous. Remove from the heat; let stand, covered, 5-10 minutes or until water is absorbed. Fluff with a fork.

2. Meanwhile, in a large nonstick skillet, heat oil over medium-high heat. Add onion; cook and stir until tender. Add the garlic; cook for 1 minute longer. Sir in remaining ingredients; heat through, stirring occasionally. Serve with couscous.

1 cup chickpea mixture with ⅔ cup couscous: 340 cal., 10g fat (1g sat. fat), 0 chol., 677mg sod., 51g carb. (9g sugars, 9g fiber), 11g pro.

BASIL POLENTA WITH RATATOUILLE

We offered a vegan menu at our wedding. Everyone raved about the polenta topped with colorful ratatouille—our version of the classic stewed vegetable dish.
—*Kimberly Hammond, Kingwood, TX*

Prep: 25 min. + chilling • **Cook:** 40 min.
Makes: 4 servings

- 4 cups water
- ½ tsp. salt, divided
- 1 cup cornmeal
- ½ cup minced fresh basil
- 1 medium eggplant, peeled and cut into ½-in. cubes
- 1 medium onion, halved and sliced
- 1 medium green pepper, julienned
- 5 Tbsp. olive oil, divided
- 4 garlic cloves, minced
- 1 can (14½ oz.) diced tomatoes, drained
- ½ cup pitted Greek olives, sliced
- 1 tsp. dried oregano
- ¼ tsp. pepper
  Fresh basil leaves

1. In a large heavy saucepan, bring water and ¼ tsp. salt to a boil. Reduce heat to a gentle boil; slowly whisk in cornmeal. Cook and stir with a wooden spoon until polenta is thickened and pulls away cleanly from the sides of pan, 15-20 minutes. Stir in basil.
2. Spread into an 8-in. square baking dish coated with cooking spray. Refrigerate for 30 minutes.
3. Meanwhile, in a large skillet, saute the eggplant, onion and green pepper in 2 Tbsp. oil until crisp-tender. Add the garlic; cook 1 minute longer. Stir in the tomatoes, olives, oregano, pepper and remaining salt. Cook and stir over medium heat until vegetables are tender, 10-12 minutes.
4. Cut polenta into 4 squares. In another large skillet, cook polenta in remaining oil in batches until golden brown, 7-8 minutes on each side. Serve polenta with ratatouille; garnish with basil.

1 polenta square with 1 cup ratatouille: 400 cal., 22g fat (3g sat. fat), 0 chol., 709mg sod., 46g carb. (9g sugars, 10g fiber), 6g pro.

CHEESE TORTELLINI WITH TOMATOES & CORN

Fresh corn and basil make this dish taste like summer. I think it's a good one for bringing to picnics or gatherings, but it's great alongside any entree for weeknight dinners.
—*Sally Maloney, Dallas, GA*

Takes: 25 min. • **Makes:** 4 servings

- 1 pkg. (9 oz.) refrigerated cheese tortellini
- 3⅓ cups fresh or frozen corn (about 16 oz.)
- 2 cups cherry tomatoes, quartered
- 2 green onions, thinly sliced
- ¼ cup minced fresh basil
- 2 Tbsp. grated Parmesan cheese
- 4 tsp. olive oil
- ¼ tsp. garlic powder
- ⅛ tsp. pepper

In a 6-qt. stockpot, cook tortellini according to the package directions, adding corn during the last 5 minutes of cooking. Drain; transfer to a large bowl. Add remaining ingredients; toss to coat.
1¾ cups: 366 cal., 12g fat (4g sat. fat), 30mg chol., 286mg sod., 57g carb. (6g sugars, 5g fiber), 14g pro.

SUMMER BOUNTY RATATOUILLE

The name says it all! Put all of your garden's surplus to good use with classic ratatouille. The rustic dish originates from the Provence region of France and is traditionally made with eggplant, tomatoes, onions, zucchini, garlic, bell peppers and fragrant herbs. It's delicious with freshly baked bread. You can also serve it over hot cooked spaghetti.
—*Phyllis Jacques, Venice, FL*

- -

Prep: 20 min. + standing • **Cook:** 1 hour
Makes: 12 servings

- 1 large eggplant, peeled and cut into 1-in. cubes
- 1½ tsp. kosher salt, divided
- 3 Tbsp. olive oil
- 2 medium sweet red peppers, cut into ½-in. strips
- 2 medium onions, peeled and chopped
- 4 garlic cloves, minced
- ¼ cup tomato paste
- 1 Tbsp. herbes de Provence
- ½ tsp. pepper
- 3 cans (14½ oz. each) diced tomatoes, undrained
- 1½ cups water
- 4 medium zucchini, quartered lengthwise and sliced ½-in. thick
- ¼ cup chopped fresh basil
- 2 Tbsp. minced fresh rosemary
- 2 Tbsp. minced fresh parsley
- 2 French bread baguettes (10½ oz. each), cubed and toasted

1. Place eggplant in a colander over a plate; toss with 1 tsp. kosher salt. Let stand for 30 minutes. Rinse and drain well.

2. In a Dutch oven, heat oil over medium-high heat; saute peppers and onions until tender, 8-10 minutes. Add the garlic; cook and stir 1 minute. Stir in tomato paste, herbs de Provence, pepper, remaining salt, tomatoes and water. Add zucchini and eggplant; bring to a boil. Reduce heat; simmer, uncovered, until flavors are blended, 40-45 minutes, stirring occasionally.

3. Stir in fresh herbs. Serve ratatouille over baguette cubes.

Note: Look for herbes de Provence in the spice aisle.

1 cup ratatouille with 1 cup bread cubes: 205 cal., 4g fat (1g sat. fat), 0 chol., 542mg sod., 38g carb. (8g sugars, 6g fiber), 7g pro.

TEST KITCHEN TIP

Salting an eggplant draws out some of the moisture, giving the flesh a denser texture. This means it will give off less moisture and absorb less fat during cooking. Salting also may cut some of the bitterness from an eggplant. To salt, place slices, cubes or strips of eggplant in a colander over a plate; sprinkle with about ½ tsp. salt and toss. Let stand for 30 minutes. Rinse, drain well and pat dry with paper towels.

PORTOBELLO POLENTA STACKS

My friends and I have recently started growing portobello mushrooms from kits we found at a farmers market. We love to try new recipes like this one with our harvest.
—*Breanne Heath, Chicago, IL*

Takes: 30 min. • **Makes:** 4 servings

1	Tbsp. olive oil
3	garlic cloves, minced
2	Tbsp. balsamic vinegar
4	large portobello mushrooms (about 5 in.), stems removed
¼	tsp. salt
¼	tsp. pepper
1	tube (18 oz.) polenta, cut into 12 slices
1	large tomato, cut crosswise into four slices
½	cup grated Parmesan cheese
2	Tbsp. minced fresh basil

1. Preheat oven to 400°. In a small saucepan, heat oil over medium heat. Add garlic; cook and stir until tender, 1-2 minutes (do not allow to brown). Stir in balsamic vinegar; remove from heat.

2. Place mushrooms in a 13x9-in. baking dish, gill side up. Brush with vinegar mixture; sprinkle with salt and pepper. Top with polenta and tomato slices; sprinkle with Parmesan cheese.

3. Bake, uncovered, until mushrooms are tender, 20-25 minutes. Sprinkle with basil.

1 serving: 219 cal., 6g fat (2g sat. fat), 9mg chol., 764mg sod., 32g carb. (7g sugars, 3g fiber), 7g pro. **Diabetic exchanges:** 1½ starch, 1 lean meat, 1 vegetable, 1 fat.

VEGGIE NICOISE SALAD

Many of my co-workers follow vegetarian diets. When we cook or eat together, the focus is on fresh produce. This colorful salad combines some of our favorite ingredients in one dish—and with eggs and kidney beans, it delivers enough protein to satisfy everyone.
—*Elizabeth Kelley, Chicago, IL*

Prep: 40 min. • **Cook:** 25 min.
Makes: 8 servings

- ⅓ cup olive oil
- ¼ cup lemon juice
- 2 tsp. minced fresh oregano
- 2 tsp. minced fresh thyme
- 1 tsp. Dijon mustard
- 1 garlic clove, minced
- ¼ tsp. coarsely ground pepper
- ⅛ tsp. salt
- 1 can (16 oz.) kidney beans, rinsed and drained
- 1 small red onion, halved and thinly sliced
- 1 lb. small red potatoes (about 9), halved
- 1 lb. fresh asparagus, trimmed
- ½ lb. fresh green beans, trimmed
- 12 cups torn romaine (about 2 small bunches)
- 6 hard-boiled large eggs, quartered
- 1 jar (6½ oz.) marinated quartered artichoke hearts, drained
- ½ cup Nicoise or kalamata olives

1. For vinaigrette, whisk together first 8 ingredients. In another bowl, toss kidney beans and onion with 1 Tbsp. vinaigrette. Set aside bean mixture and remaining vinaigrette.

2. Place potatoes in a saucepan and cover with water. Bring to a boil. Reduce the heat; simmer, covered, until tender, 10-15 minutes. Drain. While still warm, toss with 1 Tbsp. vinaigrette; set aside.

3. In a pot of boiling water, cook asparagus just until crisp-tender, 2-4 minutes. Remove with tongs and immediately drop in ice water. Drain and pat dry. In same pot of boiling water, cook green beans until crisp-tender, 3-4 minutes. Remove beans; place in ice water. Drain and pat dry.

4. To serve, toss asparagus with 1 Tbsp. of the vinaigrette; toss green beans with 2 tsp. vinaigrette. Toss torn romaine with the remaining vinaigrette; place on a platter. Arrange vegetables, kidney bean mixture, eggs, artichoke hearts and olives over top.

1 serving: 329 cal., 19g fat (4g sat. fat), 140mg chol., 422mg sod., 28g carb. (6g sugars, 7g fiber), 12g pro. **Diabetic exchanges:** 3 fat, 2 medium-fat meat, 2 vegetable, 1½ starch.

CREAMY LENTILS WITH KALE ARTICHOKE SAUTE

I've been trying to eat more meatless meals, so I experimented with this hearty saute and served it over brown rice. It was so good that even those who aren't big fans of kale gobbled it up.
—*Teri Rasey, Cadillac, MI*

Takes: 30 min. • **Makes:** 4 servings

- ½ cup dried red lentils, rinsed and sorted
- ¼ tsp. dried oregano
- ⅛ tsp. pepper
- 1¼ cups vegetable broth
- ¼ tsp. sea salt, divided
- 1 Tbsp. olive oil or grapeseed oil
- 16 cups chopped fresh kale (about 12 oz.)
- 1 can (14 oz.) water-packed artichoke hearts, drained and chopped
- 3 garlic cloves, minced
- ½ tsp. Italian seasoning
- 2 Tbsp. grated Romano cheese
- 2 cups hot cooked brown or basmati rice

1. Place first 4 ingredients and ⅛ tsp. salt in a small saucepan; bring to a boil. Reduce heat; simmer, covered, until lentils are tender and liquid is almost absorbed, 12-15 minutes. Remove from heat.

2. In a 6-qt. stockpot, heat oil over medium heat. Add kale and remaining salt; cook, covered, until kale is wilted, 4-5 minutes, stirring occasionally. Add artichoke hearts, garlic and Italian seasoning; cook and stir for 3 minutes. Remove from heat; stir in cheese.

3. Serve lentils and kale mixture over rice.

1 serving: 321 cal., 6g fat (2g sat. fat), 1mg chol., 661mg sod., 53g carb. (1g sugars, 5g fiber), 15g pro.

GREEN OLIVE HUMMUS PITAS

For a healthy on-the-go meal, combine fresh Greek salad with zesty hummus. You can also serve the spread with crackers or as a dip with cut fresh vegetables.
—Nicole Filizetti, Stevens Point, WI

Takes: 20 min. • **Makes:** 2 servings

- ¾ cup canned garbanzo beans or chickpeas, rinsed and drained
- 2 Tbsp. lemon juice
- 1 Tbsp. sliced green olives with pimientos
- 1 tsp. olive oil
- 1 garlic clove, minced
- 1 cup fresh baby spinach
- ¼ cup chopped seeded peeled cucumber
- ¼ cup crumbled feta cheese
- 2 Tbsp. chopped marinated quartered artichoke hearts
- 2 Tbsp. sliced Greek olives
- ¼ tsp. dried oregano
- 2 whole wheat pita pocket halves

1. Place the first 5 ingredients in a food processor; cover and process until smooth. Set aside.

2. In a small bowl, combine the baby spinach, chopped cucumber, feta cheese, artichokes, olives and oregano.

3. Spread bean mixture into pita halves; add salad. Serve immediately.

1 filled pita half: 292 cal., 12g fat (3g sat. fat), 8mg chol., 687mg sod., 38g carb. (3g sugars, 7g fiber), 10g pro. **Diabetic exchanges:** 2 starch, 1 lean meat, 1 fat.

MUSHROOM BOLOGNESE WITH WHOLE WHEAT PASTA

A traditional Bolognese sauce is meat-based with everything from pork to pancetta. Skipping the meat, I loaded this pasta dish with baby portobellos and veggies.
—*Amber Massey, Argyle, TX*

Prep: 10 min. • **Cook:** 35 min.
Makes: 6 servings

- 1 Tbsp. olive oil
- 1 large sweet onion, finely chopped
- 2 medium carrots, finely chopped
- 1 large zucchini, finely chopped
- ½ lb. baby portobello mushrooms, finely chopped
- 3 garlic cloves, minced
- ½ cup dry red wine or reduced-sodium chicken broth
- 1 can (28 oz.) crushed tomatoes, undrained
- 1 can (14½ oz.) diced tomatoes, undrained
- ½ cup grated Parmesan cheese
- ½ tsp. dried oregano
- ½ tsp. pepper
- ⅛ tsp. crushed red pepper flakes
  Dash ground nutmeg
- 4½ cups uncooked whole wheat rigatoni

1. In a 6-qt. stockpot coated with cooking spray, heat oil over medium-high heat. Add onion and carrots; cook and stir until tender. Add zucchini, mushrooms and garlic; cook and stir until tender. Stir in wine; bring to a boil; cook until liquid is almost evaporated.
2. Stir in crushed and diced tomatoes, cheese and seasonings; bring to a boil. Reduce heat; simmer, covered, 25-30 minutes or until slightly thickened.
3. Cook rigatoni according to package directions; drain. Serve with sauce.

1⅓ cups sauce with 1 cup pasta: 369 cal., 6g fat (2g sat. fat), 6mg chol., 483mg sod., 65g carb. (15g sugars, 12g fiber), 17g pro.

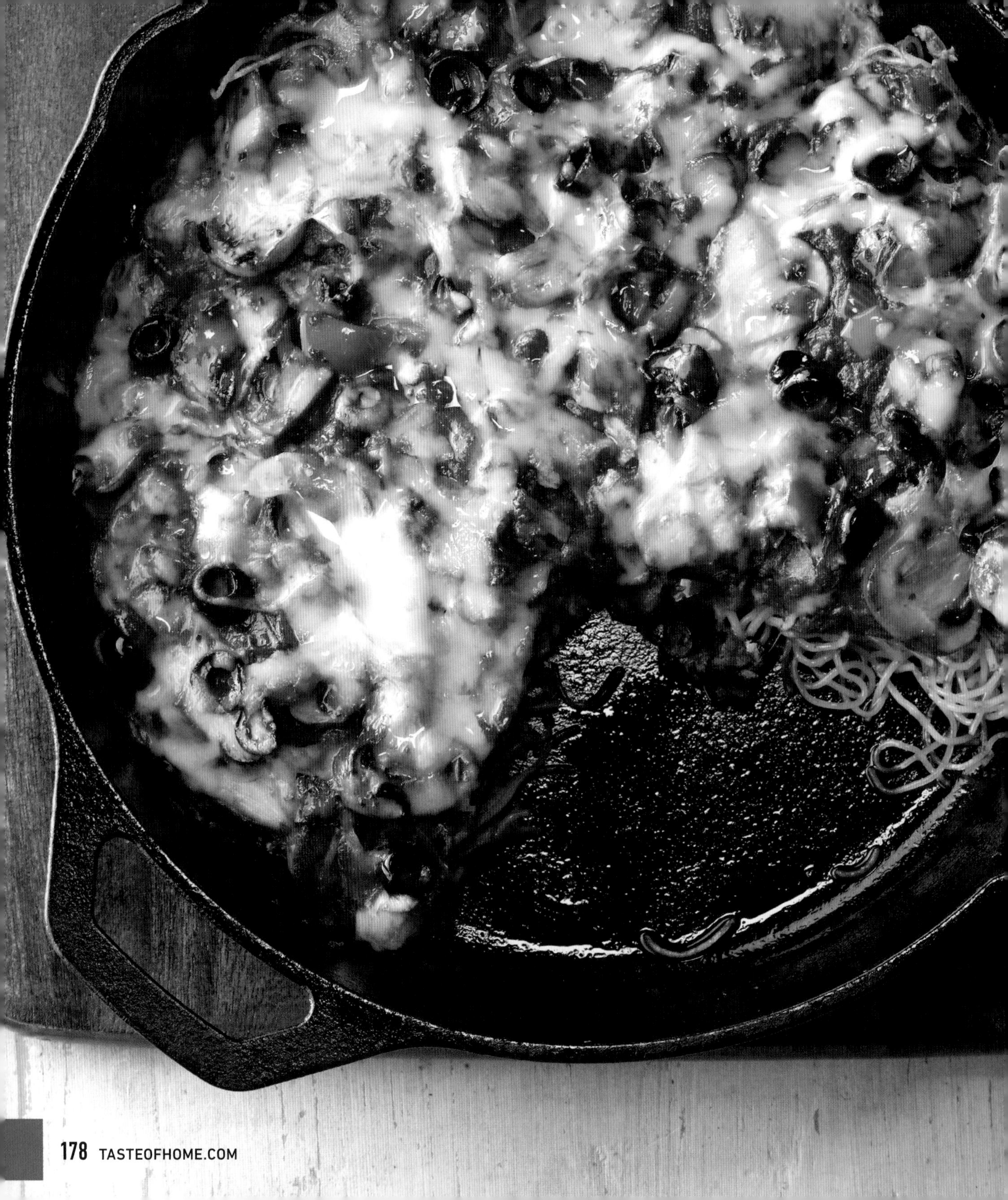

PASTA PIZZA

My family often requests this meatless main dish, which is a tempting cross between pizza and spaghetti.

—*Andrea Quick, Columbus, OH*

- -

Prep: 25 min. • **Bake:** 10 min.
Makes: 4 servings

8	oz. uncooked angel hair pasta
4	tsp. olive oil, divided
2	cups sliced fresh mushrooms
½	cup chopped green pepper
¼	cup chopped onion
1	can (15 oz.) pizza sauce
¼	cup sliced ripe olives
½	cup shredded part-skim mozzarella cheese
¼	tsp. Italian seasoning

1. Preheat oven to 400°. Cook pasta according to package directions; drain.
2. In a large cast-iron or other ovenproof skillet, heat 1 tsp. oil over medium heat. Add mushrooms, green pepper and onion; saute until tender. Remove with a slotted spoon and keep warm. Increase heat to medium-high. In same skillet, heat remaining oil. Spread pasta evenly in skillet to form a crust. Cook until lightly browned, 5-7 minutes.
3. Turn crust onto a large plate. Reduce heat to medium; slide crust back into skillet. Top with pizza sauce, sauteed vegetables and olives; sprinkle with mozzarella cheese and Italian seasoning. Bake until cheese is melted, 10-12 minutes.

1 serving: 374 cal., 10g fat (3g sat. fat), 9mg chol., 532mg sod., 56g carb. (7g sugars, 5g fiber), 14g pro.

MIMI'S LENTIL MEDLEY

I made this one summer evening by putting together what I had on hand. My husband gave it his top rating.

—*Mary Ann Hazen, Rochester Hills, MI*

- -

Prep: 15 min. • **Cook:** 25 min.
Makes: 8 servings

1	cup dried lentils, rinsed
2	cups water
2	cups sliced fresh mushrooms
1	medium cucumber, cubed
1	medium zucchini, cubed
1	small red onion, chopped
½	cup chopped soft sun-dried tomato halves (not packed in oil)
½	cup rice vinegar
¼	cup minced fresh mint
3	Tbsp. olive oil
2	tsp. honey
1	tsp. dried basil
1	tsp. dried oregano
4	cups fresh baby spinach, chopped
1	cup (4 oz.) crumbled feta cheese

1. Place lentils in a small saucepan. Add water; bring to a boil. Reduce heat; simmer, covered, 20-25 minutes or until tender. Drain and rinse in cold water.
2. Transfer to a large bowl. Add mushrooms, cucumber, zucchini, onion and tomatoes. In a small bowl, whisk vinegar, mint, oil, honey, basil and oregano. Drizzle over lentil mixture; toss to coat. Add spinach and feta cheese; toss to combine.

1¼ cups: 225 cal., 8g fat (2g sat. fat), 8mg chol., 404mg sod., 29g carb. (11g sugars, 5g fiber), 10g pro. **Diabetic exchanges:** 1½ fat, 1 starch, 1 vegetable.

MUSHROOM-BEAN BOURGUIGNON

In our family, boeuf bourguignon has been a staple for generations. I wanted a meatless alternative, so I came up with this. Serve with a French baguette and dinner's ready!

—*Sonya Labbe, West Hollywood, CA*

Prep: 15 min. • **Cook:** 1¼ hours
Makes: 10 servings (2½ qt.)

- 4 Tbsp. olive oil, divided
- 5 medium carrots, cut into 1-in. pieces
- 2 medium onions, halved and sliced
- 2 garlic cloves, minced
- 8 large portobello mushrooms, cut into 1-in. pieces
- 1 Tbsp. tomato paste
- 1 bottle (750 ml) dry red wine
- 2 cups mushroom broth or vegetable broth, divided
- 1 tsp. salt
- 1 tsp. minced fresh thyme or ½ tsp. dried thyme
- ½ tsp. pepper
- 2 cans (15½ oz. each) navy beans, rinsed and drained
- 1 pkg. (14.4 oz.) frozen pearl onions
- 3 Tbsp. all-purpose flour

1. In a Dutch oven, heat 2 Tbsp. oil over medium-high heat. Add carrots and onions; cook and stir 8-10 minutes or until onions are tender. Add garlic; cook 1 minute longer. Remove from pan.

2. In the same pan, heat 1 Tbsp. oil over medium-high heat. Add half of the mushrooms; cook and stir until lightly browned. Remove from pan; repeat with remaining oil and mushrooms.

3. Return mushrooms to pan. Add tomato paste; cook and stir 1 minute. Stir in wine, 1½ cups broth, salt, thyme, pepper and carrot mixture; bring to a boil. Reduce heat; simmer, covered, 25 minutes.

4. Add navy beans and pearl onions; cook 30 minutes longer. In a small bowl, whisk the flour and remaining broth until smooth; stir into pan. Bring to a boil; cook and stir until slightly thickened, about 2 minutes.

1 cup: 234 cal., 6g fat (1g sat. fat), 0 chol., 613mg sod., 33g carb. (6g sugars, 7g fiber), 9g pro. **Diabetic exchanges:** 2 starch, 2 vegetable, 1 lean meat, 1 fat.

WINE PAIRING

Pinot Noir. A wine from Burgundy, France, is the classic pairing, since boeuf bourguignon originated there. The stew would be tasty with a pinot noir from Italy or the U.S., too.

WHITE BEANS & BOW TIES

When we have fresh veggies, we toss them with pasta shapes like penne or bow ties. What a tasty way to enjoy a meatless meal!
—*Angela Buchanan, Longmont, CO*

Takes: 25 min. • **Makes:** 4 servings

- 2½ cups uncooked whole wheat bow tie pasta (about 6 oz.)
- 1 Tbsp. olive oil
- 1 medium zucchini, sliced
- 2 garlic cloves, minced
- 2 large tomatoes, chopped (about 2½ cups)
- 1 can (15 oz.) cannellini beans, rinsed and drained
- 1 can (2¼ oz.) sliced ripe olives, drained
- ¾ tsp. freshly ground pepper
- ½ cup crumbled feta cheese

1. Cook the pasta according to package directions. Drain, reserving ½ cup of the pasta water.
2. Meanwhile, in a large skillet, heat oil over medium-high heat; saute the zucchini until crisp-tender, 2-4 minutes. Add garlic; cook and stir 30 seconds. Stir in tomatoes, beans, olives and pepper; bring to a boil. Reduce heat; simmer, uncovered, until tomatoes are softened, 3-5 minutes, stirring occasionally.
3. Stir in pasta and enough pasta water to moisten as desired. Stir in cheese.
1½ cups: 348 cal., 9g fat (2g sat. fat), 8mg chol., 394mg sod., 52g carb. (4g sugars, 11g fiber), 15g pro.

TEST KITCHEN TIP

Boost protein in meatless pasta dishes like this one by using whole wheat noodles, adding white beans or stirring in a little cheese. Or try all three!

LENTIL LOAF

This vegetarian riff on traditional meat loaf is so flavorful, you won't even miss the meat.

—Tracy Fleming, Phoenix, AZ

- -

Prep: 35 min. • **Bake:** 45 min. + standing
Makes: 6 servings

- ¾ cup brown lentils, rinsed
- 1 can (14½ oz.) vegetable broth
- 1 Tbsp. olive oil
- 1¾ cups shredded carrots
- 1 cup finely chopped onion
- 1 cup chopped fresh mushrooms
- 2 Tbsp. minced fresh basil or 2 tsp. dried basil
- 1 Tbsp. minced fresh parsley
- 1 cup shredded part-skim mozzarella cheese
- ½ cup cooked brown rice
- 1 large egg
- 1 large egg white
- ½ tsp. salt
- ½ tsp. garlic powder
- ¼ tsp. pepper
- 2 Tbsp. tomato paste
- 2 Tbsp. water

1. Place lentils and broth in a small saucepan; bring to a boil. Reduce heat; simmer, covered, until tender, about 30 minutes.
2. Preheat oven to 350°. Line a 9x5-in. loaf pan with parchment, letting ends extend up sides. Coat paper with cooking spray.
3. In a large skillet, heat oil over medium heat; saute carrots, onion and mushrooms until tender, about 10 minutes. Stir in herbs. Transfer to a large bowl; cool slightly.
4. Add the cheese, rice, egg, egg white, seasonings and lentils to vegetables; mix well. Mix tomato paste and water; spread over loaf.
5. Bake until a thermometer inserted into the center reads 160°, 45-50 minutes. Let stand 10 minutes before slicing.
1 slice: 213 cal., 5g fat (3g sat. fat), 43mg chol., 580mg sod., 29g carb. (5g sugars, 5g fiber), 14g pro. **Diabetic exchanges:** 2 lean meat, 1½ starch, 1 vegetable, ½ fat.

MAMA RACHEL'S MEDITERRANEAN PIZZA

Pizza has been a regular weekend dinner at our house since my pizza-crazy sons, now grown, were just little guys. We laughingly call pizza an art form around here. Each one is an original!
—*Rachel Barton, Austin, TX*

- -

Prep: 35 min. + rising • **Bake:** 20 min.
Makes: 2 pizzas (6 slices each)

- 1 Tbsp. active dry yeast
- 1 cup warm water (110° to 115°)
- 1 Tbsp. sugar
- 1 Tbsp. olive oil
- ½ tsp. salt
- 2½ to 3 cups all-purpose flour
- 2 Tbsp. cornmeal

TOPPINGS

- 2 Tbsp. olive oil
- 3 garlic cloves, peeled and thinly sliced
- 2 cups shredded part-skim mozzarella cheese
- 2 large tomatoes, thinly sliced
- ⅓ cup pitted kalamata olives, thinly sliced
- ½ cup shredded Parmesan cheese
- ¼ tsp. crushed red pepper flakes
- 6 fresh basil leaves, thinly sliced

1. In a large bowl, dissolve yeast in warm water. Add the sugar, oil, salt and 1 cup flour; beat until smooth. Stir in enough remaining flour to form a stiff dough.

2. Turn dough onto a floured surface; knead until smooth and elastic, 6-8 minutes. Place in a greased bowl, turning once to grease the top. Cover with plastic wrap and let rise in a warm place until doubled, about 45 minutes.

3. Preheat oven to 400°. Grease two 12-in. pizza pans; sprinkle with cornmeal. Punch down dough; divide in half. Press to fit pans. Pinch edges to form a rim. Cover; let rest for 10 minutes. Bake 8-10 minutes or until edges are lightly browned.

4. Increase oven setting to 450°. Brush crusts with oil; top with garlic, mozzarella cheese, tomatoes, olives and Parmesan cheese. Bake 10-12 minutes or until crust is golden and cheese is melted. Sprinkle with pepper flakes and basil.

1 slice: 216 cal., 9g fat (3g sat. fat), 13mg chol., 307mg sod., 25g carb. (3g sugars, 1g fiber), 9g pro. **Diabetic exchanges:** 1½ starch, 1 medium-fat meat, 1 fat.

QUICK ITALIAN VEGGIE SKILLET

Don't know what to serve tonight? Italian flavors are a good starting point. Cannellini and garbanzo beans combine in this snappy rice dish.

—*Sonya Labbe, West Hollywood, CA*

Takes: 25 min. • **Makes:** 4 servings

- 1 can (15 oz.) no-salt-added garbanzo beans or chickpeas, rinsed and drained
- 1 can (15 oz.) no-salt-added cannellini beans, rinsed and drained
- 1 can (14½ oz.) no-salt-added stewed tomatoes, undrained
- 1 cup vegetable broth
- ¾ cup uncooked instant rice
- 1 tsp. Italian seasoning
- ¼ tsp. crushed red pepper flakes, optional
- 1 cup marinara sauce
- ¼ cup grated Parmesan cheese Minced fresh basil

In a large skillet, combine first 6 ingredients and, if desired, pepper flakes; bring to a boil. Reduce heat; simmer, covered, until rice is tender, 7-9 minutes. Stir in marinara sauce; heat through, stirring occasionally. Top with cheese and basil.

1⅓ cups: 342 cal., 4g fat (1g sat. fat), 6mg chol., 660mg sod., 59g carb. (10g sugars, 11g fiber), 16g pro.

FULL GARDEN FRITTATA

I top my veggie frittata with tomatoes and fresh mozzarella. It's breakfast for dinner!
—*Melissa Rosenthal, Vista, CA*

- -

Prep: 25 min. • **Bake:** 10 min.
Makes: 2 servings

4	large eggs
⅓	cup 2% milk
¼	tsp. salt, divided
⅛	tsp. coarsely ground pepper
2	tsp. olive oil
½	medium zucchini, chopped
½	cup chopped baby portobello mushrooms
¼	cup chopped onion
1	garlic clove, minced
2	Tbsp. minced fresh basil
1	tsp. minced fresh oregano
1	tsp. minced fresh parsley
	Toppings: Grape tomatoes, fresh mozzarella balls and sliced fresh basil

1. Preheat oven to 375°. In a bowl, whisk eggs, milk, ⅛ tsp. salt and pepper. In an 8-in. ovenproof skillet, heat oil over medium-high heat. Add zucchini, mushrooms and onion; cook and stir until tender. Add garlic, herbs and remaining salt; cook 1 minute longer. Pour in egg mixture.
2. Bake, uncovered, until the eggs are set, 10-15 minutes. Cut into 4 wedges. Serve with toppings.
2 wedges: 227 cal., 15g fat (4g sat. fat), 375mg chol., 463mg sod., 7g carb. (5g sugars, 1g fiber), 15g pro.

WINE PAIRING

Orange Wine. Made with white grapes kept in long contact with their skins, orange wine is sometimes aged in clay pots. Enjoy it with scrambled eggs, mushrooms and garden herbs.

SPINACH & ARTICHOKE PIZZA

My from-scratch pizza has a beer-flavored whole wheat crust. It's so good topped with spinach, artichoke hearts, tomatoes and fresh basil.
—Raymonde Bourgeois, Swastika, ON

- -

Prep: 25 min. • **Bake:** 20 min.
Makes: 6 slices

1½ to 1¾ cups white whole wheat flour
1½ tsp. baking powder
¼ tsp. salt
¼ tsp. each dried basil, oregano
   and parsley flakes
¾ cup beer or nonalcoholic beer
TOPPINGS
1½ tsp. olive oil
1 garlic clove, minced
2 cups shredded Italian cheese blend
2 cups fresh baby spinach
1 can (14 oz.) water-packed
   quartered artichoke hearts,
   drained and coarsely chopped
2 medium tomatoes, seeded
   and coarsely chopped
2 Tbsp. thinly sliced fresh basil

1. Preheat oven to 425°. In a large bowl, whisk 1½ cups flour, baking powder, salt and dried herbs until blended. Add beer, stirring just until moistened.
2. Turn dough onto a well-floured surface; knead gently 6-8 times, adding additional flour if needed. Press dough to fit a greased 12-in. pizza pan. Pinch edge to form a rim. Bake until crust edges are lightly browned, about 8 minutes.
3. Mix olive oil and minced garlic; spread over crust. Sprinkle with ½ cup cheese; layer with spinach, artichoke hearts and tomatoes. Sprinkle with remaining cheese. Bake until the crust is golden and cheese is melted, 8-10 minutes. Sprinkle with fresh basil.
1 slice: 290 cal., 10g fat (6g sat. fat), 27mg chol., 654mg sod., 32g carb. (1g sugars, 5g fiber), 14g pro. **Diabetic exchanges:** 2 starch, 1 medium-fat meat, 1 vegetable.

BLACK BEAN & SWEET POTATO RICE BOWLS

With three hungry boys, dinners need to be quick and filling. I like to get some veggies in, too. These healthy bowls are a family favorite because they're hearty and fun to tweak with different ingredients.
—Kim Van Dunk, Caldwell, NJ

- -

Takes: 30 min. • **Makes:** 4 servings

¾ cup uncooked long grain rice
¼ tsp. garlic salt
1½ cups water
3 Tbsp. olive oil, divided
1 large sweet potato, peeled and diced
1 medium red onion, finely chopped
4 cups chopped fresh kale
   (tough stems removed)
1 can (15 oz.) black beans,
   rinsed and drained
2 Tbsp. sweet chili sauce
   Lime wedges, optional
   Additional sweet chili sauce, optional

1. Place rice, garlic salt and water in a large saucepan; bring to a boil. Reduce the heat; simmer, covered, until water is absorbed and rice is tender, 15-20 minutes. Remove from heat; let stand 5 minutes.
2. Meanwhile, in a large skillet, heat 2 Tbsp. oil over medium-high heat; saute the sweet potato for 8 minutes. Add onion; cook and stir until potato is tender, 4-6 minutes. Add kale; cook and stir until tender, 3-5 minutes. Stir in beans; heat through.
3. Gently stir 2 Tbsp. chili sauce and the remaining oil into rice; add to potato mixture. If desired, serve bowls with lime wedges and additional chili sauce.
2 cups: 435 cal., 11g fat (2g sat. fat), 0 chol., 405mg sod., 74g carb. (15g sugars, 8g fiber), 10g pro.

FETA STEAK TACOS,
PAGE 198

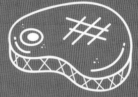

Beef, Pork & Lamb

Gather around the table and get ready to dig in.
When it comes to serving up a satisfying meal
that's full of flavor, vigor and heartiness, these
meaty options offer endless possibilities.

SPAGHETTI SQUASH MEATBALL CASSEROLE

One of our favorite comfort food dinners is spaghetti and meatballs. We're crazy about this lightened-up, healthier version featuring so many veggies. The same beloved flavors with more nutritious ingredients!
—*Courtney Stultz, Weir, KS*

Prep: 35 min. • **Bake:** 30 min.
Makes: 6 servings

- 1 medium spaghetti squash (about 4 lbs.)
- ½ tsp. salt, divided
- ½ tsp. fennel seed
- ¼ tsp. ground coriander
- ¼ tsp. dried basil
- ¼ tsp. dried oregano
- 1 lb. lean ground beef (90% lean)
- 2 tsp. olive oil
- 1 medium onion, chopped
- 1 garlic clove, minced
- 2 cups chopped collard greens
- 1 cup chopped fresh spinach
- 1 cup reduced-fat ricotta cheese
- 2 plum tomatoes, chopped
- 1 cup pasta sauce
- 1 cup shredded part-skim mozzarella cheese

1. Cut squash lengthwise in half; discard seeds. Place halves on a microwave-safe plate, cut side down. Microwave, uncovered, on high until tender, 15-20 minutes. Cool squash slightly.

2. Preheat oven to 350°. Mix ¼ tsp. salt with remaining seasonings; add to beef, mixing lightly but thoroughly. Shape into 1½-in. balls. In a large skillet, brown the meatballs over medium heat; remove from pan.

3. In same pan, heat oil over medium heat; saute onion until tender, 3-4 minutes. Add garlic; cook and stir 1 minute. Stir in collard greens, spinach, ricotta cheese and remaining salt; remove from heat.

4. Using a fork, separate strands of spaghetti squash; stir into greens mixture. Transfer to a greased 13x9-in. baking dish. Top with the tomatoes, meatballs, sauce and cheese. Bake, uncovered, until the meatballs are cooked through, 30-35 minutes.

1 serving: 362 cal., 16g fat (6g sat. fat), 69mg chol., 618mg sod., 32g carb. (7g sugars, 7g fiber), 26g pro. **Diabetic exchanges:** 3 lean meat, 2 starch, 1 fat.

READER RAVE

"One of the best spaghetti squash recipes I have found yet. Highly recommend others try it! Thanks for sharing."
—TERESA, TASTEOFHOME.COM

SMOKY ESPRESSO STEAK

This juicy steak rubbed with espresso, cocoa and pumpkin pie spice is one of my husband's favorites. We usually grill it, but broiling it in the oven works in the chilly months.
—*Deborah Biggs, Omaha, NE*

- -

Takes: 30 min. • **Makes:** 4 servings

3	tsp. instant espresso powder
2	tsp. brown sugar
1½	tsp. smoked or regular paprika
1	tsp. salt
1	tsp. baking cocoa
¼	tsp. pumpkin pie spice
¼	tsp. pepper
1	lb. beef flat iron or top sirloin steak (¾ in. thick)

1. Preheat broiler. Mix the first 7 ingredients; rub over both sides of steak. Place steak on a broiler pan; let stand 10 minutes.

2. Broil steak 3-4 in. from heat 4-6 minutes on each side or until meat reaches desired doneness (for medium-rare, a thermometer should read 135°; medium, 140°; medium-well, 145°). Let steak stand for 5 minutes before slicing.

3 oz. cooked beef: 216 cal., 12g fat (5g sat. fat), 73mg chol., 661mg sod., 4g carb. (2g sugars, 0 fiber), 22g pro.

BEEF & BLUE CHEESE PENNE

Unique and simple to prepare, this delicious pasta dish is filled with fresh flavors, and it's as healthy as it is hearty.

—Frances Pietsch, Flower Mound, TX

Takes: 30 min. • **Makes:** 4 servings

- 2 **cups uncooked whole wheat penne pasta**
- 2 **beef tenderloin steaks (6 oz. each)**
- ¼ **tsp. salt**
- ¼ **tsp. pepper**
- 5 **oz. fresh baby spinach (about 6 cups), coarsely chopped**
- 2 **cups grape tomatoes, halved**
- ⅓ **cup prepared pesto**
- ¼ **cup chopped walnuts**
- ¼ **cup crumbled Gorgonzola cheese**

1. Cook the pasta according to package directions.

2. Meanwhile, sprinkle steaks with salt and pepper. Grill steaks, covered, over medium heat or broil 4 in. from heat 5-7 minutes on each side or until meat reaches desired doneness (for medium-rare, a thermometer should read 135°; medium, 140°; medium-well, 145°).

3. Drain pasta; transfer to a large bowl. Add spinach, tomatoes, pesto and walnuts; toss to coat. Cut steak into thin slices. Serve pasta mixture with beef; sprinkle with cheese.

1 serving: 532 cal., 22g fat (6g sat. fat), 50mg chol., 434mg sod., 49g carb. (3g sugars, 9g fiber), 35g pro.

WINE PAIRING

Barbera. This light wine is one of Italy's most food-friendly. It will work nicely with the herby spinach and pesto. And barbera's acidity will brighten up the whole wheat penne and rich beef.

ORANGE-GLAZED PORK LOIN

This is one of the best pork recipes I've ever tried. My family looks forward to this roast for dinner, and guests always ask for the recipe. The flavorful rub and a glaze sparked with orange juice are also outstanding on pork chops.

—*Lynnette Miete, Alna, ME*

Prep: 10 min.
Bake: 1 hour 20 min. + standing
Makes: 16 servings

- 1   tsp. salt
- 1   garlic clove, minced
- 2   to 3 fresh thyme sprigs or
     ¼ tsp. dried thyme
- ¼   tsp. ground ginger
- ¼   tsp. pepper
- 1   boneless pork loin roast (5 lbs.)

GLAZE

- 1   cup orange juice
- ¼   cup packed brown sugar
- 1   Tbsp. Dijon mustard
- ⅓   cup cold water
- 1   Tbsp. cornstarch

1. Preheat oven to 350°. Combine the first 5 ingredients; rub over roast. Place fat side up on a rack in a shallow roasting pan. Bake, uncovered, for 1 hour.
2. Meanwhile, in a saucepan over medium heat, combine orange juice, brown sugar and mustard. In a small bowl, mix water and cornstarch until smooth. Add to orange juice mixture. Bring to a boil; cook and stir for 2 minutes. Reserve 1 cup glaze for serving; brush half of remaining glaze over roast.
3. Bake until a thermometer reads 145°, 20-40 minutes longer, brushing occasionally with remaining glaze. Let stand 10 minutes before slicing. Reheat reserved glaze; serve with roast.
4 oz. cooked pork with 1 Tbsp. glaze: 199 cal., 7g fat (2g sat. fat), 71mg chol., 212mg sod., 6g carb. (5g sugars, 0 fiber), 28g pro.
Diabetic exchanges: 4 lean meat, ½ starch.

PIZZAIOLA CHOPS

My favorite cousin shared this recipe and I tweaked it for our family. Taste as you go, and try the Italian trick of sprinkling on some oregano to give it that extra something.
—*Lorraine Caland, Shuniah, ON*

- -

Takes: 30 min. • **Makes:** 4 servings

- 2   **Tbsp. olive oil, divided**
- 4   **boneless pork loin chops (6 oz. each)**
- 1   **tsp. salt, divided**
- ¼   **tsp. pepper, divided**
- 1½ **cups sliced baby portobello mushrooms**
- 1   **medium sweet yellow pepper, coarsely chopped**
- 1   **medium sweet red pepper, coarsely chopped**
- 2   **large tomatoes, chopped**
- ½   **cup white wine or chicken broth**
- 1   **Tbsp. minced fresh oregano or ½ tsp. dried oregano**
- 2   **garlic cloves, minced**
     Hot cooked rice, optional

1. In a large skillet, heat 1 Tbsp. oil over medium-high heat. Season pork chops with ½ tsp. salt and ⅛ tsp. pepper. Brown chops on both sides. Remove from pan.

2. In same pan, heat remaining oil over medium-high heat. Add mushrooms, yellow pepper and red pepper; cook and stir until mushrooms are tender, 3-4 minutes. Add tomatoes, wine, oregano, garlic and the remaining salt and pepper. Bring to a boil. Reduce heat; simmer, uncovered, 2 minutes.

3. Return chops to pan. Cook, covered, until a thermometer inserted in pork reads 145°, 5-7 minutes. Let stand 5 minutes. If desired, serve with rice.

1 pork chop and 1 cup vegetable mixture: 351 cal., 17g fat (5g sat. fat), 82mg chol., 647mg sod., 10g carb. (4g sugars, 2g fiber), 35g pro. **Diabetic exchanges:** 5 lean meat, 1½ fat, 1 vegetable.

PEAR & POMEGRANATE LAMB TAGINE

Pomegranate, pear and orange go together so well that I decided to use them to prepare a Middle Eastern-themed tagine with lamb. This tastes delicious served over couscous, polenta, or cauliflower mashed with some feta cheese.

—*Arlene Erlbach, Morton Grove, IL*

Prep: 20 min. • **Cook:** 6 hours
Makes: 4 servings

- 2½ lbs. lamb shanks
- 2 large pears, finely chopped
- 3 cups thinly sliced shallots
- ½ cup orange juice, divided
- ½ cup pomegranate juice, divided
- 1 Tbsp. honey
- 1½ tsp. ground cinnamon
- 1 tsp. salt
- 1 tsp. ground allspice
- 1 tsp. ground cardamom
- ¼ cup pomegranate seeds
- ¼ cup minced fresh parsley
  Cooked couscous, optional

1. Place lamb in a 5- or 6-qt. oval slow cooker. Add pears and shallots. Combine ¼ cup orange juice, ¼ cup pomegranate juice, honey and seasonings; pour over shallots.
2. Cook, covered, on low for 6-8 hours or until meat is tender. Remove lamb to a rimmed serving platter; keep warm. Stir remaining orange and pomegranate juices into cooking liquid; pour over lamb. Sprinkle with pomegranate seeds and parsley. If desired, serve over couscous.
½ lamb shank with 1 cup vegetables: 438 cal., 13g fat (5g sat. fat), 99mg chol., 680mg sod., 52g carb. (28g sugars, 5g fiber), 31g pro.

FARMERS MARKET PASTA

When we moved into our house, little did we know that we had a wild asparagus patch. Twenty years later, that little patch still gives us plenty of asparagus. This recipe can be used almost any time of year, with almost any assortment of vegetables the season has to offer. By cooking without butter or oil, you can cut fat and calories, but the flavors are still there.

—Wendy Ball, Battle Creek, MI

Prep: 20 min. • **Cook:** 20 min.
Makes: 6 servings

- 9 oz. uncooked whole wheat linguine
- 1 lb. fresh asparagus, trimmed and cut into 2-in. pieces
- 2 medium carrots, thinly sliced
- 1 small red onion, chopped
- 2 medium zucchini or yellow summer squash, thinly sliced
- ½ lb. sliced fresh mushrooms
- 2 garlic cloves, minced
- 1 cup half-and-half cream
- ⅔ cup reduced-sodium chicken broth
- 1 cup frozen petite peas
- 2 cups cubed fully cooked ham
- 2 Tbsp. julienned fresh basil
- ¼ tsp. pepper
- ½ cup grated Parmesan cheese
  Optional: Additional fresh basil and Parmesan cheese

1. In a 6-qt. stockpot, cook linguine according to the package directions, adding asparagus and carrots during the last 3-5 minutes of cooking. Drain; return to pot.
2. Place a large skillet coated with cooking spray over medium heat. Add onion; cook and stir 3 minutes. Add squash, mushrooms, and garlic; cook and stir until crisp-tender, 4-5 minutes.
3. Add cream and broth; bring to a boil, stirring to loosen browned bits from pan. Reduce heat; simmer, uncovered, until sauce is thickened slightly, about 5 minutes. Stir in the peas, ham, 2 Tbsp. basil and pepper; heat through.

4. Add to linguine mixture; stir in ½ cup cheese. If desired, top with additional basil and cheese.
2 cups: 338 cal., 9g fat (4g sat. fat), 53mg chol., 817mg sod., 46g carb. (8g sugars, 8g fiber), 23g pro. **Diabetic exchanges:** 2½ starch, 2 lean meat, 1 vegetable, ½ fat.

HERB-RUBBED PORK LOIN

A savory herb rub and a mere 15 minutes of prep time turn plain pork roast into an easy, elegant entree.

—Robin Schloesser, Chester, NJ

Prep: 15 min. • **Bake:** 1 hour + standing
Makes: 12 servings

- 1 Tbsp. olive oil
- 2 tsp. each minced fresh marjoram, rosemary, sage and thyme
- 1 tsp. salt
- ½ tsp. pepper
- 1 boneless whole pork loin roast (4 lbs.)
- 1 cup water

1. In a small bowl, combine the oil, herbs, salt and pepper; rub over pork. Place roast on a rack in a large shallow roasting pan. Pour water into pan.
2. Bake, uncovered, at 350° for 1-1½ hours or until a thermometer reads 160°. Transfer to a serving platter. Let stand for 10 minutes before slicing.
4 oz. cooked pork: 198 cal., 8g fat (3g sat. fat), 75mg chol., 240mg sod., 0 carb. (0 sugars, 0 fiber), 29g pro. **Diabetic exchanges:** 4 lean meat.

FETA STEAK TACOS

These tacos have the perfect combination of Mexican and Mediterranean flavors. They're a big hit with my family.
—*Debbie Reid, Clearwater, FL*

- -

Takes: 30 min. • **Makes:** 8 servings

1   beef flat iron steak or top sirloin steak (1¼ lbs.), cut into thin strips
¼   cup Greek vinaigrette
½   cup fat-free plain Greek yogurt
2   tsp. lime juice
1   Tbsp. oil from sun-dried tomatoes
1   small green pepper, cut into thin strips
1   small onion, cut into thin strips
¼   cup chopped oil-packed sun-dried tomatoes
¼   cup sliced Greek olives
8   whole wheat tortillas (8 in.), warmed
¼   cup crumbled garlic and herb feta cheese
    Lime wedges

1. In a large bowl, toss beef with vinaigrette; let stand 15 minutes. In a small bowl, mix yogurt and lime juice.

2. In a large skillet, heat oil from sun-dried tomatoes over medium-high heat. Add the green pepper and onion; cook and stir until crisp-tender, 3-4 minutes. Remove to a small bowl; stir in sun-dried tomatoes and olives.

3. Place same skillet over medium-high heat. Add beef; cook and stir until no longer pink, 2-3 minutes. Remove from pan.

4. Serve steak and pepper mixture in tortillas; top with cheese. Serve with yogurt mixture and lime wedges.

1 taco with 1 Tbsp. yogurt mixture: 317 cal., 15g fat (4g sat. fat), 48mg chol., 372mg sod., 25g carb. (2g sugars, 3g fiber), 20g pro. **Diabetic exchanges:** 3 lean meat, 2 fat, 1½ starch.

ONE-POT BEEF & PEPPER STEW

I wanted to prepare a quick and satisfying dish one evening and came up with this recipe using things I had on hand. Since I love most things made with bell peppers, tomatoes or green chiles, those ingredients played a starring role.
—*Sandra Clark, Sierra Vista, AZ*

- -

Prep: 10 min. • **Cook:** 30 min.
Makes: 8 servings

1   lb. lean ground beef (90% lean)
3   cans (14½ oz. each) diced tomatoes, undrained
4   large green peppers, coarsely chopped
1   large onion, chopped
2   cans (4 oz. each) chopped green chiles
3   tsp. garlic powder
1   tsp. pepper
¼   tsp. salt
2   cups uncooked instant rice
    Hot pepper sauce, optional

1. In a 6-qt. stockpot, cook ground beef over medium heat 6-8 minutes or until no longer pink, breaking into crumbles; drain. Add tomatoes, green peppers, onion, chiles and seasonings; bring to a boil. Reduce heat; simmer, covered, 20-25 minutes or until vegetables are tender.

2. Prepare the rice according to package directions. Serve with stew and, if desired, pepper sauce.

1½ cups: 244 cal., 5g fat (2g sat. fat), 35mg chol., 467mg sod., 35g carb. (8g sugars, 5g fiber), 15g pro. **Diabetic exchanges:** 2 lean meat, 2 vegetable, 1½ starch.

● ❄

GREEK SLOPPY JOES

Feta is one of my favorite kinds of cheese. It's good in a burger, but truly shines in this Mediterranean-style sloppy joe.
—*Sonya Labbe, West Hollywood, CA*

- -

Takes: 25 min. • **Makes:** 6 servings

1	lb. lean ground beef (90% lean)
1	small red onion, chopped
2	garlic cloves, minced
1	can (15 oz.) tomato sauce
1	tsp. dried oregano
	Romaine leaves
6	kaiser rolls, split and toasted
½	cup crumbled feta cheese

1. In a large skillet, cook beef, red onion and garlic over medium heat until beef is no longer pink, 6-8 minutes, breaking up beef into crumbles; drain. Stir in tomato sauce and oregano. Bring to a boil. Reduce the heat; simmer, uncovered, until sauce is slightly thickened, 8-10 minutes, stirring occasionally.
2. Place romaine on roll bottoms; top with meat mixture. Sprinkle with feta cheese; replace tops.
Freeze option: Freeze cooled meat mixture in freezer containers. To use, partially thaw in refrigerator overnight. Heat through in a saucepan, stirring occasionally and adding a little water if necessary.
1 sandwich: 337 cal., 10g fat (4g sat. fat), 52mg chol., 767mg sod., 36g carb. (3g sugars, 3g fiber), 24g pro. **Diabetic exchanges:** 3 lean meat, 2 starch, 1 vegetable.

MINI MEDITERRANEAN PIZZA

I was on a mini pizza kick and had already served up Mexican and Italian variations, so I decided to try Mediterranean flavors and came up with these.

—Jenny Dubinsky, Inwood, WV

Prep: 30 min. • **Bake:** 5 min.
Makes: 4 servings

1	Tbsp. olive oil
8	oz. lean ground beef (90% lean)
¼	cup finely chopped onion
2	garlic cloves, minced
1	can (8 oz.) tomato sauce
1	tsp. minced fresh rosemary or ¼ tsp. dried rosemary, crushed
2	whole wheat pita breads (6 in.), cut in half horizontally
1	medium tomato, seeded and chopped
½	cup fresh baby spinach, thinly sliced
12	Greek pitted olives, thinly sliced
½	cup shredded part-skim mozzarella cheese
¼	cup crumbled feta cheese

1. Heat oil in a large nonstick skillet; cook the beef, onion and garlic over medium heat until meat is no longer pink, 5-6 minutes; drain. Stir in tomato sauce and rosemary; bring to a boil. Reduce heat; simmer, uncovered, until thickened, 6-9 minutes.

2. Place pita halves, cut side up, on a baking sheet. Top with meat mixture, tomato, spinach and olives. Sprinkle with cheeses. Bake at 400° until the cheeses are melted, 4-6 minutes.

1 pizza: 287 cal., 12g fat (5g sat. fat), 47mg chol., 783mg sod., 25g carb. (3g sugars, 4g fiber), 21g pro. **Diabetic exchanges:** 2 lean meat, 1½ starch, 1 fat.

TOP-RATED ITALIAN POT ROAST

I'm always collecting recipes from magazines and newspapers. This one just sounded too good not to try. You'll love the the blend of wholesome ingredients and aromatic spices.

—*Karen Burdell, Lafayette, CO*

Prep: 30 min. • **Cook:** 6 hours
Makes: 8 servings

- 1 cinnamon stick (3 in.)
- 6 whole peppercorns
- 4 whole cloves
- 3 whole allspice berries
- 2 tsp. olive oil
- 1 boneless beef chuck roast (2 lbs.)
- 2 celery ribs, sliced
- 2 medium carrots, sliced
- 1 large onion, chopped
- 4 garlic cloves, minced
- 1 cup dry sherry or reduced-sodium beef broth
- 1 can (28 oz.) crushed tomatoes
- ¼ tsp. salt
  Hot cooked egg noodles and minced parsley, optional

1. Place cinnamon stick, peppercorns, cloves and allspice on a double thickness of cheesecloth. Gather corners of cloth to enclose spices; tie securely with string.

2. In a large skillet, heat oil over medium-high heat. Brown roast on all sides; transfer to a 4-qt. slow cooker. Add celery, carrots and spice bag.

3. Add onion to same skillet; cook and stir until tender. Add garlic; cook 1 minute longer. Add sherry, stirring to loosen browned bits from pan. Bring to a boil; cook and stir until liquid is reduced to ⅔ cup. Stir in tomatoes and salt; pour over roast and vegetables.

4. Cook, covered, on low 6-7 hours or until meat and vegetables are tender. Remove roast from slow cooker; keep warm. Discard spice bag; skim fat from sauce. Serve roast and sauce with noodles and parsley if desired.

Freeze option: Place sliced pot roast in freezer containers; top with sauce. Cool and freeze. To use, partially thaw in refrigerator overnight. Heat through in a covered saucepan, stirring gently and adding a little broth if necessary.

3 oz. cooked beef with ⅔ cup sauce: 251 cal., 12g fat (4g sat. fat), 74mg chol., 271mg sod., 11g carb. (2g sugars, 3g fiber), 24g pro.

Diabetic exchanges: 3 lean meat, 2 vegetable, ½ fat.

LAMB MARSALA

Lamb was a special treat for my family when I was growing up. I've had this recipe for more than 30 years and still enjoy it today. Marsala wine, garlic and oregano make each bite of this succulent dish irresistible.

—*Bonnie Silverstein, Denver, CO*

Prep: 10 min. • **Bake:** 1 hour
Makes: 6 servings

- ¾ cup Marsala wine or ½ cup chicken broth, ¼ cup white grape juice and 1 Tbsp. white wine vinegar
- 1 garlic clove, minced
- 1 Tbsp. dried oregano
- 1 Tbsp. olive oil
- 1 boneless leg of lamb (2½ lbs.), rolled and tied
- ½ tsp. salt
- ¼ tsp. pepper
- 1 lb. fresh mushrooms, quartered

1. In a small bowl, combine the wine, garlic and oregano; set aside. Rub oil over lamb, then sprinkle with salt and pepper. Place roast on a rack in a shallow roasting pan; spoon some of wine mixture over roast. Set aside remaining wine mixture.

2. Bake, uncovered, at 325° for 1-1½ hours or until meat reaches desired doneness (for medium-rare, a thermometer should read 135°; medium, 140°; medium-well, 145°), basting occasionally with some of reserved wine mixture. Remove from the oven; cover loosely with foil for 10-15 minutes.

3. Meanwhile, pour the pan drippings into a measuring cup; skim fat. In a large skillet coated with cooking spray, saute mushrooms until tender. Add the pan drippings and any remaining wine mixture; heat through. Slice lamb and serve with mushroom sauce.

1 serving: 330 cal., 13g fat (5g sat. fat), 114mg chol., 296mg sod., 7g carb. (4g sugars, 1g fiber), 38g pro. **Diabetic exchanges:** 5 lean meat, 1 vegetable.

ASPARAGUS HAM DINNER

I've been making this for my family for years now, and it's always well received. With asparagus, tomato, pasta and chunks of ham, it's a tempting blend of tastes and textures.
—*Rhonda Zavodny, David City, NE*

- -

Takes: 25 min. • **Makes:** 6 servings

- 2 **cups uncooked corkscrew or spiral pasta**
- ¾ **lb. fresh asparagus, cut into 1-in. pieces**
- 1 **medium sweet yellow pepper, julienned**
- 1 **Tbsp. olive oil**
- 6 **medium tomatoes, diced**
- 6 **oz. boneless fully cooked ham, cubed**
- ¼ **cup minced fresh parsley**
- ½ **tsp. salt**
- ½ **tsp. dried oregano**
- ½ **tsp. dried basil**
- ⅛ **to ¼ tsp. cayenne pepper**
- ¼ **cup shredded Parmesan cheese**

Cook pasta according to package directions. Meanwhile, in a large cast-iron or other heavy skillet, saute asparagus and yellow pepper in oil until crisp-tender. Add tomatoes and ham; heat through. Drain pasta; add to vegetable mixture. Stir in parsley and seasonings. Sprinkle with cheese.

1⅓ cups: 204 cal., 5g fat (1g sat. fat), 17mg chol., 561mg sod., 29g carb. (5g sugars, 3g fiber), 12g pro.

WINE PAIRING

Assyrtiko. If you've never had a wine from Greece, here's a tasty place to start. This refreshing white wine pairs with springtime foods like asparagus, ham and herbs. It has citrus, mineral and savory flavors.

BEEF BARLEY SKILLET

This versatile dish goes together fast since it's made with quick-cooking barley. You can make it with ground turkey or chicken, and any color bell pepper that you have on hand.
—*Irene Tetreault, South Hadley, MA*

Takes: 30 min. • **Makes:** 4 servings

- 1 lb. lean ground beef (90% lean)
- 1 small onion, chopped
- ¼ cup chopped celery
- ¼ cup chopped green pepper
- 1 can (14½ oz.) diced tomatoes, undrained
- 1½ cups water
- ¾ cup quick-cooking barley
- ½ cup chili sauce
- 1 tsp. Worcestershire sauce
- ½ tsp. dried marjoram
- ⅛ tsp. pepper
- Chopped parsley, optional

In a large skillet, cook ground beef, onion, celery and green pepper over medium-high heat until the beef is no longer pink and vegetables are tender, breaking up beef into crumbles, 5-7 minutes; drain. Stir in remaining ingredients. Bring to a boil; reduce heat. Simmer, uncovered, until barley is tender, 5-10 minutes. If desired, top with parsley.
1½ cups: 362 cal., 10g fat (4g sat. fat), 71mg chol., 707mg sod., 41g carb. (11g sugars, 8g fiber), 27g pro. **Diabetic exchanges:** 3 lean meat, 2 starch, 1 vegetable.

TEST KITCHEN TIP

Barley is a flavorful, chewy alternative to white rice. Pearl barley has had the double outer hull and bran layer removed. Quick-cooking barley is precooked pearl barley. Store barley in an airtight container in a cool, dry place. Barley also can be stored in the refrigerator or freezer.

ROSEMARY PORK TENDERLOIN

I started growing rosemary in my garden after I discovered this pork recipe. My husband and I think it's restaurant-quality, and we look forward to making it after work.
—*Judy Learned, Boyertown, PA*

Prep: 15 min. + standing • **Grill:** 20 min.
Makes: 4 servings

- 1 garlic clove, minced
- ¾ tsp. salt
- 1 Tbsp. olive oil
- 2 tsp. minced fresh rosemary
- ¼ tsp. pepper
- 1 pork tenderloin (1 lb.)

1. Place garlic on a cutting board; sprinkle with salt. Using the flat side of a knife, mash garlic. Continue to mash until it reaches a paste consistency. Transfer to a small bowl.
2. Stir in the oil, rosemary and pepper; brush over pork. Let stand for 20 minutes.
3. Grill pork on a lightly oiled rack, covered, over medium heat or broil 4 in. from the heat until a thermometer reads 145°, 9-11 minutes on each side. Let meat stand for 5 minutes before slicing.
3 oz. cooked pork: 163 cal., 7g fat (2g sat. fat), 63mg chol., 488mg sod., 0 carb. (0 sugars, 0 fiber), 23g pro. **Diabetic exchanges:** 3 lean meat, ½ fat.

WEEKNIGHT PASTA

This is a good recipe to make when short on time. Lovely herb accents enhance this easy gluten-free spaghetti and sauce.
—*Marv Salter, West Hills, CA*

Prep: 15 min. • **Cook:** 20 min.
Makes: 2 servings

- ½ lb. lean ground beef (90% lean)
- 1 cup sliced fresh mushrooms
- ⅓ cup chopped onion
- 1 garlic clove, minced
- 1 cup gluten-free reduced-sodium beef broth
- ⅔ cup water
- ⅓ cup tomato paste
- ½ tsp. dried basil
- ½ tsp. dried oregano
- ⅛ tsp. pepper
- 3 oz. uncooked gluten-free spaghetti, broken in half
- 2 tsp. grated Parmesan cheese

1. In a large skillet, cook the ground beef, mushrooms, onion and garlic over medium heat until the meat is no longer pink and the vegetables are tender; drain.
2. Stir in the broth, water, tomato paste, seasonings and spaghetti. Bring to a boil. Reduce the heat; cover and simmer until spaghetti is tender, 15-20 minutes. Sprinkle with cheese.
Note: Read all ingredient labels for possible gluten content prior to use. Ingredient formulas can change, and production facilities vary among brands. If you're concerned that your produce may contain gluten, contact the company.
1½ cups: 412 cal., 11g fat (4g sat. fat), 75mg chol., 335mg sod., 46g carb. (6g sugars, 4g fiber), 31g pro. **Diabetic exchanges:** 3 lean meat, 2½ starch, 2 vegetable.

❄ GRILLED GREEK PORK CHOPS

My in-laws taught me a lot about cooking, so any time I come across a great new recipe, I enjoy making it for them. These bright, lemony chops quickly became a favorite.
—*Geri Lipczynski, Oak Lawn, IL*

Prep: 15 min. + marinating • **Grill:** 10 min.
Makes: 4 servings

- 2 Tbsp. olive oil
- 4 tsp. lemon juice
- 1 Tbsp. Worcestershire sauce
- 2 tsp. dried oregano
- 1 tsp. salt
- 1 tsp. onion powder
- 1 tsp. garlic powder
- 1 tsp. pepper
- ½ tsp. ground mustard
- 4 boneless pork loin chops (¾ in. thick and 4 oz. each)

1. In a large bowl, mix the first 9 ingredients. Add pork chops and turn to coat. Cover; refrigerate 8 hours or overnight.
2. Drain pork, discarding marinade. Grill chops, covered, over medium heat or broil 4 in. from heat until a thermometer reads 145°, 4-5 minutes per side. Let stand for 5 minutes before serving.
Freeze option: Freeze chops with marinade in a freezer container. To use, thaw in refrigerator overnight. Drain pork, discarding marinade. Grill as directed.
1 pork chop: 193 cal., 10g fat (3g sat. fat), 55mg chol., 349mg sod., 2g carb. (0 sugars, 1g fiber), 22g pro. **Diabetic exchanges:** 3 lean meat, ½ fat.
Greek Chicken Breasts: Substitute 4 boneless skinless chicken breasts (6 oz. each) for the pork. Proceed as directed. Grill or broil until a thermometer reads 170°, 5-7 minutes on each side.

SWEET POTATO STEW

Beef broth and herbs pair nicely with the sweet potatoes' subtle sweetness in this hearty stew that's perfect for fall.
—*Helen Vail, Glenside, PA*

- -

Prep: 20 min. • **Cook:** 20 min.
Makes: 4 servings

- 2 cans (14½ oz. each) reduced-sodium beef broth
- ¾ lb. lean ground beef (90% lean)
- 2 medium sweet potatoes, peeled and cut into ½-in. cubes
- 1 small onion, finely chopped
- ½ cup V8 juice
- 1 Tbsp. golden raisins
- 1 garlic clove, minced
- ½ tsp. dried thyme
  Dash cayenne pepper

In a large saucepan, bring broth to a boil. Crumble beef into broth. Cook, covered, for 3 minutes, stirring occasionally. Add remaining ingredients; return to a boil. Reduce heat; simmer, uncovered, until meat is no longer pink and potatoes are tender, about 15 minutes.

1¼ cups: 265 cal., 7g fat (3g sat. fat), 58mg chol., 532mg sod., 29g carb. (13g sugars, 4g fiber), 20g pro. **Diabetic exchanges:** 2 starch, 2 lean meat.

LAMB PITAS WITH YOGURT SAUCE

The spiced lamb in these stuffed pita pockets goes perfectly with cool cucumber slices and creamy yogurt.

—Angela Leinenbach, Mechanicsville, VA

Prep: 35 min. • **Cook:** 6 hours
Makes: 8 servings

- 2 Tbsp. olive oil
- 2 lbs. lamb stew meat (¾-in. pieces)
- 1 large onion, chopped
- 1 garlic clove, minced
- ⅓ cup tomato paste
- ½ cup dry red wine
- 1¼ tsp. salt, divided
- 1 tsp. dried oregano
- ½ tsp. dried basil
- 1 medium cucumber
- 1 cup plain yogurt
- 16 pita pocket halves, warmed
- 4 plum tomatoes, sliced

1. In a large skillet, heat oil over medium-high heat; brown lamb in batches. Transfer lamb to a 3- or 4-qt. slow cooker, reserving the drippings in skillet.

2. In drippings, saute onion over medium heat until tender, 4-6 minutes. Add garlic and tomato paste; cook and stir 2 minutes. Stir in wine, 1 tsp. salt, oregano and basil. Add to lamb. Cook, covered, on low until lamb is tender, 6-8 hours.

3. To serve, dice enough cucumber to measure 1 cup; thinly slice remaining cucumber. Combine diced cucumber with yogurt and remaining salt. Fill pita halves with lamb mixture, tomatoes, sliced cucumbers and yogurt mixture.

Freeze option: Freeze cooled lamb mixture in freezer containers. To use, partially thaw in refrigerator overnight. Heat through in a saucepan, stirring occasionally; add a little broth or water if necessary.

2 filled pita halves: 383 cal., 11g fat (3g sat. fat), 78mg chol., 766mg sod., 39g carb. (5g sugars, 3g fiber), 31g pro. **Diabetic exchanges:** 3 lean meat, 2½ starch, 1 fat.

5i ⏱

GLAZED PORK CHOPS

When I was a new mom, I needed tasty, healthy meals I could whip up fast. These juicy chops won me over. Since this is a one-pan dish, cleanup's a breeze, too.
—*Kristin Tanis, Hatfield, PA*

Takes: 30 min. • **Makes:** 4 servings

- 4 bone-in pork loin chops (¾ in. thick and 7 oz. each)
- ⅓ cup plus 1 Tbsp. cider vinegar, divided
- 3 Tbsp. soy sauce
- 3 garlic cloves, minced
- 1½ tsp. cornstarch

1. In a large nonstick skillet, brown pork chops over medium heat, about 2 minutes per side. Mix ⅓ cup vinegar, soy sauce and garlic; pour over chops. Bring to a boil. Reduce heat; simmer, covered, until a thermometer inserted in pork reads 145°, 7-9 minutes.

2. Mix cornstarch and remaining vinegar until smooth; stir into pan. Bring to a boil; cook and stir until sauce is thickened, about 1 minute.

1 pork chop with 2 Tbsp. sauce: 224 cal., 8g fat (3g sat. fat), 86mg chol., 754mg sod., 2g carb. (0 sugars, 0 fiber), 32g pro. **Diabetic exchanges:** 4 lean meat.

READER RAVE

"Really rich flavors. The pork came out tender and moist. The whole family loved it, even the ones who are finicky about pork!"
—HECTOR3918, TASTEOFHOME.COM

⑤j

ITALIAN PORK & POTATO CASSEROLE

This dish's aroma when baking brings back fond memories of home. My mother created the recipe years ago, using ingredients she had on hand.

—*Theresa Kreyche, Tustin, CA*

Prep: 10 min. • **Bake:** 45 min.
Makes: 6 servings

- 6   **cups sliced red potatoes**
- 3   **Tbsp. water**
- 1   **garlic clove, minced**
- ½   **tsp. salt**
- ⅛   **tsp. pepper**
- 6   **boneless pork loin chops (6 oz. each)**
- 1   **jar (24 oz.) marinara sauce**
- ¼   **cup shredded Parmesan cheese**

1. Place potatoes and water in a microwave-safe dish. Cover and microwave on high until almost tender, about 5 minutes; drain.

2. Place potatoes in a 13x9-in. baking dish coated with cooking spray. Sprinkle with garlic, salt and pepper. Top with pork chops and marinara sauce. Cover and bake at 350° until a thermometer inserted in pork reads 145° and potatoes are tender, 40-45 minutes.

3. Sprinkle with cheese. Bake, uncovered, until cheese is melted, 3-5 minutes longer. Let stand 5 minutes before serving.

1 pork chop with 1 cup potatoes and ½ cup sauce: 412 cal., 11g fat (4g sat. fat), 84mg chol., 506mg sod., 38g carb. (10g sugars, 4g fiber) 39g pro.

GREEK-STYLE STUFFED PEPPERS

A bounty of bell peppers combines with traditional Greek ingredients to create a dish that bursts with color and fresh flavor.
—Renee Murby, Johnston, RI

Prep: 30 min. • **Cook:** 4½ hours
Makes: 8 servings

- 2 Tbsp. olive oil
- 1 small fennel bulb, chopped
- 1 small red onion, chopped
- 1 pkg. (10 oz.) frozen chopped spinach, thawed and squeezed dry
- 3 garlic cloves, minced
- 2 each medium sweet yellow, orange, red and green peppers
- 1 can (28 oz.) crushed tomatoes, divided
- 1 lb. ground lamb
- 1 cup cooked barley
- 1 cup crumbled feta cheese, plus more for serving
- ½ cup Greek olives, chopped
- 1½ tsp. dried oregano
- ½ tsp. salt
- ½ tsp. crushed red pepper flakes
- ½ tsp. pepper
  Chopped fresh parsley, optional

1. In a large skillet, heat oil over medium-high heat. Add fennel and onion; cook and stir until tender, 6-8 minutes. Add spinach and garlic; cook 1 minute longer. Cool slightly.
2. Cut and reserve tops from peppers; remove seeds. Pour 1 cup crushed tomatoes into bottom of a 6- or 7-qt. slow cooker. In large bowl, combine remaining ingredients; add fennel mixture. Spoon mixture into peppers; place in slow cooker. Pour remaining crushed tomatoes over peppers; replace pepper tops. Cook, covered, on low until peppers are tender, 4½-5½ hours. If desired, serve peppers with additional feta and chopped parsley.
1 stuffed pepper: 313 cal., 16g fat (6g sat. fat), 45mg chol., 684mg sod., 26g carb. (11g sugars, 8g fiber), 17g pro.

5i ⏱

LEMON-GARLIC PORK CHOPS

My son James created these zesty chops spiced with paprika and cayenne. He keeps the spice rub in a jar to use with pork or chicken breasts.

—Molly Seidel, Edgewood, NM

- -

Takes: 20 min. • **Makes:** 4 servings

- 2 Tbsp. lemon juice
- 2 garlic cloves, minced
- 1 tsp. salt
- 1 tsp. paprika
- ½ tsp. pepper
- ¼ tsp. cayenne pepper
- 4 boneless pork loin chops (6 oz. each)

1. Preheat broiler. In a small bowl, mix the first 6 ingredients; brush over pork chops. Place in a 15x10x1-in. baking pan.
2. Broil 4-5 in. from heat until a thermometer reads 145°, 4-5 minutes on each side. Let stand 5 minutes before serving.
1 pork chop: 233 cal., 10g fat (4g sat. fat), 82mg chol., 638mg sod., 2g carb. (0 sugars, 0 fiber), 33g pro. **Diabetic exchanges:** 5 lean meat.

LAMB CHOPS WITH MINT SALSA

This flavorful entree is well seasoned with an herbal rub of basil, garlic, rosemary and thyme. Serve the tender slices of meat with a refreshing salsa that will have even non-lamb lovers licking their lips.

—Taste of Home Test Kitchen

- -

Prep: 15 min. + chilling • **Bake:** 20 min.
Makes: 8 servings (2 cups salsa)

- 5 tsp. olive oil
- 2 garlic cloves, minced
- 1 tsp. each dried basil, thyme and rosemary, crushed
- ½ tsp. salt
- ¼ tsp. pepper
- 2 racks of lamb (8 ribs each)

MINT SALSA
- 1 cup minced fresh mint
- 1 small cucumber, peeled, seeded and chopped
- ½ cup seeded chopped tomato
- ⅓ cup finely chopped onion
- ⅓ cup chopped sweet yellow pepper
- 1 jalapeno pepper, seeded and chopped
- 3 Tbsp. lemon juice
- 2 Tbsp. sugar
- 2 garlic cloves, minced
- ¾ tsp. ground ginger
- ¼ tsp. salt

1. In a small bowl, combine the oil, garlic and seasonings. Rub over lamb. Place in a roasting pan; cover and refrigerate for 1 hour. In a bowl, combine the salsa ingredients; cover and refrigerate until serving.
2. Bake lamb, uncovered, at 425° until meat reaches desired doneness (for medium-rare, a thermometer should read 135°; medium, 140°; medium-well, 145°), for 20-30 minutes. Cover loosely with foil; let stand 5-10 minutes before slicing. Serve with mint salsa.
Note: Wear disposable gloves when cutting hot peppers; the oils can burn skin. Avoid touching your face.
2 lamb chops with ¼ cup salsa: 184 cal., 10g fat (3g sat. fat), 49mg chol., 270mg sod., 7g carb. (4g sugars, 1g fiber), 15g pro. **Diabetic exchanges:** 2 lean meat, ½ starch, ½ fat.

WINE PAIRING

Cabernet Sauvignon. Choose a fruity cabernet (or a cab-merlot blend) from a warm climate like California. Cabs taste good with fresh mint, and they are wonderful with flavorful meats like this.

POTATO-TOPPED GROUND BEEF SKILLET

I love recipes I can cook and serve in the same skillet. Compared to other ground beef skillet recipes, the depth of flavor in this one is amazing, and I never have leftovers when I take it to potlucks. If your butcher has chili grind beef, which is coarsely ground, go for that—it lends an extra meaty texture.

—Fay Moreland, Wichita Falls, TX

- -

Prep: 25 min. • **Cook:** 45 min.
Makes: 8 servings

- 2   lbs. lean ground beef (90% lean)
- ½   tsp. salt
- ¼   tsp. pepper
- 1   Tbsp. olive oil
- 1   large onion, chopped
- 4   medium carrots, sliced
- ½   lb. sliced fresh mushrooms
- 4   garlic cloves, minced
- 2   Tbsp. all-purpose flour
- 2   tsp. herbes de Provence
- 1¼   cups dry red wine or reduced-sodium beef broth
- 1   can (14½ oz.) reduced-sodium beef broth

TOPPING

- 1¼   lbs. red potatoes (about 4 medium), cut into ¼-in. slices
- 1   Tbsp. olive oil
- ¼   tsp. salt
- ⅛   tsp. pepper
- ⅓   cup shredded Parmesan cheese Minced fresh parsley, optional

1. In a broiler-safe 12-in. skillet, cook and crumble beef over medium-high heat until no longer pink, 6-8 minutes. Stir in salt and pepper; remove from pan.

2. In same pan, heat oil over medium-high heat; saute onion, carrots, mushrooms and garlic until onion is tender, 4-6 minutes. Stir in flour and herbs; cook 1 minute. Stir in the wine; bring to a boil. Cook 1 minute, stirring to loosen browned bits from pan. Add beef and broth; return to a boil. Reduce heat; simmer, covered, until flavors are blended, about 30 minutes, stirring occasionally. Remove from heat.

3. Meanwhile, place potatoes in a large saucepan; add water to cover. Bring to a boil. Reduce heat; cook, uncovered, until tender, 10-12 minutes. Drain; cool slightly.

4. Preheat broiler. Arrange potatoes over stew, overlapping slightly; brush lightly with oil. Sprinkle with salt and pepper, then cheese. Broil 5-6 in. from heat until potatoes are lightly browned, 6-8 minutes. Let stand 5 minutes. If desired, sprinkle with parsley.

1¼ cups: 313 cal., 14g fat (5g sat. fat), 74mg chol., 459mg sod., 18g carb. (4g sugars, 3g fiber), 26g pro. **Diabetic exchanges:** 3 lean meat, 1 vegetable, ½ starch, ½ fat.

TEST KITCHEN TIP

Common olive oil works better when cooking at a high heat than virgin or extra virgin oil. While these higher grades have ideal flavor for cold foods, they start to smoke at a lower temperature.

SPICE-RUBBED LAMB CHOPS

Lamb chops rank among my all-time favorite things to eat. My girls, Hanna and Amani, love watching me make my delicious chops, but they love eating them even more.

—Nareman Dietz, Beverly Hills, MI

- -

Prep: 15 min. + chilling • **Bake:** 5 min.
Makes: 2 servings

2	tsp. lemon juice
2	tsp. Worcestershire sauce
1½	tsp. pepper
1¼	tsp. ground cumin
1¼	tsp. curry powder
1	garlic clove, minced
½	tsp. sea salt
½	tsp. onion powder
½	tsp. crushed red pepper flakes
4	lamb rib chops
1	Tbsp. olive oil

1. Mix first 9 ingredients; spread over chops. Refrigerate, covered, overnight.
2. Preheat oven to 450°. In an ovenproof skillet, heat oil over medium-high heat; brown chops, about 2 minutes per side. Transfer to oven; roast until desired doneness (for medium-rare, a thermometer should read 135°; medium, 140°), 3-4 minutes.
2 lamb chops: 290 cal., 17g fat (4g sat. fat), 90mg chol., 620mg sod., 5g carb. (1g sugars, 2g fiber), 29g pro. **Diabetic exchanges:** 4 lean meat, 1½ fat.

MEDITERRANEAN POT ROAST DINNER

I first made this recipe one cold winter day. My family (adults, kids and dogs) were having a blast sledding and playing in the snow, and when we came inside supper was ready! This pot roast is perfect served with mashed potatoes, rice or dinner rolls.

—Holly Battiste, Barrington, NJ

Prep: 30 min. • **Cook:** 8 hours
Makes: 8 servings

- 2 lbs. potatoes (about 6 medium), peeled and cut into 2-in. pieces
- 5 medium carrots (about ¾ lb.), cut into 1-in. pieces
- 2 Tbsp. all-purpose flour
- 1 boneless beef chuck roast (3 to 4 lbs.)
- 1 Tbsp. olive oil
- 8 large fresh mushrooms, quartered
- 2 celery ribs, chopped
- 1 medium onion, thinly sliced
- ¼ cup sliced Greek olives
- ½ cup minced fresh parsley, divided
- 1 can (14½ oz.) fire-roasted diced tomatoes, undrained
- 1 Tbsp. minced fresh oregano or 1 tsp. dried oregano
- 1 Tbsp. lemon juice
- 2 tsp. minced fresh rosemary or ½ tsp. dried rosemary, crushed
- 2 garlic cloves, minced
- ¾ tsp. salt
- ¼ tsp. pepper
- ¼ tsp. crushed red pepper flakes, optional

1. Place potatoes and carrots in a 6-qt. slow cooker. Sprinkle flour over all surfaces of roast. In a large skillet, heat oil over medium-high heat. Brown roast on all sides. Place over vegetables.

2. Add mushrooms, celery, onion, olives and ¼ cup parsley to slow cooker. In a small bowl, mix remaining ingredients; pour over top.

3. Cook, covered, on low 8-10 hours or until meat and vegetables are tender. Remove beef. Stir remaining parsley into vegetables. Serve beef with vegetables.

5 oz. cooked beef with 1 cup vegetables: 422 cal., 18g fat (6g sat. fat), 111mg chol., 538mg sod., 28g carb. (6g sugars, 4g fiber), 37g pro.
Diabetic exchanges: 5 lean meat, 1½ starch, 1 vegetable, ½ fat.

ROASTED BEEF TENDERLOIN

Roast beef marinated in port wine and spices makes a simple but elegant roast.

—*Schelby Thompson, Camden Wyoming, DE*

Prep: 10 min. + marinating
Bake: 40 min. + standing
Makes: 12 servings

- ½ cup port wine or ½ cup beef broth plus 1 Tbsp. balsamic vinegar
- ½ cup reduced-sodium soy sauce
- 2 Tbsp. olive oil
- 4 to 5 garlic cloves, minced
- 1 tsp. dried thyme
- 1 tsp. pepper
- ½ tsp. hot pepper sauce
- 1 beef tenderloin roast (3 lbs.)
- 1 bay leaf

1. For the marinade, whisk together first 7 ingredients. Place roast, bay leaf and ¾ cup marinade into a large bowl and turn to coat. Cover and refrigerate 8 hours or overnight. Reserve remaining marinade for basting; cover and refrigerate.

2. Preheat oven to 425°. Place tenderloin on a rack in a roasting pan; discard bay leaf and marinade. Roast until meat reaches desired doneness (for medium-rare, a thermometer should read 135°; medium, 140°; medium-well, 145°), for 40-50 minutes, basting occasionally with the reserved marinade during the last 15 minutes.

3. Remove roast from oven; tent with foil. Let stand 10 minutes before slicing.

3 oz. cooked beef: 193 cal., 8g fat (3g sat. fat), 49mg chol., 257mg sod., 2g carb. (1g sugars, 0 fiber), 25g pro.

WINE PAIRING

Merlot. Red wine goes well with beef tenderloin. Merlot is a good choice here; it's soft and fruit-forward to echo the port marinade.

ANCHO GARLIC STEAKS WITH SUMMER SALSA

The first time I tasted this, I was amazed how well the blueberries and watermelon went with the peppery steak. Use whatever fruits are in season so you can serve this anytime.

—Veronica Callaghan, Glastonbury, CT

- -

Takes: 30 min. • **Makes:** 4 servings

- 2 **boneless beef top loin steaks** (1¼ in. thick and 8 oz. each)
- 2 tsp. ground ancho chili pepper
- 1 tsp. garlic salt

SALSA

- 1 cup seeded diced watermelon
- 1 cup fresh blueberries
- 1 medium tomato, chopped
- ¼ cup finely chopped red onion
- 1 Tbsp. minced fresh mint
- 1½ tsp. grated fresh gingerroot
- ¼ tsp. salt

1. Rub steaks with chili pepper and garlic salt. Grill, covered, over medium heat or broil 4 in. from heat until the meat reaches the desired doneness (for medium-rare, a thermometer should read 135°; medium, 140°; medium-well, 145°), 7-9 minutes on each side.

2. In a bowl, combine salsa ingredients. Cut steak into slices; serve with salsa.

Note: Top loin steak may be labeled as strip steak, Kansas City steak, New York strip steak, ambassador steak or boneless club steak in your region.

3 oz. cooked beef with ½ cup salsa: 195 cal., 5g fat (2g sat. fat), 50mg chol., 442mg sod., 10g carb. (7g sugars, 2g fiber), 25g pro. **Diabetic exchanges:** 3 lean meat, ½ fruit.

MEDITERRANEAN PORK & ORZO

On a busy day, this meal in a bowl is one of my go-to recipes. It's quick to put together, leaving me more time to relax at the table.
—*Mary Relyea, Canastota, NY*

Takes: 30 min. • **Makes:** 6 servings

1½	lbs. pork tenderloin
1	tsp. coarsely ground pepper
2	Tbsp. olive oil
3	qt. water
1¼	cups uncooked orzo pasta
¼	tsp. salt
1	pkg. (6 oz.) fresh baby spinach
1	cup grape tomatoes, halved
¾	cup crumbled feta cheese

1. Rub pork with pepper; cut into 1-in. cubes. In a large nonstick skillet, heat the oil over medium heat. Add pork; cook and stir until no longer pink, 8-10 minutes.
2. Meanwhile, in a Dutch oven, bring water to a boil. Stir in orzo and salt; cook, uncovered, for 8 minutes. Stir in spinach; cook until orzo is tender and spinach is wilted, 45-60 seconds longer. Drain.
3. Add tomatoes to pork; heat through. Stir in orzo mixture and cheese.
1⅓ cups: 372 cal., 11g fat (4g sat. fat), 71mg chol., 306mg sod., 34g carb. (2g sugars, 3g fiber), 31g pro. **Diabetic exchanges:** 3 lean meat, 2 starch, 1 vegetable, 1 fat.

SKEWERLESS STOVETOP KABOBS

My family loves this quick and easy recipe so much, we never have any leftovers. It's also great on the grill.
—*Jennifer Mitchell, Altoona, PA*

- -

Takes: 30 min. • **Makes:** 4 servings

1 pork tenderloin (1 lb.), cut into ¾-in. cubes
¾ cup fat-free Italian salad dressing, divided
2 large green peppers, cut into ¾-in. pieces
2 small zucchini, cut into ½-in. slices
1 large sweet onion, cut into wedges
½ lb. medium fresh mushrooms, halved
1 cup cherry tomatoes
¼ tsp. pepper
⅛ tsp. seasoned salt

1. In a large cast-iron or other heavy skillet, cook pork over medium-high heat in ¼ cup salad dressing until no longer pink. Remove from pan.
2. In same pan, cook peppers, zucchini, onion, mushrooms, tomatoes, pepper and seasoned salt in remaining salad dressing until vegetables are tender. Return pork to skillet; heat through.

2 cups: 236 cal., 5g fat (2g sat. fat), 65mg chol., 757mg sod., 22g carb. (12g sugars, 4g fiber), 27g pro. **Diabetic exchanges:** 3 lean meat, 2 starch.

SPICY LAMB CURRY

I've tweaked this curry over the years using a blend of aromatic spices. Fenugreek seeds are common in Middle Eastern cuisine and can be found in specialty spice stores.
—*Janis Kracht, Slaterville Springs, NY*

- -

Prep: 25 min. + marinating • **Cook:** 1 hour
Makes: 6 servings

3 Tbsp. ground cumin
2 Tbsp. ground ginger
1 Tbsp. ground coriander
1 Tbsp. ground fenugreek
4 garlic cloves, minced
1 tsp. ground cloves
½ tsp. ground cinnamon
2 lbs. lamb stew meat, cut into ¾-in. pieces
1 Tbsp. olive oil
2 large onions, chopped
½ cup water
2 Tbsp. paprika
2 Tbsp. tomato paste
1 tsp. salt
1 tsp. ground mustard
1 tsp. chili powder
1 cup (8 oz.) plain yogurt
3 cups hot cooked brown rice
Optional toppings: Cubed fresh pineapple, flaked coconut and toasted sliced almonds

1. In a large bowl, combine first 7 ingredients. Add the lamb; turn to coat. Cover; refrigerate for 8 hours or overnight.
2. In a Dutch oven, brown meat in oil in batches; remove and keep warm. In the same pan, cook onions in drippings until tender. Add the water, paprika, tomato paste, salt, mustard and chili powder.
3. Return lamb to pan. Bring to a boil. Reduce heat; cover and simmer for 1-1½ hours or until meat is tender. Remove from the heat; stir in yogurt. Serve with rice. Top with the pineapple, coconut and almonds if desired.
Note: Ground fenugreek is available from Penzeys Spices. Visit *penzeys.com* or call 800-741-7787.

¾ cup curry with ½ cup rice: 419 cal., 14g fat (4g sat. fat), 104mg chol., 534mg sod., 36g carb. (5g sugars, 6g fiber), 37g pro.

MUSHROOM & SPINACH SAUTE,
PAGE 224

Side Dishes

Let these standout dishes be the difference between a good entree and a great meal. Go ahead and go back for seconds! These bright sides are too good to pass up.

MUSHROOM & SPINACH SAUTE

Fresh veggies and garlic combine to make this super-fast dish that's perfect for two, but easy to double or triple for a crowd.
—*Pauline Howard, Lago Vista, TX*

- -

Takes: 10 min. • **Makes:** 2 servings

- 2 tsp. olive oil
- 2 cups sliced fresh mushrooms
- 2 garlic cloves, minced
- 1 pkg. (5 to 6 oz.) fresh baby spinach
- ⅛ tsp. salt
- ⅛ tsp. pepper

In a large skillet, heat oil over medium-high heat. Add mushrooms; saute until tender, about 2 minutes. Add garlic; cook 1 minute longer. Add spinach in batches; cook and stir until wilted, about 1 minute. Season with salt and pepper. Serve immediately.

¾ cup: 76 cal., 5g fat (1g sat. fat), 0mg chol., 208mg sod., 6g carb. (2g sugars, 2g fiber), 4g pro. **Diabetic exchanges:** 1 vegetable, 1 fat.

LEMON PARMESAN ORZO

A hint of lemon and a generous helping of chopped parsley make this orzo one of my family's most requested springtime recipes. It goes well with chicken, pork or fish, and you could eat it on its own for a light lunch.
—*Leslie Palmer, Swampscott, MA*

- -

Takes: 20 min. • **Makes:** 4 servings

- 1 cup uncooked whole wheat orzo pasta
- 1 Tbsp. olive oil
- ¼ cup grated Parmesan cheese
- 2 Tbsp. minced fresh parsley
- ½ tsp. grated lemon zest
- ¼ tsp. salt
- ¼ tsp. pepper

Cook orzo according to package directions; drain. Transfer to a small bowl; drizzle with oil. Stir in remaining ingredients.

½ cup: 191 cal., 6g fat (1g sat. fat), 4mg chol., 225mg sod., 28g carb. (0 sugars, 7g fiber), 7g pro. **Diabetic exchanges:** 2 starch, ½ fat.

STEAMED KALE

This steamed kale tastes amazing and is packed with vitamins. It's a wonderful accompaniment to almost any entree. I use garlic, red pepper and balsamic vinegar to keep my family coming back for more!

—*Mary Bilyeu, Ann Arbor, MI*

- -

Prep: 15 min. • **Cook:** 25 min.
Makes: 4 servings

1	**bunch kale**
1	**Tbsp. olive oil**
3	**garlic cloves, minced**
⅔	**cup water**
¼	**tsp. salt**
⅛	**tsp. crushed red pepper flakes**
1	**Tbsp. balsamic vinegar**

1. Trim kale, discarding the thick ribs and stems. Chop leaves. In a Dutch oven, saute kale leaves in oil until wilted. Add garlic; cook 1 minute longer.

2. Stir in the water, salt and pepper flakes. Bring to a boil. Reduce heat; cover and simmer for 20-25 minutes or until kale is tender. Remove from heat; stir in vinegar.

¾ cup: 61 cal., 4g fat (1g sat. fat), 0 chol., 171mg sod., 6g carb. (1g sugars, 1g fiber), 2g pro. **Diabetic exchanges:** 1 vegetable, ½ fat.

LEMON-GARLIC LIMA BEANS

When I was growing up on Cyprus, my mom would often make this side dish to have with roast lamb. I wasn't a big fan of lima beans when I was a kid, but now I love them. They remind me of home.

—*Paris Paraskeva, San Francisco, CA*

- -

Prep: 15 min. + soaking • **Cook:** 1¼ hours
Makes: 6 servings

- 1 **lb. dried lima beans**
- 2 **bay leaves**
- 3 **Tbsp. extra virgin olive oil, divided**
- 1 **medium onion, chopped**
- 4 **garlic cloves, thinly sliced**
- ¼ **cup chopped fresh parsley**
- 2 **Tbsp. lemon juice**
- 1 **Tbsp. chopped fresh oregano**
- 2 **tsp. grated lemon zest**
- ½ **tsp. salt**
- ¼ **tsp. pepper**
  Additional chopped fresh parsley

1. Rinse and sort beans; soak according to package directions. Drain and rinse beans, discarding liquid.

2. Place beans in a large saucepan; add bay leaves and water to cover by 2 in. Bring to a boil. Reduce heat; simmer, covered, until beans are tender, 1¼-1½ hours. Drain.

3. In a large skillet, heat 1 Tbsp. oil over medium heat. Add onion; cook and stir until tender, 3-4 minutes. Add garlic; cook 1 minute longer. Add next 6 ingredients. Stir in drained beans and remaining oil; toss to combine. Sprinkle with additional parsley.

½ cup: 326 cal., 8g fat (1g sat. fat), 0 chol., 209mg sod., 51g carb. (7g sugars, 16g fiber), 16g pro.

SCENTED RICE IN BAKED PUMPKIN

This beautiful, delicious and healthy side is a showpiece that always delights family and friends. Feel free to use different grains, squash, fruit and nuts to suit your tastes— it's impossible to go wrong!

—*Lynn Heisel, Jackson, MO*

Prep: 30 min. • **Bake:** 35 min.
Makes: 2 servings

- 1 small pie pumpkin (about 2 lbs.)
- 1 Tbsp. olive oil
- ½ cup uncooked brown rice
- 1 cup water
- ¼ cup coarsely chopped pecans, toasted
- 3 dried apricots, chopped
- 2 Tbsp. raisins
- ¼ tsp. salt
- ¼ tsp. curry powder
- ⅛ tsp. ground cinnamon
- ⅛ tsp. ground cardamom, optional
- ⅛ tsp. ground cumin

1. Wash pumpkin; cut into 6 wedges. Remove loose fibers and seeds from the inside and discard or save seeds for toasting. Brush pumpkin wedges with olive oil. Place onto an ungreased 15x10x1-in. baking sheet. Bake at 400° for 35-40 minutes or until tender.
2. Meanwhile, in a small saucepan, bring rice and water to a boil. Reduce heat; cover and simmer for 20-25 minutes or until liquid is absorbed and rice is tender. Stir in the pecans, apricots, raisins, salt, curry, cinnamon and, if desired, cardamom. Set 4 pumpkin wedges aside for another use. Sprinkle cumin onto remaining wedges; top with rice mixture.
Note: Use the leftover roasted pie pumpkin any way you would used cooked winter squash: puree and use in soup, mash for a side dish, or cube and stir into stuffing or pilaf.
1 serving: 389 cal., 15g fat (2g sat. fat), 0 chol., 309mg sod., 62g carb. (13g sugars, 5g fiber), 7g pro.

BALSAMIC-GLAZED ZUCCHINI

I am a member of an organic Community Supported Agriculture farm. Once I received the most delicious garden-fresh garlic and zucchini in a seasonal box, which led to my discovery of this amazing recipe.
—*Joe Cherry, Metuchen, NJ*

- -

Takes: 15 min. • **Makes:** 4 servings

- 1 Tbsp. olive oil
- 3 medium zucchini, cut into ½-in. slices
- 2 garlic cloves, minced
- ¼ tsp. salt
- ¼ cup balsamic vinegar

1. In a large skillet, heat oil over medium-high heat. Add zucchini; cook and stir until tender, 5-7 minutes. Add the garlic and salt; cook 1 minute longer. Remove from pan.

2. Add vinegar to same pan; bring to a boil. Cook until reduced by half. Add the zucchini; toss to coat.

⅔ cup: 65 cal., 4g fat (1g sat. fat), 0 chol., 166mg sod., 8g carb. (5g sugars, 2g fiber), 2g pro. **Diabetic exchanges:** 1 vegetable, 1 fat.

ROASTED ITALIAN GREEN BEANS & TOMATOES

Roasting green beans and tomatoes allows their flavors to shine through. The vibrant colors of this dish light up our holiday table.
—*Brittany Allyn, Mesa, AZ*

- -

Takes: 25 min. • **Makes:** 8 servings

- 1½ **lbs. fresh green beans,**
  trimmed and halved
- 1 **Tbsp. olive oil**
- 1 **tsp. Italian seasoning**
- ½ **tsp. salt**
- 2 **cups grape tomatoes, halved**
- ½ **cup grated Parmesan cheese**

1. Preheat oven to 425°. Place the green beans in a 15x10x1-in. baking pan coated with cooking spray. Mix oil, Italian seasoning and salt; drizzle over beans. Toss to coat. Roast 10 minutes, stirring once.

2. Add tomatoes to pan. Roast until beans are crisp-tender and the tomatoes are softened, 4-6 minutes longer. Sprinkle with cheese.

¾ cup: 70 cal., 3g fat (1g sat. fat), 4mg chol., 231mg sod., 8g carb. (3g sugars, 3g fiber), 4g pro. **Diabetic exchanges:** 1 vegetable, ½ fat.

SAUTEED SQUASH WITH TOMATOES & ONIONS

My favorite meals showcase my love of family and food. This zucchini with tomatoes is like a scaled-down ratatouille—comforting, simple and delicious!

—*Adan Franco, Milwaukee, WI*

Takes: 20 min. • **Makes:** 8 servings

- 2 Tbsp. olive oil
- 1 medium onion, finely chopped
- 4 medium zucchini, chopped
- 2 large tomatoes, finely chopped
- 1 tsp. salt
- ¼ tsp. pepper

1. In a large skillet, heat oil over medium-high heat. Add onion; cook and stir until tender, 2-4 minutes. Add zucchini; cook and stir for 3 minutes.
2. Stir in tomatoes, salt and pepper; cook and stir until squash is tender, 4-6 minutes longer. Serve with a slotted spoon.
¾ cup: 60 cal., 4g fat (1g sat. fat), 0 chol., 306mg sod., 6g carb. (4g sugars, 2g fiber), 2g pro. **Diabetic exchanges:** 1 vegetable, ½ fat.

ROASTED BROCCOLI & CAULIFLOWER

Whenever we make a time-consuming main dish, it gives us the opportunity to whip up this quick broccoli and cauliflower side. The veggies are an especially good fit when you're watching calories.

—*Debra Tolbert, Deville, LA*

Takes: 25 min. • **Makes:** 8 servings

- 4 cups fresh cauliflowerets
- 4 cups fresh broccoli florets
- 10 garlic cloves, peeled and halved
- 2 Tbsp. olive oil
- ½ tsp. salt
- ½ tsp. pepper

Preheat oven to 425°. In a large bowl, combine all ingredients; toss to coat. Transfer to 2 greased 15x10x1-in. baking pans. Roast 15-20 minutes or until tender.
¾ cup: 58 cal., 4g fat (1g sat. fat), 0 chol., 173mg sod., 6g carb. (2g sugars, 2g fiber), 2g pro. **Diabetic exchanges:** 1 vegetable, ½ fat.

GRILLED EGGPLANT WITH FETA RELISH

I created this impressive eggplant with feta as a light dish for my vegetarian friends. It's an easy accompaniment that stands out.
—*Amanda Dekrey, Fargo, ND*

Takes: 25 min. • **Makes:** 8 servings

- 3 Tbsp. balsamic vinaigrette
- 1 tsp. garlic powder
- 1 cup (4 ounces) crumbled feta cheese
- ⅔ cup chopped seeded peeled cucumber
- ½ cup chopped seeded plum tomato
- ¼ cup finely chopped red onion
- 8 slices eggplant (¾ inch thick)
- 2 Tbsp. olive oil
- 1 tsp. salt
- ½ tsp. pepper
  Minced fresh basil or parsley, optional

1. In a small bowl, whisk the vinaigrette and garlic powder until combined. Stir in feta, cucumber, tomato and onion. Refrigerate, covered, until serving.
2. Brush eggplant with oil; sprinkle with salt and pepper. Grill, covered, over medium heat or broil 4 in. from heat 4-5 minutes on each side or until tender. Top eggplant with feta mixture. If desired, sprinkle with basil.
1 eggplant slice with 3 Tbsp. relish: 105 cal., 7g fat (2g sat. fat), 8mg chol., 499mg sod., 8g carb. (4g sugars, 3g fiber), 4g pro.

OLIVE OIL MASHED POTATOES WITH PANCETTA

In this tasty side, classic American mashed potatoes take a trip to Italy with the flavors of olive oil, garlic and pancetta. No one will be able to resist going back for seconds!
—*Bryan Kennedy, Kaneohe, HI*

Takes: 30 min. • **Makes:** 8 servings

- 3 lbs. Yukon Gold potatoes, peeled and cubed
- 3 slices pancetta or bacon, chopped
- 1 Tbsp. plus ¼ cup olive oil, divided
- 4 garlic cloves, minced
- ⅓ cup minced fresh parsley
- ½ tsp. salt
- ½ tsp. pepper

1. Place potatoes in a large saucepan and cover with water. Bring to a boil. Reduce heat; cover and simmer until tender, 15-20 minutes.
2. Meanwhile, in a large skillet, cook pancetta in 1 Tbsp. oil over medium heat until crisp. Add garlic; cook for 1 minute longer. Remove from the heat.
3. Drain potatoes; transfer to a large bowl. Mash potatoes with remaining oil. Stir in the parsley, pancetta mixture, salt and pepper.
⅔ cup: 206 cal., 11g fat (2g sat. fat), 7mg chol., 313mg sod., 23g carb. (2g sugars, 2g fiber), 4g pro. **Diabetic exchanges:** 2 fat, 1½ starch.

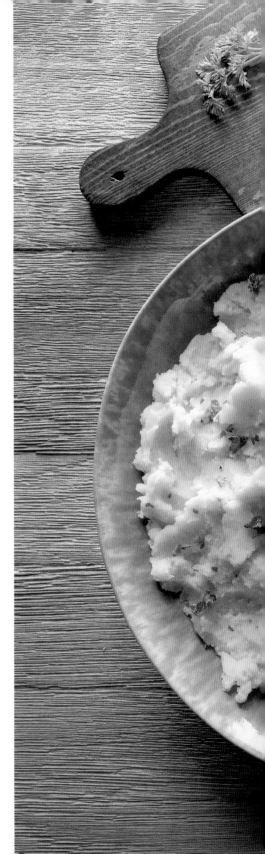

LEMONY GREEN BEANS

The beauty of this recipe is you can throw it together in minutes using ingredients you probably already have on hand. It tastes amazing, too. What's not to love?
—*Jennifer Capoano, Carlstadt, NJ*

Takes: 20 min. • **Makes:** 6 servings

  ¼ cup chicken broth
  2 Tbsp. olive oil
1½ lbs. fresh green beans, trimmed
  ¾ tsp. lemon-pepper seasoning
     Lemon wedges

In a large skillet, heat chicken broth and oil over medium-high heat. Add green beans; cook and stir until crisp-tender. Sprinkle with lemon pepper. Serve with lemon wedges.
1 serving: 76 cal., 5g fat (1g sat. fat), 0 chol., 88mg sod., 8g carb. (3g sugars, 4g fiber), 2g pro. **Diabetic exchanges:** 1 vegetable, 1 fat.

PESTO PASTA & POTATOES

Although this healthy pasta dish is pretty simple to begin with, the cooking method makes it even simpler: You can throw the green beans and pasta into one big pot.
—*Laura Flowers, Moscow, ID*

Takes: 30 min. • **Makes:** 12 servings

- 1½ lbs. small red potatoes, halved
- 12 oz. uncooked whole grain spiral pasta
- 3 cups cut fresh or frozen green beans
- 1 jar (6½ oz.) prepared pesto
- 1 cup grated Parmigiano-Reggiano cheese

1. Place potatoes in a large saucepan; add water to cover. Bring to a boil. Reduce heat; cook, uncovered, until tender, 8-10 minutes. Drain; transfer to a large bowl.

2. Meanwhile, cook pasta according to package directions, adding green beans during the last 5 minutes of cooking. Drain, reserving ¾ cup pasta water, and add to potatoes. Toss with pesto, cheese and enough pasta water to moisten.

¾ cup: 261 cal., 10g fat (3g sat. fat), 11mg chol., 233mg sod., 34g carb. (2g sugars, 5g fiber), 11g pro. **Diabetic exchanges:** 2 starch, 2 fat.

READER RAVE

"I haven't made a lot of pesto dishes. This was refreshing and delicious!"
—QUEENLALISA, TASTEOFHOME.COM

HERB & SUN-DRIED TOMATO MUFFINS

My mom often made these yummy muffins instead of bread or buns. Now I love to bake them and serve alongside soup or chili.
—*Elizabeth King, Duluth, MN*

Prep: 20 min. • **Bake:** 20 min.
Makes: 1 dozen

- 2 cups all-purpose flour
- 2 tsp. baking powder
- 1 tsp. snipped fresh dill or ¼ tsp. dill weed
- 1 tsp. minced fresh thyme or ¼ tsp. dried thyme
- ½ tsp. baking soda
- ½ tsp. salt
- ½ tsp. pepper
- 1 large egg
- 1¼ cups 2% milk
- ¼ cup olive oil
- ½ cup shredded cheddar cheese
- ½ cup oil-packed sun-dried tomatoes, finely chopped

1. Preheat oven to 375°. In a large bowl, mix first 7 ingredients. In another bowl, whisk the egg, milk and olive oil. Add to the flour mixture; stir just until moistened. Fold in the cheese and tomatoes.

2. Fill greased muffin cups three-fourths full. Bake 18-20 minutes or until a toothpick inserted in center comes out clean. Cool 5 minutes before removing from pan to a wire rack. Serve warm.

1 muffin: 161 cal., 8g fat (2g sat. fat), 25mg chol., 277mg sod., 18g carb. (2g sugars, 1g fiber), 5g pro. **Diabetic exchanges:** 1½ fat, 1 starch.

ROSEMARY BEETS

We're a family of beet eaters. For a simple side dish, I use a slow cooker and let the beets mellow with rosemary and thyme.
—*Nancy Heishman, Las Vegas, NV*

Prep: 20 min. • **Cook:** 6 hours
Makes: 8 servings

⅓ cup honey
¼ cup white balsamic vinegar
1 Tbsp. minced fresh rosemary or 1 tsp. dried rosemary, crushed
2 tsp. minced fresh thyme or ¾ tsp. dried thyme
1 Tbsp. olive oil
2 garlic cloves, minced
¾ tsp. salt
½ tsp. Chinese five-spice powder
½ tsp. coarsely ground pepper
5 large fresh beets (about 3½ lbs.), peeled and trimmed
1 medium red onion, chopped
1 medium orange, peeled and chopped
1 cup crumbled feta cheese

1. In a small bowl, whisk the first 9 ingredients until blended. Place beets in a greased 4-qt. slow cooker. Add onion and orange. Pour honey mixture over top.

2. Cook, covered, on low 6-8 hours or until beets are tender. Remove beets; cut into wedges. Return to slow cooker. Serve warm, or refrigerate and serve cold. Serve with a slotted spoon; sprinkle with cheese.

¾ cup: 200 cal., 4g fat (2g sat. fat), 8mg chol., 511mg sod., 37g carb. (31g sugars, 5g fiber), 6g pro. **Diabetic exchanges:** 2 vegetable, 1 starch, 1 fat.

THYMED ZUCCHINI SAUTE

Simple and flavorful, this side is a tasty and healthy way to use up all those zucchini that take over your garden. The best part is it's ready in no time!
—*Bobby Taylor, Ulster Park, NY*

- -

Takes: 15 min. • **Makes:** 4 servings

1 Tbsp. olive oil
1 lb. medium zucchini, quartered
   lengthwise and halved
¼ cup finely chopped onion
½ vegetable bouillon cube, crushed
2 Tbsp. minced fresh parsley
1 tsp. minced fresh thyme
   or ¼ tsp. dried thyme

In a large skillet, heat oil over medium-high heat. Add zucchini, onion and bouillon; cook and stir 4-5 minutes or until the zucchini is crisp-tender. Sprinkle with herbs.
Note: This recipe was prepared with Knorr vegetable bouillon.
¾ cup: 53 cal., 4g fat (1g sat. fat), 0 chol., 135mg sod., 5g carb. (2g sugars, 2g fiber), 2g pro. **Diabetic exchanges:** 1 vegetable, ½ fat.

READER RAVE

"Very delicious! I would say it makes 2 servings, and I feel that I still want to eat more of it! I used 3 zucchinis, a tablespoon of chicken bouillon, dried thyme and sweet onion. I am looking forward to cooking this again!"
—LICHEVAS, TASTEOFHOME.COM

GRILLED SUMMER VEGETABLE & COUSCOUS SALAD

My husband and I live in Southern California, where we grow a variety of summer veggies and fresh herbs. This delightful change-of-pace salad features the eggplant and bell peppers we grow, and some of the herbs we keep in hanging pots. It's great as a side with any type of grilled meat or fish. If you want to serve it as a vegetarian main dish, add some crumbled goat cheese or feta cheese.

—Patricia Levenson, Santa Ana, CA

Prep: 35 min. • **Grill:** 10 min.
Makes: 10 servings

DRESSING
- ½ cup olive oil
- ⅓ cup balsamic vinegar
- 4 tsp. capers, drained
- 4 tsp. lemon juice
- 2 garlic cloves, minced
- ¾ tsp. Dijon mustard
- 1¼ tsp. minced fresh rosemary or ½ tsp. dried rosemary, crushed
- 1¼ tsp. minced fresh thyme or ½ tsp. dried thyme
- ⅛ tsp. salt
- ⅛ tsp. pepper

SALAD
- 1 pkg. (10 oz.) uncooked couscous
- 2 medium zucchini or yellow summer squash, halved lengthwise
- 2 medium sweet yellow or red peppers, quartered
- 1 Japanese eggplant, halved lengthwise
- 2 Tbsp. olive oil
- ¼ tsp. salt
- ¼ tsp. pepper
- 1 cup grape tomatoes, halved
- ½ cup Greek olives, pitted and sliced
- 1 Tbsp. minced fresh parsley or 1 tsp. dried parsley flakes
- 1 Tbsp. minced fresh basil or 1 tsp. dried basil

1. In a small bowl, whisk first 10 ingredients. Refrigerate until serving.

2. Cook couscous according to the package directions. Meanwhile, brush the zucchini, yellow peppers and eggplant with olive oil; sprinkle with salt and pepper. Grill, covered, over medium heat until the vegetables are crisp-tender, 10-12 minutes, turning once.

3. Chop grilled vegetables; place in a large bowl. Add the tomatoes, olives, parsley, basil and couscous. Pour dressing over salad and toss to coat. Serve warm or chilled.

¾ cup: 272 cal., 16g fat (2g sat. fat), 0 chol., 244mg sod., 29g carb. (5g sugars, 3g fiber), 5g pro. **Diabetic exchanges:** 2 fat, 1½ starch, 1 vegetable.

TEST KITCHEN TIP

Couscous is a commercially produced grain product usually made from semolina and shaped into tiny beads. It originated in the Middle East and North Africa. Found in the rice or pasta section of the grocery store, it is available in regular or quick-cooking forms. Serve as a side dish, or in salads where you would use rice or pasta.

ROASTED ROSEMARY CAULIFLOWER

Roasting the cauliflower brings out its flavor. Even folks who aren't big fans are likely to enjoy it this way.

—*Joann Fritzler, Belen, NM*

Takes: 30 min. • **Makes:** 6 servings

- 1 medium head cauliflower (about 2½ lbs.), broken into florets
- 2 Tbsp. olive oil
- 2 tsp. minced fresh rosemary or ¾ tsp. dried rosemary, crushed
- ½ tsp. salt

Preheat oven to 450°. Toss all ingredients; spread in a greased 15x10x1-in. pan. Roast until tender and lightly browned, 20-25 minutes, stirring occasionally.

¾ cup: 65 cal., 5g fat (1g sat. fat), 0 chol., 226mg sod., 5g carb. (2g sugars, 2g fiber), 2g pro. **Diabetic exchanges:** 1 vegetable, 1 fat.

ROASTED GREEN VEGETABLE MEDLEY

Roasting veggies like broccoli, green beans and Brussels sprouts is a great way to serve them, and almost any veggie combo works! For a slightly heartier dish, add thinly sliced potatoes and cook a few minutes longer.
—*Suzan Crouch, Grand Prairie, TX*

- -

Prep: 20 min. • **Bake:** 20 min.
Makes: 10 servings

- 1 lb. fresh green beans, trimmed and cut into 2-in. pieces
- 4 cups fresh broccoli florets
- 10 small fresh mushrooms, halved
- 8 fresh Brussels sprouts, halved
- 2 medium carrots, cut into ¼-in. slices
- 1 medium onion, halved and sliced
- 3 to 5 garlic cloves, thinly sliced
- 4 Tbsp. olive oil, divided
- ½ cup grated Parmesan cheese
- 3 Tbsp. julienned fresh basil leaves, optional
- 2 Tbsp. minced fresh parsley
- 1 Tbsp. grated lemon zest
- 2 Tbsp. lemon juice
- ¼ tsp. salt
- ¼ tsp. pepper

1. Preheat oven to 425°. Place the first 7 ingredients in a large bowl; toss with 2 Tbsp. oil. Divide between two 15x10x1-in. pans coated with cooking spray.

2. Roast until tender, 20-25 minutes, stirring occasionally. Transfer to a large bowl. Mix remaining ingredients with remaining oil; toss with vegetables.

1 serving: 109 cal., 7g fat (1g sat. fat), 3mg chol., 96mg sod., 10g carb. (3g sugars, 3g fiber), 4g pro. **Diabetic exchanges:** 1 vegetable, 1 fat.

MEDITERRANEAN SLOW-COOKER MASHED POTATOES

I love to use my slow cooker when family comes over. On Sundays when I make my special turkey meat loaf, this is a no-fuss side that tastes amazing!
—*Kristen Heigl, Staten Island, NY*

- -

Prep: 20 min. • **Cook:** 2 hours
Makes: 10 servings

- 4 lbs. red potatoes, cubed
- 1 cup sour cream
- ½ cup butter, softened
- 3 garlic cloves, minced
- 2 Tbsp. snipped fresh dill
- ¾ tsp. salt
- ½ tsp. pepper
- 1 cup crumbled feta cheese

Place potatoes in a 6-qt. stockpot; add water to cover. Bring to a boil. Reduce the heat; cook, uncovered, until tender, 10-15 minutes. Drain and coarsely mash. Combine the next 6 ingredients in a greased 5-qt. slow cooker; stir in mashed potatoes and feta until well combined. Cook, covered, on low until heated through, 2-3 hours.

¾ cup: 287 cal., 15g fat (10g sat. fat), 46mg chol., 377mg sod., 30g carb. (3g sugars, 4g fiber), 6g pro.

HOMEMADE PASTA

Try your hand at homemade pasta with this spinach dough. We promise it's easier than you think. You don't even need a pasta maker or any other special equipment to create this healthy dish.
—Taste of Home *Test Kitchen*

- -

Prep: 30 min. + standing
Cook: 10 min./batch
Makes: 8 servings

- 1 **pkg. (10 oz.) frozen chopped spinach, thawed and squeezed dry**
- ¼ **cup packed fresh parsley sprigs**
- 3½ **to 4 cups all-purpose flour**
- ½ **tsp. salt**
- 4 **large eggs**
- 3 **Tbsp. water**
- 1 **Tbsp. olive oil**
  Marinara sauce

1. Place the spinach and parsley in a food processor; cover and process until finely chopped. Add 3½ cups flour and salt; process until blended. Add the eggs, water and olive oil. Process until the dough forms a ball, 15-20 seconds.

2. Turn onto a floured surface; knead until smooth and elastic, 8-10 minutes, adding remaining flour if necessary. Cover dough and let rest for 30 minutes. Divide the dough into fourths.

3. On a floured surface, roll each portion to ⅟₁₆-in. thickness. Dust top of dough with flour to prevent sticking; cut into ¼-in. slices. Separate the slices; allow noodles to dry on kitchen towels for at least 1 hour before cooking.

4. To cook, fill a Dutch oven three-fourths full with water. Bring to a boil. Add noodles in batches; cook, uncovered, until tender, 8-10 minutes. Drain. Serve with sauce.

1 cup: 259 cal., 5g fat (1g sat. fat), 106mg chol., 211mg sod., 43g carb. (1g sugars, 3g fiber), 10g pro.

5i

ROASTED BRUSSELS SPROUTS WITH CRANBERRIES

There's no fuss here—both the preparation and cooking are so quick. I like to sprinkle dried cranberries on top and stir them in, but feel free to let your imagination take over and get creative with whatever you want to add! Try sprinkling raisins or walnuts on top, or even sliced oranges.

—*Ellen Ruzinsky, Yorktown Heights, NY*

- -

Prep: 15 min. • **Bake:** 20 min.
Makes: 12 servings

  3 **lbs. fresh Brussels sprouts,
       trimmed and halved**
  3 **Tbsp. olive oil**
  1 **tsp. kosher salt**
  ½ **tsp. pepper**
  ½ **cup dried cranberries**

Preheat oven to 425°. Divide Brussels sprouts between 2 greased 15x10x1-in. baking pans. Drizzle with oil; sprinkle with salt and pepper. Toss to coat. Roast until tender, stirring occasionally, 20-25 minutes. Transfer to a large bowl; stir in cranberries.

½ cup: 94 cal., 4g fat (1g sat. fat), 0 chol., 185mg sod., 14g carb. (6g sugars, 5g fiber), 4g pro. **Diabetic exchanges:** 1 vegetable, 1 fat.

SICILIAN STEAMED LEEKS

I love the challenge of developing recipes for my garden-fresh leeks, a delicious yet underused vegetable. This Italian dish is a family favorite.

—Roxanne Chan, Albany, CA

- -

Takes: 20 min. • **Makes:** 6 servings

- 6 medium leeks (white portion only), halved lengthwise, cleaned
- 1 large tomato, chopped
- 1 small navel orange, peeled, sectioned and chopped
- 2 Tbsp. minced fresh parsley
- 2 Tbsp. sliced Greek olives
- 1 tsp. capers, drained
- 1 tsp. red wine vinegar
- 1 tsp. olive oil
- ½ tsp. grated orange zest
- ½ tsp. pepper
  Crumbled feta cheese

In a Dutch oven, place steamer basket over 1 in. of water. Place leeks in basket. Bring water to a boil. Reduce heat to maintain a low boil; steam, covered, until leeks are tender, 8-10 minutes. Meanwhile, combine the next 9 ingredients. Transfer leeks to a serving platter. Spoon tomato mixture over top; sprinkle with cheese.

1 serving: 83 cal., 2g fat (0 sat. fat), 0 chol., 77mg sod., 16g carb. (6g sugars, 3g fiber), 2g pro. **Diabetic exchanges:** 1 starch, ½ fat.

GREEK-STYLE SQUASH

Here's a great way to use up summer squash. You can almost taste the sunshine in this fast, colorful vegetable dish. The foil packets make for easy cleanup.

—Betty Washburn, Reno, NV

- -

Prep: 15 min. • **Grill:** 30 min.
Makes: 4 servings

- 2 small yellow summer squash, thinly sliced
- 2 small zucchini, thinly sliced
- 1 medium tomato, seeded and chopped
- ¼ cup pitted ripe olives
- 2 Tbsp. chopped green onion
- 2 tsp. olive oil
- 1 tsp. lemon juice
- ¾ tsp. garlic salt
- ¼ tsp. dried oregano
- ⅛ tsp. pepper
- 2 Tbsp. grated Parmesan cheese

1. Place the yellow squash, zucchini, tomato, olives and onion on a double thickness of heavy-duty foil (about 17x18 in.). Combine oil, lemon juice, garlic salt, oregano and pepper; drizzle over vegetables. Fold foil around mixture and seal tightly.
2. Grill, covered, over medium heat until vegetables are tender, 30-35 minutes. Open foil carefully to allow steam to escape. Transfer vegetables to a serving bowl. Sprinkle with cheese.

¾ cup: 80 cal., 5g fat (1g sat. fat), 2mg chol., 479mg sodium, 8g carb. (0 sugars, 3g fiber), 4g pro. **Diabetic exchanges:** 2 vegetable, ½ fat.

WHITE BALSAMIC BLUEBERRY,
CORN & FETA SALAD,
PAGE 248

SOUPS & SALADS

Between warm, comforting creations and cool, refreshing dishes, these light bowls will give you all the mouthwatering flavors of a colorful meal on the Mediterranean coast.

WHITE BALSAMIC BLUEBERRY, CORN & FETA SALAD

I'm not typically a huge fan of summer corn, but when it comes to this refreshing salad, I can't put my fork down.
—*Colleen Delawder, Herndon, VA*

Prep: 30 min. + soaking • **Grill:** 20 min.
Makes: 10 servings

- 8 medium ears sweet corn
- 3 Tbsp. olive oil
- 3 Tbsp. white balsamic vinegar
- 1 Tbsp. minced fresh chives, plus more for garnish
- ¾ tsp. kosher salt
- ¼ tsp. pepper
- 1 cup fresh blueberries
- ½ cup crumbled feta cheese

1. Carefully peel back corn husks to within 1 in. of bottoms; remove silk. Rewrap corn in husks; secure with kitchen string. Place in a stockpot; cover with cold water. Soak for 20 minutes; drain.

2. Grill corn, covered, over medium heat about 20 minutes or until tender, turning often. Cut string and peel back husks. Cool slightly. Cut corn from cobs; transfer to a large bowl.

3. In a small bowl, whisk the oil, vinegar, chives, salt and pepper. Pour over corn; toss to coat. Gently fold in blueberries and feta. Garnish with additional chives as desired.

¾ cup: 133 cal., 6g fat (1g sat. fat), 3mg chol., 210mg sod., 19g carb. (8g sugars, 2g fiber), 4g pro. **Diabetic exchanges:** 1 starch, 1 fat.

MANESTRA TOMATO SOUP

My recipe for *manestra*, which means "orzo" in Greek, is straightforward and easy to make. You only need a few steps to transform a handful of simple ingredients into a creamy one-pot wonder in about 30 minutes.
—*Kiki Vagianos, Melrose, MA*

Prep: 10 min. • **Cook:** 25 min.
Makes: 4 servings

- 2 Tbsp. olive oil
- 1 medium onion, chopped
- 1¼ cups uncooked whole wheat orzo pasta
- 2 cans (14½ oz. each) whole tomatoes, undrained, coarsely chopped
- 3 cups reduced-sodium chicken broth
- 2 tsp. dried oregano
- ¼ tsp. salt
- ¼ tsp. pepper
  Crumbled feta cheese and minced fresh basil, optional

1. In large saucepan, heat oil over medium heat; saute onion until tender, 3-5 minutes. Add orzo; cook and stir until lightly toasted.

2. Stir in tomatoes, broth and seasonings; bring to a boil. Reduce heat; simmer, covered, until orzo is tender, 15-20 minutes, stirring occasionally. If desired, top with feta cheese and basil.

Freeze option: Freeze cooled soup in freezer containers. To use, partially thaw in refrigerator overnight. Heat through in a saucepan, stirring occasionally; add broth or water if necessary.

1 cup: 299 cal., 8g fat (1g sat. fat), 0 chol., 882mg sod., 47g carb. (7g sugars, 12g fiber), 11g pro.

SHAVED FENNEL SALAD

This salad tastes even more impressive than it looks. It's got an incredible crunch thanks to the cucumbers, radishes and apples, and the finish of fennel fronds adds just the faintest hint of licorice flavor.
—*William Milton III, Clemson, SC*

Takes: 15 min. • **Makes:** 8 servings

- 1 large fennel bulb, fronds reserved
- 1 English cucumber
- 1 medium Honeycrisp apple
- 2 Tbsp. extra virgin olive oil
- ½ tsp. kosher salt
- ¼ tsp. coarsely ground pepper
- 2 radishes, thinly sliced

With a mandoline or vegetable peeler, cut the fennel, cucumber and apple into very thin slices. Transfer to a large bowl; toss with olive oil, salt and pepper. Top with radishes and reserved fennel fronds to serve.

¾ cup: 55 cal., 4 g fat (1 g sat. fat), 0 chol., 138 mg sod., 6 g carb. (4 g sugars, 2 g fiber), 1 g pro. **Diabetic exchanges:** 1 vegetable, 1 fat.

GREEK-STYLE LENTIL SOUP

This is a warm, comforting soup, and the fact that lentils are so good for you is certainly a bonus! Add cooked meat if you'd like.
—*Mary Smith, Columbia, MO*

Prep: 20 min. • **Cook:** 5 hours
Makes: 12 servings (3 qt.)

- 4 cups water
- 4 cups vegetable broth
- 2 cups dried lentils, rinsed
- 2 medium carrots, chopped
- 1 small onion, chopped
- 1 celery rib, chopped
- 1 tsp. dried oregano, divided
- 1 cup chopped fresh spinach
- ½ cup tomato sauce
- 1 can (2¼ oz.) sliced ripe olives, drained
- 3 Tbsp. red wine vinegar
- 2 garlic cloves, minced
- ½ tsp. salt
- ¼ tsp. pepper
  Chopped red onion, chopped parsley and lemon wedges, optional

1. Place the water, broth, lentils, carrots, onion, celery and ½ tsp. oregano in a 5- or 6-qt. slow cooker. Cook, covered, on low until lentils are tender, 4-5 hours.
2. Stir in the spinach, tomato sauce, olives, vinegar, garlic, salt, pepper and remaining ½ tsp. oregano. Cook, covered, on low until spinach is wilted, about 1 hour longer. If desired, serve with red onion, parsley and lemon wedges.

1 cup: 134 cal., 1g fat (0 sat. fat), 0 chol., 420mg sod., 24g carb. (2g sugars, 4g fiber), 9g pro. **Diabetic exchanges:** 1½ starch, 1 lean meat.

TEST KITCHEN TIP

If lentils aren't in your regular meal rotation, they should be. They're not only easy on the budget but good for you—each serving is packed with fiber, protein, B vitamins and more.

KOHLRABI, CUCUMBER & TOMATO SALAD

This chilled, refreshing salad is wonderful on hot days. It has a nice crunch and a delicious balance of sweet and spicy flavors.

—*Kristina Segarra, Yonkers, NY*

Prep: 20 min. + chilling • **Cook:** 10 min.
Makes: 6 servings

- 2 **Tbsp. olive oil**
- 1 **medium red onion, finely chopped**
- 2 **pickled hot cherry peppers, seeded and finely chopped**
- 2 **garlic cloves, minced**
- 2 **Tbsp. cider vinegar**
- 1 **tsp. salt**
- 1 **kohlrabi, peeled and cut into ½-in. pieces**
- 2 **large yellow tomatoes, seeded and chopped**
- 2 **mini cucumbers, cut into ½-in. pieces**
- 2 **Tbsp. minced fresh cilantro**

1. In a small skillet, heat oil over medium-high heat. Add onion; cook and stir 2-3 minutes or until crisp-tender. Add peppers and garlic; cook 2 minutes longer. Stir in vinegar and salt; remove from heat.

2. In a large bowl, combine the kohlrabi, tomatoes and cucumbers. Pour in onion mixture; gently toss to coat. Chill for 1 hour. Sprinkle with cilantro before serving.

Note: Kirby cucumbers are a good choice in this recipe. The pickled peppers don't add a lot of heat, but you can cut them back or eliminate them altogether. You can use cherry tomatoes or other favorite vegetables you may have in the garden.

¾ cup: 59 cal., 4g fat (1g sat. fat), 0 chol., 372mg sod., 6g carb. (2g sugars, 2g fiber), 2g pro. **Diabetic exchanges:** 1 vegetable, ½ fat.

ITALIAN SALAD WITH LEMON VINAIGRETTE

For a delicious Italian twist on salad, I mix greens with red onion, mushrooms, olives, pepperoncini, lemon juice and seasoning. Add tomatoes and carrots if you'd like.
—*Deborah Loop, Clinton Township, MI*

- -

Takes: 20 min.
Makes: 8 servings (½ cup vinaigrette)

- 1   pkg. (5 oz.) spring mix salad greens
- 1   small red onion, thinly sliced
- 1   cup sliced fresh mushrooms
- 1   cup assorted olives, pitted and coarsely chopped
- 8   pepperoncini
      Optional toppings: Chopped tomatoes, shredded carrots and grated Parmesan cheese

VINAIGRETTE
- ⅓   cup extra virgin olive oil
- 3   Tbsp. lemon juice
- 1   tsp. Italian seasoning
- ¼   tsp. salt
- ¼   tsp. pepper

1. In a large bowl, combine first 5 ingredients; toss lightly. If desired, add toppings.
2. In a small bowl, whisk all the vinaigrette ingredients until blended. Serve with salad.
1¼ cups: 109 cal., 11g fat (1g sat. fat), 0 chol., 343mg sod., 4g carb. (1g sugars, 1g fiber), 1g pro. **Diabetic exchanges:** 2 fat, 1 vegetable.

SALMON DILL SOUP

My husband loves salmon so much he could eat it every day, so when I get salmon, I try to make it into a special dish that will be a treat for both of us. According to him, this is the best soup I have ever made.
—*Hidemi Walsh, Plainfield, IN*

- -

Takes: 30 min. • **Makes:** 2 servings

- 1 **large potato, peeled and cut into 1½-in. pieces**
- 1 **large carrot, cut into ½-in.-thick slices**
- 1½ **cups water**
- 1 **cup reduced-sodium chicken broth**
- 5 **medium fresh mushrooms, halved**
- 1 **Tbsp. all-purpose flour**
- ¼ **cup reduced-fat evaporated milk**
- ¼ **cup shredded part-skim mozzarella cheese**
- ½ **lb. salmon fillet, cut into 1½-in. pieces**
- ¼ **tsp. pepper**
- ⅛ **tsp. salt**
- 1 **Tbsp. chopped fresh dill**

1. Place the first 4 ingredients in a saucepan; bring to a boil. Reduce heat to medium; cook, uncovered, until the vegetables are tender, 10-15 minutes.

2. Add mushrooms. In a small bowl, mix flour and milk until smooth; stir into soup. Return to a boil; cook and stir until mushrooms are tender. Reduce heat to medium; stir in cheese until melted.

3. Reduce heat to medium-low. Add salmon; cook, uncovered, until fish just begins to flake easily with a fork, 3-4 minutes. Stir in pepper and salt. Sprinkle with dill.

2½ cups: 398 cal., 14g fat (4g sat. fat), 71mg chol., 647mg sod., 37g carb. (7g sugars, 3g fiber), 30g pro. **Diabetic exchanges:** 3 lean meat, 2½ starch.

HAZELNUT ASPARAGUS SOUP

My heart is so happy when bundles of tender asparagus become available in the spring. No one would ever guess this restaurant-quality soup can be prepared in about 30 minutes.
—*Cindy Beberman, Orland Park, IL*

- -

Prep: 20 min. • **Cook:** 15 min.
Makes: 4 servings (3 cups)

1	Tbsp. olive oil
½	cup chopped sweet onion
3	garlic cloves, sliced
	Dash crushed red pepper flakes
2½	cups cut fresh asparagus (about 1½ lbs.), trimmed
2	cups vegetable broth
⅓	cup whole hazelnuts, toasted
2	Tbsp. chopped fresh basil
2	Tbsp. lemon juice
½	cup unsweetened almond milk
2	tsp. gluten-free reduced-sodium tamari soy sauce
¼	tsp. salt
	Shaved asparagus, optional

1. In a large saucepan, heat oil over medium heat. Add onion, garlic and pepper flakes; cook and stir until onion is softened, 4-5 minutes. Add asparagus and broth; bring to a boil. Reduce heat; simmer, covered, until asparagus is tender, 6-8 minutes. Remove from heat; cool slightly.

2. Place hazelnuts, basil and lemon juice in a blender. Add asparagus mixture. Process until smooth and creamy. Return to saucepan. Stir in almond milk, tamari sauce and salt. Heat through, taking care not to boil soup. If desired, top with shaved asparagus.

Note: To toast nuts, bake in a shallow pan in a 350° oven for 5-10 minutes or cook in a skillet over low heat until lightly browned, stirring occasionally. Reduced-sodium soy sauce may be used in place of the tamari soy sauce.

¾ cup: 164 cal., 13g fat (1g sat. fat), 0 chol., 623mg sod., 11g carb. (4g sugars, 4g fiber), 5g pro. **Diabetic exchanges:** 2½ fat, ½ starch.

GARDEN BOUNTY PANZANELLA

To make this colorful dish in a snap, use your favorite prepared salad dressing and pick up sliced veggies at the grocery store salad bar.
—*Jannine Fisk, Malden, MA*

- -

Prep: 15 min. • **Cook:** 20 min.
Makes: 16 servings

¼	cup olive oil
12	oz. French or ciabatta bread, cut into 1-in. cubes (about 12 cups)
4	large tomatoes, coarsely chopped
1	English cucumber, coarsely chopped
1	medium green pepper, cut into 1-in. pieces
1	medium sweet yellow pepper, cut into 1-in. pieces
1	small red onion, halved and thinly sliced
½	cup coarsely chopped fresh basil
¼	cup grated Parmesan cheese
¾	tsp. kosher salt
¼	tsp. coarsely ground pepper
½	cup Italian salad dressing

1. In a large skillet, heat 2 Tbsp. oil over medium heat. Add half of the bread cubes; cook and stir until toasted, about 8 minutes. Remove from pan. Repeat with remaining oil and bread cubes.

2. Combine the bread cubes, tomatoes, cucumber, peppers, onion, basil, cheese, salt and pepper. Toss with dressing.

1 cup: 131 cal., 6g fat (1g sat. fat), 1mg chol., 310mg sod., 18g carb. (3g sugars, 2g fiber), 3g pro.

WINE PAIRING

Cabernet Franc. Serve this light-bodied red with a slight chill by popping it in the fridge for 30-40 minutes before serving. Cab franc is a nice companion to garden vegetables and herbs.

SPRING GREEK PASTA SALAD

For a light meal or side, we toss rotini with cucumber, zucchini and sweet peppers. Make it into a main dish by adding grilled chicken.
—*Christine Schenher, Exeter, CA*

- -

Takes: 30 min.
Makes: 16 servings

- 4 cups veggie rotini or other spiral pasta (about 12 oz.)

VINAIGRETTE
- ¼ cup olive oil
- 3 Tbsp. lemon juice
- 2 Tbsp. balsamic vinegar
- 1 Tbsp. water
- 3 garlic cloves, minced
- 1 tsp. salt
- ¼ tsp. pepper
- 3 Tbsp. minced fresh oregano or 1 Tbsp. dried oregano

SALAD
- 3 large tomatoes, seeded and chopped
- 1 medium sweet red pepper, chopped
- 1 small cucumber, seeded and chopped
- 1 small zucchini, chopped
- 1 small red onion, halved and thinly sliced
- ⅓ cup sliced pitted Greek olives, optional
- 1 cup (4 oz.) crumbled feta cheese

1. Cook pasta according to the package directions. Drain; rinse with cold water and drain well.
2. In a small bowl, whisk oil, lemon juice, vinegar, water, garlic, salt and pepper until blended. Stir in oregano.
3. In a large bowl, combine pasta, vegetables and, if desired, olives. Add vinaigrette and cheese; toss to combine. Refrigerate, covered, until serving.
¾ cup: 142 cal., 5g fat (1g sat. fat), 4mg chol., 219mg sod., 20g carb. (3g sugars, 2g fiber), 5g pro. **Diabetic exchanges:** 1 starch, 1 fat.

LEMONY MUSHROOM-ORZO SOUP

Here's a versatile soup that works well as an appetizer or a side for a sandwich lunch. It's loaded with mushrooms and orzo pasta, with a hint of lemon to brighten the flavor.
—*Edrie O'Brien, Denver, CO*

- -

Takes: 30 min. • **Makes:** 2 servings

- 2½ cups sliced fresh mushrooms
- 2 green onions, chopped
- 1 Tbsp. olive oil
- 1 garlic clove, minced
- 1½ cups reduced-sodium chicken broth
- 1½ tsp. minced fresh parsley
- ¼ tsp. dried thyme
- ⅛ tsp. pepper
- ¼ cup uncooked orzo pasta
- 1½ tsp. lemon juice
- ⅛ tsp. grated lemon zest

1. In a small saucepan, saute the mushrooms and onions in oil until tender. Add garlic; cook 1 minute longer. Stir in the broth, parsley, thyme and pepper.
2. Bring to a boil. Stir in orzo, lemon juice and zest. Cook until pasta is tender, 5-6 minutes.
1 cup: 191 cal., 8g fat (1g sat. fat), 0 chol., 437mg sod., 24g carb. (4g sugars, 2g fiber), 9g pro. **Diabetic exchanges:** 1½ fat, 1 starch, 1 vegetable.

WINE PAIRING

Pinot Grigio. The popular Italian white is a natural with lemony dishes and chicken soup. Get one from the Alto Adige region (it's a bit more robust than others from Italy), or from the U.S., where the grape is called pinot gris.

ARTICHOKE TOMATO SALAD

For a little zip, crumble feta over the top of this salad. Or add shredded rotisserie chicken for a beautiful main dish.

—*Deborah Williams, Peoria, AZ*

Takes: 20 min. • **Makes:** 8 servings

- 5 large tomatoes (about 2 lbs.), cut into wedges
- ¼ tsp. salt
- ¼ tsp. pepper
- 1 jar (7½ oz.) marinated quartered artichoke hearts, drained
- 1 can (2¼ oz.) sliced ripe olives, drained
- 2 Tbsp. minced fresh parsley
- 2 Tbsp. white wine vinegar
- 2 garlic cloves, minced

Arrange tomato wedges on a large platter; sprinkle with salt and pepper. In a small bowl, toss remaining ingredients; spoon mixture over tomatoes.

¾ cup: 74 cal., 5g fat (1g sat. fat), 0 chol., 241mg sod., 7g carb. (3g sugars, 2g fiber), 1g pro. **Diabetic exchanges:** 1 vegetable, 1 fat.

GOLDEN SUMMER PEACH SOUP

Since peaches and tomatoes are in season together, I like to blend them into a cool, delicious soup. Leftovers keep well in the fridge—but they rarely last long!

—*Julie Hession, Las Vegas, NV*

Prep: 20 min. + chilling • **Makes:** 8 servings

- 3 cups sliced peeled fresh or frozen peaches, thawed
- 3 medium yellow tomatoes, chopped
- 1 medium sweet yellow pepper, chopped
- 1 medium cucumber, peeled and chopped
- ½ cup chopped sweet onion
- 1 garlic clove, minced
- ⅓ cup lime juice
- 2 Tbsp. rice vinegar
- 1 Tbsp. marinade for chicken
- 1 tsp. salt
- ¼ tsp. hot pepper sauce
- 1 to 3 tsp. sugar, optional
  Chopped peaches, cucumber and tomatoes

1. Place the first 6 ingredients in a food processor; process until blended. Add lime juice, vinegar, marinade for chicken, salt and hot pepper sauce; process until smooth. If desired, stir in sugar.

2. Refrigerate, covered, at least 4 hours. Top servings with additional chopped peaches, cucumber and tomatoes.

Note: This recipe was tested with Lea & Perrins Marinade for Chicken.

⅔ cup: 56 cal., 0 fat (0 sat. fat), 0 chol., 342mg sod., 13g carb. (8g sugars, 2g fiber), 2g pro.

Diabetic exchanges: 1 vegetable, ½ fruit.

SOUR CREAM CUCUMBERS

It's been a tradition at our house to serve this alongside other Hungarian specialties that my mom learned to make from the women at church. In the summer months, fresh-picked cucumbers from the garden make this tasty dish even more delightful.

—Pamela Eaton, Monclova, OH

Prep: 15 min. + chilling • **Makes:** 8 servings

- ½ cup sour cream
- 3 Tbsp. white vinegar
- 1 Tbsp. sugar
  Pepper to taste
- 4 medium cucumbers, peeled if desired and thinly sliced
- 1 small sweet onion, thinly sliced and separated into rings

In a large bowl, whisk the sour cream, white vinegar, sugar and pepper until blended. Add sliced cucumbers and onion; toss to coat. Refrigerate, covered, at least 4 hours. Serve with a slotted spoon.

¾ cup: 62 cal., 3g fat (2g sat. fat), 10mg chol., 5mg sod., 7g carb. (5g sugars, 2g fiber), 2g pro. **Diabetic exchanges:** 1 vegetable, ½ fat.
Cucumbers with Dill: Omit first 4 ingredients. Mix ¾ cup white vinegar, ⅓ cup snipped fresh dill, ⅓ cup sugar and ¾ tsp. pepper. Stir in cucumbers.

ITALIAN CABBAGE SOUP

After doing yardwork on a cold and windy day, we love to warm up with this light but hearty soup. It's brimming with cabbage, veggies and white beans. Pass the crusty bread, please!

—*Jennifer Stowell, Deep River, IA*

Prep: 15 min. • **Cook:** 6 hours
Makes: 8 servings (2 qt.)

- 4 cups chicken stock
- 1 can (6 oz.) tomato paste
- 1 small head cabbage (about 1½ lbs.), shredded
- 4 celery ribs, chopped
- 2 large carrots, chopped
- 1 small onion, chopped
- 1 can (15½ oz.) great northern beans, rinsed and drained
- 2 garlic cloves, minced
- 2 fresh thyme sprigs
- 1 bay leaf
- ½ tsp. salt
  Shredded Parmesan cheese, optional

1. In a 5- or 6-qt. slow cooker, whisk together stock and tomato paste. Stir in vegetables, beans, garlic and seasonings. Cook, covered, on low until vegetables are tender, 6-8 hours.
2. Remove the thyme sprigs and bay leaf. If desired, serve with cheese.

1 cup: 111 cal., 0g fat (0g sat. fat), 0mg chol., 537mg sod., 21g carb. (7g sugars, 6g fiber), 8g pro. **Diabetic exchanges:** 1 starch.

MEDITERRANEAN BROWN RICE SALAD

My family and friends love this healthy, fresh, gluten-free salad. It's so light and refreshing, and it's a good way to get younger kids to eat veggies, too. Whether you love Greek food or just want a simple salad bursting with flavor, this recipe will not disappoint. If you'd like, replace the brown rice with orzo.
—*Sarah Hawkins, Wanatah, IN*

- -

Prep: 30 min. • **Cook:** 35 min. + chilling
Makes: 14 servings

- 1½ cups uncooked long grain brown rice
- 3½ cups water
- 2 Tbsp. white vinegar
- 2 Tbsp. balsamic vinegar
- 1 garlic clove, minced
- ¾ tsp. pepper
- ½ tsp. salt
- ½ cup olive oil
- ¼ cup chopped fresh basil
- 6 oz. fresh baby spinach (about 8 cups), coarsely chopped
- 16 oz. cherry tomatoes, halved
- 6 green onions, thinly sliced
- 2 cups (8 oz.) crumbled feta cheese

1. In a saucepan, combine rice and water; bring to a boil. Reduce heat; simmer, covered, until rice is tender and liquid is absorbed, 35-40 minutes.
2. Meanwhile, place vinegars, garlic, pepper and salt in bowl and whisk together. While whisking, gradually add oil in a steady stream. Stir in basil.
3. Place spinach in a large bowl; add cooked rice. Stir in tomatoes, green onions and dressing; toss until spinach is wilted. Gently stir in feta. Loosely cover and refrigerate 2 hours or until cold.

¾ cup: 55 cal., 3g fat (2g sat. fat), 10mg chol., 291mg sod., 3g carb. (1g sugars, 1g fiber), 4g pro.

MICHIGAN CHERRY SALAD

This recipe reminds me of what I love about my home state: apple picking with my children, buying greens at the farmers market and tasting cherries on vacations.
—*Jennifer Gilbert, Brighton, MI*

- -

Takes: 15 min. • **Makes:** 8 servings

    7 oz. fresh baby spinach (about 9 cups)
    3 oz. spring mix salad greens
       (about 5 cups)
    1 large apple, chopped
    ½ cup coarsely chopped
       pecans, toasted
    ½ cup dried cherries
    ¼ cup crumbled Gorgonzola cheese
DRESSING
    ¼ cup fresh raspberries
    ¼ cup red wine vinegar
    3 Tbsp. cider vinegar
    3 Tbsp. cherry preserves
    1 Tbsp. sugar
    2 Tbsp. olive oil

1. In a large bowl, combine first 6 ingredients.
2. Place the raspberries, vinegars, preserves and sugar in a blender. While processing, gradually add the olive oil in a steady stream. Drizzle over salad; toss to coat.
1½ cups: 172 cal., 10g fat (2g sat. fat), 3mg chol., 78mg sod., 21g carb. (16g sugars, 3g fiber), 3g pro.

WINE PAIRING

Ciliegiolo. The name means "cherry" in Italian, and the wine is such a pale red that it looks like rosé. From the seaside cliffs in northwest Italy, the wine is bright, lively, fun and tastes like—you guessed it—cherries. You also can substitute a French Beaujolais, which is easy to find. Chill slightly.

CHICKEN TORTELLINI SOUP

This simple recipe is like an Italian twist on chicken noodle soup. The tortellini and Italian herbs make it look and taste special.
—*Jean Atherly, Red Lodge, MT*

- -

Takes: 30 min.
Makes: 8 servings (about 2 qt.)

    2 cans (14½ oz. each) chicken broth
    2 cups water
    ¾ lb. boneless skinless chicken
       breasts, cut into 1-in. cubes
    1½ cups frozen mixed vegetables
    1 pkg. (9 oz.) refrigerated
       cheese tortellini
    2 celery ribs, thinly sliced
    1 tsp. dried basil
    ½ tsp. garlic salt
    ½ tsp. dried oregano
    ¼ tsp. pepper

1. In a large saucepan, bring broth and water to a boil; add chicken. Reduce heat; cook for 10 minutes.
2. Add the remaining ingredients; cook until chicken is no longer pink and vegetables are tender, 10-15 minutes longer.
1 cup: 170 cal., 4g fat (2g sat. fat), 37mg chol., 483mg sod., 20g carb. (2g sugars, 3g fiber), 14g pro. **Diabetic exchanges:** 2 lean meat, 1 starch.

SUMMER'S BOUNTY SOUP

This chunky soup packed with garden-fresh veggies is so versatile. You can add or omit just about any vegetable to make the most of what you have.

—*Victoria Hahn, Northampton, PA*

- -

Prep: 20 min. • **Cook:** 7 hours
Makes: 14 servings (about 3½ qt.)

- 4 medium tomatoes, chopped
- 2 medium potatoes, peeled and cubed
- 2 cups halved fresh green beans
- 2 small zucchini, cubed
- 1 medium yellow summer squash, cubed
- 4 small carrots, thinly sliced
- 2 celery ribs, thinly sliced
- 1 cup cubed peeled eggplant
- 1 cup sliced fresh mushrooms
- 1 small onion, chopped
- 1 Tbsp. minced fresh parsley
- 1 Tbsp. salt-free garlic and herb seasoning
- 4 cups reduced-sodium V8 juice

Combine all ingredients in a 5-qt. slow cooker. Cook, covered, on low 7-8 hours or until vegetables are tender.

1 cup: 67 cal., 0 fat (0 sat. fat), 0 chol., 62mg sod., 15g carb. (6g sugars, 3g fiber), 2g pro.
Diabetic exchanges: 2 vegetable.

SUMMER ORZO

I'm always looking for fun ways to use the fresh veggies that come in my Community Supported Agriculture box, and this salad is a favorite creation of mine. I like to improvise with whatever ingredients I have on hand—feel free to do the same here!

—*Shayna Marmar, Philadelphia, PA*

- -

Prep: 30 min. + chilling • **Makes:** 16 servings

- 1 pkg. (16 oz.) orzo pasta
- ¼ cup water
- 1½ cups fresh or frozen corn
- 24 cherry tomatoes, halved
- 2 cups (8 oz.) crumbled feta cheese
- 1 medium cucumber, seeded and chopped
- 1 small red onion, finely chopped
- ¼ cup minced fresh mint
- 2 Tbsp. capers, drained and chopped, optional
- ½ cup olive oil
- ¼ cup lemon juice
- 1 Tbsp. grated lemon zest
- 1½ tsp. salt
- 1 tsp. pepper
- 1 cup sliced almonds, toasted

1. Cook orzo according to package directions for al dente. Drain orzo; rinse with cold water and drain well. Transfer to a large bowl.
2. In a large nonstick skillet, heat water over medium heat. Add corn; cook and stir until crisp-tender, 3-4 minutes. Add to orzo; stir in tomatoes, feta cheese, cucumber, onion, mint and, if desired, capers. In a small bowl, whisk oil, lemon juice, lemon zest, salt and pepper until blended. Pour over the orzo mixture; toss to coat. Refrigerate 30 minutes.
3. Just before serving, stir in almonds.

¾ cup: 291 cal., 15g fat (4g sat. fat), 15mg chol., 501mg sod., 28g carb. (3g sugars, 3g fiber), 11g pro.

GARDEN TOMATO SALAD

When I was younger, my mom often made this cool, refreshing mix of tomatoes and cucumbers. Now I make this memorable salad whenever tomatoes are in reach.
—*Shannon Copley, Upper Arlington, OH*

- -

Takes: 15 min. • **Makes:** 8 servings

- 3 large tomatoes, cut into wedges
- 1 large sweet onion, cut into thin wedges
- 1 large cucumber, sliced

DRESSING

- ¼ cup olive oil
- 2 Tbsp. cider vinegar
- 1 garlic clove, minced
- 1 tsp. minced fresh basil
- 1 tsp. minced chives
- ½ tsp. salt

In a large bowl, combine tomatoes, onion and cucumber. In a small bowl, whisk dressing ingredients until blended. Drizzle over salad; gently toss to coat. Serve immediately.

1 cup: 92 cal., 7g fat (1g sat. fat), 0 chol., 155mg sod., 7g carb. (5g sugars, 1g fiber), 1g pro. **Diabetic exchanges:** 1½ fat, 1 vegetable.

SWEET POTATO & CHICKPEA SALAD

Take this colorful, versatile dish to the buffet at a family gathering, or enjoy it on its own as a healthy and satisfying meal.

—Brenda Gleason, Hartland, WI

Prep: 15 min. • **Bake:** 20 min.
Makes: 8 servings

- 2 medium sweet potatoes (about 1 lb.), peeled and cubed
- 1 Tbsp. olive oil
- ½ tsp. salt
- ¼ tsp. pepper
- 1 can (15 oz.) chickpeas or garbanzo beans, rinsed and drained

DRESSING
- 2 Tbsp. seasoned rice vinegar
- 4 tsp. olive oil
- 1 Tbsp. minced fresh gingerroot
- 1 garlic clove, minced
- ¼ tsp. salt
- ¼ tsp. pepper

SALAD
- 4 cups spring mix salad greens
- ¼ cup crumbled feta cheese

1. In a large bowl, combine the sweet potatoes, oil, salt and pepper; toss to coat. Transfer to a 15x10x1-in. baking pan coated with cooking spray. Roast at 425° until tender, 20-25 minutes, stirring once.
2. In a large bowl, combine chickpeas and sweet potatoes. In a small bowl, whisk the dressing ingredients. Add to sweet potato mixture; toss to coat. Serve mixture over salad greens; top with cheese.

½ cup sweet potato mixture with ½ cup greens and 1½ tsp. cheese: 134 cal., 6g fat (1g sat. fat), 2mg chol., 466mg sod., 18g carb. (6g sugars, 4g fiber), 4g pro. **Diabetic exchanges:** 1 starch, 1 fat.

SO-EASY GAZPACHO

My daughter got this recipe from a friend a few years ago. Now I serve it often as an appetizer. It certainly is the talk of the party!
—*Lorna Sirtoli, Cortland, NY*

Prep: 10 min. + chilling • **Makes:** 5 servings

- 2 cups tomato juice
- 4 medium tomatoes, peeled and finely chopped
- ½ cup chopped seeded peeled cucumber
- ⅓ cup finely chopped onion
- ¼ cup olive oil
- ¼ cup cider vinegar
- 1 tsp. sugar
- 1 garlic clove, minced
- ¼ tsp. salt
- ¼ tsp. pepper

In a large bowl, combine all ingredients. Cover and refrigerate until chilled, at least 4 hours.
1 cup: 146 cal., 11g fat (2g sat. fat), 0 chol., 387mg sod., 11g carb. (8g sugars, 2g fiber), 2g pro. **Diabetic exchanges:** 2 vegetable, 2 fat.
Black Bean Zucchini Gazpacho: Substitute 2 large tomatoes for the 4 medium. Add 1 can (15 oz.) drained rinsed black beans, 2 medium zucchini, chopped, and ¼ tsp. cayenne pepper.
Refreshing Gazpacho: Increase tomato juice to 4½ cups. Add 2 chopped celery ribs, 1 finely chopped red onion, 1 each chopped medium sweet red pepper and green pepper, ¼ cup minced fresh cilantro, 2 Tbsp. lime juice, 2 tsp. sugar and 1 tsp. Worcestershire sauce. Serve with cubed avocado if desired.

SPINACH & WHITE BEAN SOUP

For me, soup is love, comfort, happiness and memories. With all its veggies and beans, this hearty bowl appeals to my kitchen-sink style of cooking.

—*Annette Palermo, Beach Haven, NJ*

- -

Takes: 30 min. • **Makes:** 6 servings

- 2 tsp. olive oil
- 3 garlic cloves, minced
- 3 cans (15 oz. each) cannellini beans, rinsed and drained, divided
- ¼ tsp. pepper
- 1 carton (32 oz.) vegetable or reduced-sodium chicken broth
- 4 cups chopped fresh spinach (about 3 oz.)
- ¼ cup thinly sliced fresh basil
  Shredded Parmesan cheese, optional

1. In a large saucepan, heat oil over medium heat. Add garlic; cook and stir 30-45 seconds or until tender. Stir in 2 cans of beans, pepper and broth.

2. Puree mixture using an immersion blender, or puree in a blender and return to pan. Stir in remaining can of beans; bring to a boil. Reduce heat; simmer, covered, 15 minutes, stirring occasionally.

3. Stir in spinach and basil; cook, uncovered, 2-4 minutes or until the spinach is wilted. If desired, serve with cheese.

Note: Reduced-sodium vegetable broth isn't widely available, but the organic versions of big-brand broths are typically lower in sodium than their conventional counterparts.

1¼ cups: 192 cal., 2g fat (0 sat. fat), 0 chol., 886mg sod., 33g carb. (1g sugars, 9g fiber), 9g pro.

ISRAELI PEPPER TOMATO SALAD

This salad, which is traditionally eaten at breakfast, lends itself to endless variety. You can add foods like olives, beets or potatoes.
—*Sandy Long, Lees Summit, MO*

- -

Prep: 25 min. + chilling • **Makes:** 9 servings

6	medium tomatoes, seeded and chopped
1	each medium sweet red, yellow and green pepper, chopped
1	medium cucumber, seeded and chopped
1	medium carrot, chopped
3	green onions, thinly sliced
1	jalapeno pepper, seeded and chopped
2	Tbsp. each minced fresh cilantro, parsley, dill and mint
¼	cup lemon juice
2	Tbsp. olive oil
3	garlic cloves, minced
½	tsp. salt
¼	tsp. pepper

In a large bowl, combine the tomatoes, sweet peppers, cucumber, carrot, green onions, jalapeno and herbs. In a small bowl, whisk together the remaining ingredients. Pour over the tomato mixture; toss to coat evenly. Cover and refrigerate for at least 1 hour. Serve with a slotted spoon.

Note: Wear disposable gloves when cutting hot peppers; the oils can burn skin. Avoid touching your face.

1 cup: 64 cal., 3g fat (0 sat. fat), 0 chol., 143mg sod., 8g carb. (5g sugars, 3g fiber), 2g pro.
Diabetic exchanges: 1 vegetable, ½ fat.

MEDITERRANEAN SHRIMP ORZO SALAD

This pretty crowd-pleaser always stands out on the buffet table. With plenty of shrimp, artichoke hearts, olives, peppers and herbs, it's a tasty change of pace from pasta salads. I serve it with a from-scratch vinaigrette.
—Ginger Johnson, Pottstown, PA

Takes: 30 min. • **Makes:** 8 servings

- 1 pkg. (16 oz.) orzo pasta
- ¾ pound peeled and deveined cooked shrimp (31-40 per lb.), cut into thirds
- 1 can (14 oz.) water-packed quartered artichoke hearts, rinsed and drained
- 1 cup finely chopped green pepper
- 1 cup finely chopped sweet red pepper
- ¾ cup finely chopped red onion
- ½ cup pitted Greek olives
- ½ cup minced fresh parsley
- ⅓ cup chopped fresh dill
- ¾ cup Greek vinaigrette

1. Cook orzo pasta according to package directions. Drain; rinse with cold water and drain well.

2. In a large bowl, combine orzo, shrimp, vegetables, olives and herbs. Add Greek vinaigrette and toss to coat. Refrigerate, covered, until serving.

1½ cups: 397 cal., 12g fat (2g sat. fat), 65mg chol., 574mg sod., 52g carb. (4g sugars, 3g fiber), 18g pro.

POTATO CLAM CHOWDER

I came across this recipe in one of my antique cookbooks. It's a timeless classic I like to prepare for friends and family throughout the year, but especially during the holidays.
—Betty Ann Morgan, Upper Marlboro, MD

Prep: 10 min. • **Cook:** 35 min.
Makes: 6 servings

- 2 cans (6½ oz. each) minced clams
- 2 bacon strips, chopped
- 1 medium onion, chopped
- 2 Tbsp. all-purpose flour
- 1 cup water
- 1¾ lbs. potatoes (about 4 medium), peeled and cut into ¾-in. cubes
- ½ tsp. salt
- ¼ to ½ tsp. dried thyme
- ¼ tsp. dried savory
- ⅛ tsp. pepper
- 2 cups 2% milk
- 2 Tbsp. minced fresh parsley

1. Drain the clams, reserving clam juice. In a large saucepan, cook bacon over medium heat until crisp, stirring occasionally. Remove the bacon with a slotted spoon; drain on paper towels.

2. Add onion to drippings; cook and stir 4-6 minutes or until tender. Stir in flour until blended. Gradually stir in water and reserved clam juice; cook and stir until bubbly.

3. Add potatoes and seasonings; bring to a boil, stirring frequently. Reduce heat; simmer, covered, 20-25 minutes or until potatoes are tender, stirring occasionally.

4. Stir in milk, minced parsley and clams; heat through. Top with bacon.

1 cup: 201 cal., 6g fat (2g sat. fat), 34mg chol., 615mg sod., 27g carb. (6g sugars, 2g fiber), 11g pro. **Diabetic exchanges:** 2 starch, 2 lean meat.

GRILLED ROMAINE TOSS

I often double this fantastic salad, and even then it's always history by the end of the day. When you can't grill outside, simply prepare it under the broiler.
—*Trisha Kruse, Eagle, ID*

Prep: 25 min. • **Grill:** 10 min.
Makes: 10 servings

- ¼ cup olive oil
- 3 Tbsp. sugar
- 1 tsp. dried rosemary, crushed
- 1 tsp. dried thyme
- ¼ tsp. salt
- ¼ tsp. pepper
- 8 plum tomatoes, quartered
- 2 large sweet onions, thinly sliced

GRILLED ROMAINE
- 4 romaine hearts
- 2 Tbsp. olive oil
- ¼ tsp. salt
- ¼ tsp. pepper

DRESSING
- ¼ cup olive oil
- ¼ cup balsamic vinegar
- 3 garlic cloves, peeled and halved
- 2 Tbsp. brown sugar
- ¼ cup grated Parmesan cheese

1. In a large bowl, combine first 6 ingredients. Add the tomatoes and onions; toss to coat. Transfer mixture to a grill wok or basket. Grill, covered, over medium heat for 8-12 minutes or until tender, stirring frequently. Set aside.
2. For grilled romaine, cut romaine hearts in half lengthwise, leaving ends intact. Brush with oil; sprinkle with salt and pepper. Place romaine halves cut sides down on grill. Grill, covered, over medium heat for 3-4 minutes each side or until slightly charred and wilted.
3. For dressing, place the oil, vinegar, garlic and brown sugar in a food processor; cover and process until smooth.
4. Coarsely chop romaine; divide among 10 salad plates. Top with tomato mixture; drizzle with dressing. Sprinkle with cheese.
Note: If you do not have a grill wok or basket, use a disposable foil pan. Poke holes in the bottom of the pan with a meat fork to allow liquid to drain.
1 cup: 198 cal., 14g fat (2g sat. fat), 2mg chol., 164mg sod., 16g carb. (12g sugars, 2g fiber), 3g pro.

QUINOA TABBOULEH

When my mom and sister developed several food allergies, we had to modify some of our recipes. I substituted quinoa for couscous in this tabbouleh—now we make it all the time.
—*Jennifer Klann, Corbett, OR*

Prep: 35 min. + chilling • **Makes:** 8 servings

- 2 cups water
- 1 cup quinoa, rinsed
- 1 can (15 oz.) black beans, rinsed and drained
- 1 small cucumber, peeled and chopped
- 1 small sweet red pepper, chopped
- ⅓ cup minced fresh parsley
- ¼ cup lemon juice
- 2 Tbsp. olive oil
- ½ tsp. salt
- ½ tsp. pepper

1. In a large saucepan, bring water to a boil. Add quinoa. Reduce heat; cover and simmer until liquid is absorbed, 12-15 minutes. Remove from the heat; fluff with a fork. Transfer to a bowl; cool completely.
2. Add the beans, cucumber, red pepper and parsley. In a small bowl, whisk the remaining ingredients; drizzle over salad and toss to coat. Refrigerate until chilled.
Note: Look for quinoa in the cereal, rice or organic food aisle.
¾ cup: 159 cal., 5g fat (1g sat. fat), 0 chol., 255mg sod., 24g carb. (1g sugars, 4g fiber), 6g pro. **Diabetic exchanges:** 1½ starch, 1 fat.

HEARTY VEGETABLE SPLIT PEA SOUP

This slow-cooked soup is my secret weapon on busy days. It's delicious served with oyster crackers tossed in a bit of melted butter and herbs, and then lightly toasted in the oven.
—*Whitney Jensen, Spring Lake, MI*

- -

Prep: 10 min. • **Cook:** 7 hours
Makes: 8 servings (2 qt.)

- 1   pkg. (16 oz.) dried green split peas, rinsed
- 1   large carrot, chopped
- 1   celery rib, chopped
- 1   small onion, chopped
- 1   bay leaf
- 1½ tsp. salt
- ½   tsp. dried thyme
- ½   tsp. pepper
- 6   cups water

In a 3- or 4-qt. slow cooker, combine all the ingredients. Cook, covered, on low 7-9 hours or until peas are tender. Stir before serving. Discard bay leaf.

Freeze option: Freeze cooled soup in freezer containers. To use, partially thaw in refrigerator overnight. Heat through in a saucepan, stirring occasionally, and add water if necessary.

1 cup: 202 cal., 1g fat (0 sat. fat), 0 chol., 462mg sod., 36g carb. (5g sugars, 15g fiber), 14g pro.

CHICKEN WILD RICE SOUP WITH SPINACH

I stir together this creamy bowl of goodness when my family and I crave something warm and comforting. Reduced-fat and reduced-sodium ingredients make it a lighter option.
—Deborah Williams, Peoria, AZ

Prep: 10 min. • **Cook:** 5¼ hours
Makes: 6 servings (about 2 qt.)

- 3 cups water
- 1 can (14½ oz.) reduced-sodium chicken broth
- 1 can (10¾ oz.) reduced-fat reduced-sodium condensed cream of chicken soup, undiluted
- ⅔ cup uncooked wild rice
- 1 garlic clove, minced
- ½ tsp. dried thyme
- ½ tsp. pepper
- ¼ tsp. salt
- 3 cups cubed cooked chicken breast
- 2 cups fresh baby spinach

1. In a 3-qt. slow cooker, mix the first 8 ingredients until blended. Cook, covered, on low until rice is tender, 5-7 hours.
2. Stir in cubed chicken and spinach. Cook, covered, on low until heated through, about 15 minutes longer.

1¼ cups: 212 cal., 3g fat (1g sat. fat), 56mg chol., 523mg sod., 19g carb. (4g sugars, 2g fiber), 25g pro. **Diabetic exchanges:** 3 lean meat, 1 starch.

MELON WITH SERRANO-MINT SYRUP

I created this recipe to use the mint I grow. The serrano pepper is a nice contrast to the sweetness of the syrup and the fruit. You can double the syrup recipe to keep in the fridge for a few days for the next salad.

—Jennifer Fisher, Austin, TX

- -

Takes: 30 min. + chilling
Makes: 12 servings

⅓	cup sugar
⅓	cup water
¼	cup lemon juice
3	Tbsp. honey
½	tsp. minced serrano pepper
¼	cup minced fresh mint
1	Tbsp. grated lemon zest
4	cups each cubed watermelon, cantaloupe and honeydew

1. In a small saucepan, bring sugar, water, lemon juice, honey and serrano pepper to a boil; cook for 3-5 minutes or until slightly thickened. Remove from the heat; stir in the mint and lemon zest. Cool completely.

2. Strain syrup; discard the pepper, mint and lemon zest. In a large bowl, combine melons. Add syrup; gently toss to coat. Refrigerate fruit salad, covered, at least 2 hours, stirring several times.

Note: Wear disposable gloves when cutting hot peppers; the oils can burn skin. Avoid touching your face.

1 cup: 92 cal., 0 fat (0 sat. fat), 0 chol., 13mg sod., 25g carb. (23g sugars, 1g fiber), 1g pro.
Diabetic exchanges: 1 fruit, ½ starch.

WINE PAIRING

Gewurztraminer. Its name comes from the German word for "spice," and this wine both tastes like spices and works well with spicy cuisines such as Thai. The fruity, aromatic refresher is made all over the world.

MINTED BEET SALAD

We have neighbors who share the vegetables they grow in their garden, and every year my husband and I look forward to their beets. My interest in Mediterranean food inspired this particular dish—the vinegar and oil dressing with fresh mint tones down the sweetness of the beets, and the olives add a salty touch.
—Barb Estabrook, Appleton, WI

Prep: 20 min. • **Cook:** 15 min. + chilling
Makes: 6 servings

- 5   medium fresh beets (about 2 lbs.)
- 2   Tbsp. water
- 2   Tbsp. champagne vinegar or rice vinegar
- 2   Tbsp. olive oil
- ½   tsp. salt
- ¼   tsp. coarsely ground pepper
- ¼   cup pitted kalamata olives, quartered
- 2   Tbsp. thinly sliced fresh mint, divided

1. Scrub beets; trim tops to 1 in. Place in a single layer in a large microwave-safe dish. Drizzle with water. Microwave, covered, on high 14-15 minutes or until easily pierced with a fork, turning once; let stand 5 minutes.

2. When cool enough to handle, peel and cut beets into ¾-in. pieces. In a bowl, whisk vinegar, oil, salt and pepper until blended. Add olives, beets and 1 Tbsp. mint; toss to coat. Refrigerate, covered, at least 1 hour or until cold. Top with remaining mint.

½ cup: 123 cal., 6g fat (1g sat. fat), 0 chol., 406mg sod., 16g carb. (12g sugars, 3g fiber), 3g pro. **Diabetic exchanges:** 1 vegetable, 1 fat.

SPICY SWEET POTATO KALE CANNELLINI SOUP

While I prefer heartier soups in the winter, sometimes I want a meatless alternative to the classic beef stew. This recipe is a healthier option that keeps me warm on chilly days!
—*Marybeth Mank, Mesquite, TX*

- -

Prep: 25 min. • **Cook:** 40 min.
Makes: 12 servings (3 qt.)

- 2 Tbsp. olive oil
- 1 medium onion, finely chopped
- 3 garlic cloves, minced
- 3 lbs. sweet potatoes (about 5 medium), cubed
- 2 medium Granny Smith apples, peeled and chopped
- 1 tsp. honey
- 1 tsp. rubbed sage
- ¾ to 1 tsp. crushed red pepper flakes
- ½ tsp. salt
- ¼ tsp. pepper
- 3 cans (14½ oz. each) vegetable broth
- 2 cans (15 oz. each) cannellini beans, rinsed and drained
- 3 cups chopped fresh kale
- ½ cup heavy whipping cream
  Optional toppings: Olive oil, giardiniera and shredded Parmesan cheese

1. In a 6-qt. stockpot, heat oil over medium-high heat. Add onion; cook and stir until tender, 6-8 minutes. Add the minced garlic; cook 1 minute longer. Stir in sweet potatoes, apples, honey, seasonings and broth. Bring to a boil. Reduce heat; simmer, covered, until potatoes are tender, 25-30 minutes.
2. Puree soup using an immersion blender or cool soup slightly and puree in batches in a blender; return to pan. Add beans and kale; cook, uncovered, over medium heat until kale is tender, 10-15 minutes, stirring occasionally. Stir in cream. Serve with toppings as desired.
1 cup: 250 cal., 6g fat (3g sat. fat), 14mg chol., 615mg sod., 44g carb. (16g sugars, 7g fiber), 5g pro. **Diabetic exchanges:** 3 starch, 1 lean meat, ½ fat.

CRUNCHY LEMON-PESTO GARDEN SALAD

I love using fresh vegetables straight from the garden to prepare this salad. If I pick the squash and cucumbers early enough, their skins are so tender that there's no need to remove them! Best yet, it's easily adaptable—any veggie can be swapped in for equally delicious results!
—*Carmell Childs, Clawson, UT*

- -

Takes: 25 min. • **Makes:** 6 servings

- 5 Tbsp. prepared pesto
- 1 Tbsp. lemon juice
- 2 tsp. grated lemon zest
- 1½ tsp. Dijon mustard
- ¼ tsp. garlic salt
- ¼ tsp. pepper
- 2½ cups yellow summer squash, thinly sliced
- 1¾ cups mini cucumber, thinly sliced
- ¾ cup fresh peas
- ½ cup shredded Parmesan cheese
- ¼ cup thinly sliced green onions
- 5 thick-sliced bacon strips, cooked and crumbled

In a bowl, whisk together first 6 ingredients until blended. In another bowl, combine squash, cucumber, peas, Parmesan and green onions. Pour dressing over salad; toss to coat. Top with bacon to serve.

¾ cup: 159 cal., 11g fat (3g sat. fat), 13mg chol., 586mg sod., 8g carb. (4g sugars, 2g fiber), 8g pro. **Diabetic exchanges:** 2 fat, 1 vegetable.

BEAN & BULGUR CHILI

A hot bowl of this zesty three-bean chili hits the spot any time of year.
—*Tari Ambler, Shorewood, IL*

- -

Prep: 25 min. • **Cook:** 40 min.
Makes: 10 servings (3½ qt.)

- 2 large onions, chopped
- 2 celery ribs, chopped
- 1 large green pepper, chopped
- 4 tsp. olive oil
- 4 garlic cloves, minced
- 1 large carrot, shredded
- 2 Tbsp. chili powder
- 1 tsp. dried oregano
- ½ tsp. coarsely ground pepper
- ½ tsp. ground cumin
- ⅛ tsp. ground cinnamon
- ⅛ tsp. ground allspice
- 2 cans (14½ oz. each) no-salt-added diced tomatoes, undrained
- 1 can (14½ oz.) fire-roasted diced tomatoes, undrained
- 1 can (16 oz.) kidney beans, rinsed and drained
- 1 can (15 oz.) pinto beans, rinsed and drained
- 1 can (15 oz.) black beans, rinsed and drained
- 1 can (14 oz.) vegetable broth
- ⅓ cup tomato paste
- 1 cup bulgur
  Reduced-fat sour cream, optional

1. In a Dutch oven over medium heat, cook the onions, celery and green pepper in oil until tender. Add garlic; cook 1 minute longer. Stir in carrot and seasonings; cook and stir 1 minute longer.

2. Stir in the tomatoes, beans, broth and tomato paste. Bring to a boil. Reduce heat; cover and simmer for 30 minutes.

3. Meanwhile, cook bulgur according to package directions. Stir into chili; heat through. Garnish with sour cream if desired.

1⅓ cups: 240 cal., 3g fat (0 sat. fat), 0 chol., 578mg sod., 45g carb. (9g sugars, 12g fiber), 11g pro.

PORTOBELLO GNOCCHI SALAD

Pan-sauteing the gnocchi eliminates the need to boil it and creates a wonderful, crispy coating. The baby bellos lend an additional earthiness to this Italian-influenced salad.
—*Fran Fehling, Staten Island, NY*

- -

Takes: 25 min. • **Makes:** 14 servings

- 1   pkg. (16 oz.) potato gnocchi
- 2   Tbsp. plus ⅓ cup olive oil, divided
- ½   lb. sliced baby portobello mushrooms
- 3   tsp. lemon juice
- 3   large plum tomatoes, seeded and chopped
- 1   can (15 oz.) garbanzo beans or chickpeas, rinsed and drained
- 1   pkg. (5 oz.) fresh baby arugula or fresh baby spinach, coarsely chopped
- ½   cup pitted Greek olives, cut in half
- ⅓   cup minced fresh parsley
- 2   Tbsp. capers, drained and chopped
- 2   tsp. grated lemon zest
- ½   tsp. salt
- ¼   tsp. coarsely ground pepper
- ½   cup crumbled feta cheese
- ¼   cup chopped walnuts, toasted

1. In large nonstick skillet over medium-high heat, cook gnocchi in 1 Tbsp. oil until lightly browned, 6-8 minutes, turning once. Remove from the skillet; cool slightly.
2. In the same skillet, saute mushrooms in 1 Tbsp. oil until tender. Place mushrooms and gnocchi in a serving bowl. Add lemon juice and remaining oil; gently toss to coat.
3. Add the tomatoes, garbanzo beans, arugula, olives, parsley, capers, lemon zest, salt and pepper; toss to combine. Garnish with cheese and walnuts.
Note: Look for potato gnocchi in the pasta or frozen foods section.
¾ cup: 204 cal., 12g fat (2g sat. fat), 5mg chol., 425mg sod., 21g carb. (3g sugars, 3g fiber), 5g pro. **Diabetic exchanges:** 2 fat, 1½ starch.

GYRO SOUP

If you like lamb, don't pass up this Greek-style soup. Seasoned with the classic flavors of rosemary, marjoram and mint, this bowl will transport you straight to the Mediterranean!
—*Bridget Klusman, Otsego, MI*

- -

Prep: 25 min. • **Cook:** 6 hours
Makes: 6 servings (2¼ qt.)

- 2   lbs. ground lamb
- 5   cups water
- 1   can (14½ oz.) diced tomatoes, undrained
- 1   medium onion, chopped
- ¼   cup red wine
- 6   garlic cloves, minced
- 3   Tbsp. minced fresh mint or 1 Tbsp. dried mint
- 1   Tbsp. dried marjoram
- 1   Tbsp. dried rosemary, crushed
- 1½ tsp. salt
- ½   tsp. pepper
     Optional toppings: Plain Greek yogurt and crumbled feta cheese

1. In a large skillet, cook and crumble lamb over medium-high heat until no longer pink, 8-10 minutes. Using a slotted spoon, transfer lamb to a 4- or 5-qt. slow cooker. Stir in the water, tomatoes, onion, wine, garlic, herbs, salt and pepper.
2. Cook, covered, on low until the flavors are blended, 6-8 hours. Serve with optional toppings as desired.
Freeze option: Freeze cooled soup in freezer containers. To use, partially thaw in refrigerator overnight. Heat through in a saucepan, stirring occasionally.
1½ cups: 329 cal., 20g fat (8g sat. fat), 100mg chol., 784mg sod., 7g carb. (3g sugars, 2g fiber), 27g pro.

PROVENCAL BEAN SALAD

Lightly coated in reduced-fat tarragon mayonnaise, this refreshing salad will perk up any meal. Every bite bursts with flavor!
—*Suzanne Banfield, Basking Ridge, NJ*

Takes: 25 min.
Makes: 12 servings

- ¾ lb. fresh green beans, trimmed
- ¾ lb. fresh wax beans, trimmed
- 1 lb. grape tomatoes, halved
- 1 can (15 oz.) cannellini beans, rinsed and drained
- ½ cup pitted Greek olives
- ½ cup reduced-fat mayonnaise
- 1 Tbsp. minced fresh tarragon or 1 tsp. dried tarragon
- 1 Tbsp. lemon juice
- 1 garlic clove, minced
- ½ tsp. salt
  Dash pepper

1. In a large saucepan, bring 4 cups water to a boil. Add green and wax beans; cover and cook for 3 minutes. Drain and immediately place beans in ice water. Drain and pat dry.
2. Place the beans, tomatoes, kidney beans and olives in a large bowl. In a small bowl, whisk the remaining ingredients; pour over salad and toss to coat.

¾ cup: 102 cal., 5g fat (1g sat. fat), 4mg chol., 321mg sod., 12g carb. (1g sugars, 4g fiber), 3g pro. **Diabetic exchanges:** 1 vegetable, 1 fat, ½ starch.

ITALIAN-STYLE LENTIL SOUP

I cook with lentils often because they're a nutritious, inexpensive source of protein. This low-fat soup is one of my favorite ways to use them. To make it even heartier, add ground beef, cooked sausage or leftover cubed chicken.

—*Rachel Keller, Roanoke, VA*

Prep: 20 min. • **Cook:** 40 min.
Makes: 6 servings

- 2 tsp. olive oil
- 2 medium onions, chopped
- 2 celery ribs, thinly sliced
- 1 medium carrot, chopped
- 1 cup dried lentils, rinsed
- ¼ cup minced fresh parsley
- 1 Tbsp. reduced-sodium beef bouillon granules
- ½ tsp. pepper
- 5¼ cups water
- 1 can (6 oz.) tomato paste
- 2 Tbsp. white vinegar
- 2 tsp. brown sugar
- ½ tsp. salt
- 2 Tbsp. shredded Parmesan cheese

1. In a large saucepan coated with cooking spray, heat oil over medium heat. Add the onions, celery and carrot; cook and stir until vegetables are crisp-tender.

2. Stir in lentils, parsley, bouillon, pepper and water; bring to a boil. Reduce heat; simmer, covered, 20-25 minutes or until lentils are tender, stirring occasionally.

3. Stir in tomato paste, vinegar, brown sugar and salt; heat through. Serve with cheese.

Freeze option: Freeze cooled soup in freezer containers. To use, partially thaw in refrigerator overnight. Heat through in a saucepan, stirring occasionally; add a little water if necessary.

Note: Unlike dried beans, lentils don't have to be soaked before using. They are a good source of iron, most B vitamins and fiber.

1 cup: 122 cal., 2g fat (1g sat. fat), 1mg chol., 420mg sod., 21g carb. (11g sugars, 6g fiber), 6g pro. **Diabetic exchanges:** 2 vegetable, 1 starch.

ZUCCHINI & SUMMER SQUASH SALAD

Take advantage of the abundant zucchini and squash crops every summer with this light, flavorful dish! It's so cool and refreshing.
—*Paula Wharton, El Paso, TX*

Prep: 25 min. + chilling • **Makes:** 12 servings

- 4   medium zucchini
- 2   yellow summer squash
- 1   medium sweet red pepper
- 1   medium red onion
- 1   cup fresh sugar snap peas, trimmed and halved
- ⅓   cup olive oil
- ¼   cup balsamic vinegar
- 2   Tbsp. reduced-fat mayonnaise
- 4   tsp. fresh sage or 1 tsp. dried sage leaves
- 2   tsp. honey
- 1   tsp. garlic powder
- 1   tsp. celery seed
- 1   tsp. dill weed
- ½   tsp. salt
- ½   tsp. pepper

Thinly slice zucchini, squash, red pepper and onion; place in a large bowl. Add snap peas. In a small bowl, whisk remaining ingredients until blended. Pour over vegetables; toss to coat. Refrigerate, covered, at least 3 hours.

¾ cup: 101 cal., 7g fat (1g sat. fat), 1mg chol., 124mg sod., 8g carb. (6g sugars, 2g fiber), 2g pro. **Diabetic exchanges:** 1½ fat, 1 vegetable.

RED POTATO SALAD WITH LEMONY VINAIGRETTE

At our house, this beloved dish is a zippy upgrade on typical mayo-based salads.
—*Elizabeth Dehart, West Jordan, UT*

Prep: 15 min. • **Cook:** 20 min. + chilling
Makes: 12 servings

- 3 lbs. red potatoes, cubed (about 10 cups)
- ⅓ cup olive oil
- 2 Tbsp. lemon juice
- 2 Tbsp. red wine vinegar
- 1½ tsp. salt
- ¼ tsp. pepper
- 2 Tbsp. minced fresh parsley
- 1 garlic clove, minced
- ½ tsp. dried oregano
- ½ cup pitted Greek olives, chopped
- ⅓ cup chopped red onion
- ½ cup shredded Parmesan cheese

1. Place potatoes in a 6-qt. stockpot; add water to cover. Bring to a boil. Reduce heat; cook, uncovered, 10-15 minutes or until tender. Drain; transfer to a large bowl.

2. In a small bowl, whisk the oil, lemon juice, vinegar, salt and pepper until blended; stir in parsley, garlic and oregano. Drizzle over the potatoes; toss to coat. Gently stir in the olives and onion. Refrigerate, covered, for at least 2 hours before serving.

3. Just before serving, stir in cheese.

¾ cup: 168 cal., 9g fat (2g sat. fat), 2mg chol., 451mg sod., 20g carb. (1g sugars, 2g fiber), 4g pro. **Diabetic exchanges:** 2 fat, 1½ starch.

CRAN-ORANGE COUSCOUS SALAD

I often create healthy salads using a variety of filling grains. This tender couscous version is amped up with the bright flavors of oranges, cranberries, basil and a touch of fennel.
—*Kristen Heigl, Staten Island, NY*

- -

Prep: 25 min. • **Cook:** 15 min.
Makes: 12 servings

- 3 **cups uncooked pearl (Israeli) couscous**
- 2 **cans (14 oz. each) garbanzo beans or chickpeas, rinsed and drained**
- 2 **large navel oranges, peeled and chopped**
- 2 **cups fresh baby spinach**
- 1 **cup crumbled goat cheese**
- 1 **small red onion, chopped**
- ¾ **cup dried cranberries**
- ½ **cup fennel bulb, thinly sliced, fronds reserved**
- ½ **cup chopped pecans, toasted**
- 8 **fresh basil leaves, chopped, plus more for garnish**

VINAIGRETTE
- ½ **cup olive oil**
- ¼ **cup orange juice**
- ¼ **cup balsamic vinegar**
- 1 **Tbsp. grated orange zest**
- 2 **tsp. honey**
- 1 **tsp. salt**
- ½ **tsp. pepper**

Prepare couscous according to package directions. Fluff with a fork; cool. In a large bowl, combine the couscous and the next 9 ingredients. In a small bowl, whisk together vinaigrette ingredients until blended. Pour dressing over salad; toss to coat. Garnish with additional basil and reserved fennel fronds.

¾ cup: 403 cal., 16g fat (3g sat. fat), 12mg chol., 335mg sod., 57g carb. (15g sugars, 5g fiber), 10g pro.

GINGER PLUM TART,
PAGE 288

YIAYIA'S SENSIBLE SWEETS

Dessert—it's everyone's favorite course, and nobody makes it like Grandma! Most of these irresistible sweets call for just a little butter or sugar, so you can indulge without guilt—just the way Grandma would want it.

GINGER PLUM TART

Sweet cravings, begone: This free-form plum tart is done in only 35 minutes. And it's extra awesome when served warm.
—Taste of Home *Test Kitchen*

- -

Prep: 15 min. • **Bake:** 20 min. + cooling
Makes: 8 servings

- 1 sheet refrigerated pie crust
- 3½ cups sliced fresh plums (about 10 medium)
- 3 Tbsp. plus 1 tsp. coarse sugar, divided
- 1 Tbsp. cornstarch
- 2 tsp. finely chopped crystallized ginger
- 1 large egg white
- 1 Tbsp. water

1. Preheat oven to 400°. On a work surface, unroll crust. Roll to a 12-in. circle. Transfer to a parchment-lined baking sheet.
2. In a large bowl, toss plums with 3 Tbsp. sugar and cornstarch. Arrange plums on crust to within 2 in. of edges; sprinkle with ginger. Fold crust edge over plums, pleating as you go.
3. In a small bowl, whisk egg white and water; brush over folded crust. Sprinkle with the remaining sugar.
4. Bake until crust is golden brown, 20-25 minutes. Cool on pan on a wire rack. Serve warm or at room temperature.
1 piece: 190 cal., 7g fat (3g sat. fat), 5mg chol., 108mg sod., 30g carb. (14g sugars, 1g fiber), 2g pro. **Diabetic exchanges:** 1½ starch, 1 fat, ½ fruit.

RICOTTA-RAISIN COFFEE CAKE

These few ingredients come together quickly so I can have a warm coffee cake to serve overnight guests for breakfast. If you don't have or don't like cardamom, substitute any sweet spice. I recommend ground nutmeg, cinnamon or allspice.
—Carol Gaus, Elk Grove Village, IL

- -

Prep: 15 min. + rising
Bake: 20 min. + cooling • **Makes:** 12 servings

- 1 loaf (1 lb.) frozen bread dough, thawed
- 1 cup part-skim ricotta cheese
- ¼ cup honey
- ¼ tsp. ground cardamom
- ¼ tsp. almond extract
- 1 cup golden raisins
- ¼ cup confectioners' sugar
- 2 to 3 tsp. fat-free milk

1. On a lightly floured surface, roll dough into a 15x9-in. rectangle. In a small bowl, combine cheese, honey, cardamom and the almond extract. Spread filling to within ½ in. of edges. Sprinkle with raisins. Roll up jelly-roll style, starting with a long side; pinch seam to seal. Pinch ends together to form a ring.
2. Place seam side down in a parchment-lined 9-in. round baking pan. Cover and let rise until doubled, about 30 minutes.
3. Preheat oven to 350°. With a sharp knife, make 12 shallow slashes in top of coffee cake. Bake 20-25 minutes or until golden brown. Cool on a wire rack. In a small bowl, combine the confectioners' sugar and milk; drizzle over cake.
1 slice: 203 cal., 3g fat (1g sat. fat), 6mg chol., 240mg sod., 37g carb. (18g sugars, 2g fiber), 7g pro.

PUMPKIN PIE CUSTARD

Instead of pumpkin pie, try this flavorful, light holiday dessert. My husband's aunt shared the recipe after she brought this treat to a family party.
—*Nancy Zimmerman,*
Cape May Court House, NJ

- -

Prep: 20 min. • **Bake:** 35 min. + chilling
Makes: 10 servings

- 1   **can (15 oz.) canned pumpkin**
- 1   **can (12 oz.) fat-free evaporated milk**
- 8   **large egg whites**
- ½   **cup fat-free milk**
- ¾   **cup sugar**
- ¼   **tsp. salt**
- 1   **tsp. ground cinnamon**
- ½   **tsp. ground ginger**
- ¼   **tsp. ground cloves**
- ¼   **tsp. ground nutmeg**
       Sweetened whipped cream and
       additional cinnamon, optional

1. Preheat oven to 350°. Place ten 6-oz. ramekins or custard cups coated with cooking spray in a 15x10x1-in. baking pan.
2. In a large bowl, beat first 4 ingredients until smooth. Add sugar, salt and spices; mix well. Divide among ramekins.
3. Bake until a knife inserted in the center comes out clean, 40-45 minutes. Cool on a wire rack; serve or refrigerate within 2 hours. If desired, top with whipped cream and sprinkle with cinnamon.
1 serving: 120 cal., 0 fat (0 sat. fat), 2mg chol., 151mg sod., 24g carb. (21g sugars, 2g fiber), 7g pro. **Diabetic exchanges:** 1½ starch.

5i

LIGHT & CREAMY CHOCOLATE PUDDING

This pudding delivers exactly what its name promises—a light and creamy texture. It uses soy milk, so it's a smart choice if you're lactose intolerant.
—*Deborah Williams, Peoria, AZ*

Prep: 10 min. • **Cook:** 15 min. + chilling
Makes: 4 servings

- 3 Tbsp. cornstarch
- 2 Tbsp. sugar
- 2 Tbsp. baking cocoa
- ⅛ tsp. salt
- 2 cups chocolate soy milk
- 1 tsp. vanilla extract

1. In a small heavy saucepan, mix cornstarch, sugar, cocoa and salt. Whisk in milk. Cook and stir over medium heat until thickened and bubbly. Reduce heat to low; cook and stir 2 minutes longer.
2. Remove from heat. Stir in vanilla. Cool 15 minutes, stirring occasionally.
3. Transfer to dessert dishes. Refrigerate, covered, 30 minutes or until cold.
½ cup: 127 cal., 2g fat (0 sat. fat), 0 chol., 112mg sod., 25g carb. (16g sugars, 1g fiber), 3g pro. **Diabetic exchanges:** 1½ starch.

WINE PAIRING

Ruby Port. This fortified (higher-alcohol—about 20%) wine from Portugal has red berry flavors. It's amazing with chocolate desserts. Pour just a small glass, as a little goes a long way.

GRAPEFRUIT YOGURT CAKE

We eat grapefruit for breakfast and in winter fruit salads, so why not for dessert? My sweet-tart cake is easy and delicious!

—*Maiah Miller, Montclair, VA*

- -

Prep: 10 min. • **Bake:** 25 min. + cooling
Makes: 12 servings

- 1½ cups all-purpose flour
- 2 tsp. baking powder
- ¼ tsp. salt
- 3 large eggs, room temperature
- 1 cup fat-free plain yogurt
- ⅓ cup sugar
- 5 Tbsp. grated grapefruit zest
- ¼ cup agave nectar or honey
- ½ tsp. vanilla extract
- ¼ cup canola oil

GLAZE
- ½ cup confectioners' sugar
- 2 to 3 tsp. grapefruit juice
  Grapefruit wheels and fresh mint leaves, optional
  Fresh mint leaves

1. Preheat oven to 350°. Whisk together flour, baking powder and salt. Combine the next 7 ingredients. Gradually stir the flour mixture into yogurt mixture, then pour into a 9-in. round baking pan coated with cooking spray. Bake until a toothpick inserted in the center of cake comes out clean, 25-30 minutes. Cool.

2. For glaze, mix confectioners' sugar with enough grapefruit juice to reach desired consistency; drizzle glaze over top, allowing some to flow over sides. Top cake with grapefruit and mint if desired.

Freeze option: Omit glaze. Securely wrap cooled cake in plastic and foil; freeze. To use, thaw at room temperature. Prepare glaze; top as directed.

1 slice: 187 cal., 6g fat (1g sat. fat), 47mg chol., 159mg sod., 30g carb. (17g sugars, 1g fiber), 4g pro. **Diabetic exchanges:** 2 starch, 1 fat.

TEST KITCHEN TIP

Any citrus works well in this cake. If grapefruit isn't your thing, use lemon, orange or lime. You can also substitute melted coconut oil for the canola oil.

DOUBLE-NUT STUFFED FIGS

We have a diabetic in our family, so we're always looking for dessert recipes everyone can enjoy. These figs are sweet and delicious without compromising on good nutrition.
—*Bob Bailey, Columbus, OH*

- -

Prep: 20 min. • **Bake:** 30 min.
Makes: 3 dozen

36	dried Calimyrna figs
⅔	cup finely chopped pecans
⅔	cup finely chopped walnuts
7	Tbsp. agave nectar, divided
3	Tbsp. baking cocoa
¼	tsp. ground cinnamon
⅛	tsp. ground cloves
½	cup pomegranate juice
4½	tsp. lemon juice

1. Preheat oven to 350°. Remove stems from figs. Cut an X in the top of each fig, about two-thirds of the way down.
2. In a small bowl, combine pecans, walnuts, 3 Tbsp. agave nectar, cocoa, cinnamon and cloves; spoon into figs. Arrange in a 13x9-in. baking dish coated with cooking spray.
3. In a small bowl, mix pomegranate juice, lemon juice and remaining agave nectar; drizzle over figs. Bake, covered, 20 minutes. Bake, uncovered, 8-10 minutes longer or until heated through, basting occasionally with cooking liquid.

1 stuffed fig: 98 cal., 3g fat (0 sat. fat), 0 chol., 3mg sod., 17g carb. (13g sugars, 3g fiber), 1g pro. **Diabetic exchanges:** 1 starch, ½ fat.

⑤ⱼ

FROZEN GREEK VANILLA YOGURT

This recipe proves it's simple and easy to make your own frozen Greek yogurt. You might even want to get the kids in on the fun.
—Taste of Home *Test Kitchen*

- -

Prep: 15 min+ chilling
Process: 15 min+ freezing • **Makes:** 2½ cups

3	cups reduced-fat plain Greek yogurt
¾	cup sugar
1½	tsp. vanilla extract
1	Tbsp. cold water
1	Tbsp. lemon juice
1	tsp. unflavored gelatin

1. Line a strainer or colander with 4 layers of cheesecloth or 1 coffee filter; place over a bowl. Place yogurt in prepared strainer; cover yogurt with sides of cheesecloth. Refrigerate 2-4 hours.

2. Remove the yogurt from cheesecloth to a bowl; discard strained liquid. Add sugar and vanilla to yogurt, stirring until the sugar is dissolved.

3. In a small microwave-safe bowl, combine cold water and lemon juice; sprinkle with gelatin and let stand 1 minute. Microwave on high for 30 seconds. Stir and let mixture stand 1 minute or until gelatin is completely dissolved; cool slightly. Stir gelatin mixture into yogurt. Cover and refrigerate until cold, about 40 minutes.

4. Pour yogurt mixture into cylinder of ice cream freezer; freeze according to the manufacturer's directions.

5. Transfer frozen yogurt to a freezer container. Freeze 2-4 hours or until firm enough to scoop.

½ cup: 225 cal., 3g fat (2g sat. fat), 8mg chol., 57mg sod., 36g carb. (36g sugars, 0 fiber), 14g pro.

⑤

BELLINI ICE

This ice is fashioned after the Bellini, a peach and white Italian wine sparkler. Pairing ripe sweet peaches with tart white grape juice creates a fantastic flavor combination. For a refreshing summer dessert, place some fresh peach slices in a large wine goblet, top with Bellini ice, and garnish with a kiwi slice.
—*Deirdre Cox, Kansas City, MO*

- -

Prep: 10 min. + freezing • **Makes:** 6 servings

- 2 medium peaches, peeled and quartered
- 2 cups white grape juice
- 1 cup lemon-lime carbonated water
- ¼ cup lime juice
  Fresh peach slices, optional

1. Place peaches in a food processor. Cover and process until pureed. Transfer to an 11x7-in. dish. Stir in grape juice, carbonated water and lime juice. Freeze for 1 hour; stir with a fork.
2. Freeze 2-3 hours longer or until completely frozen, stirring every 30 minutes. Stir with a fork just before serving; spoon into dessert dishes. Garnish with peach slices if desired.
1 serving: 65 cal., 0 fat (0 sat. fat), 0 chol., 5mg sod., 16g carb. (14g sugars, 1g fiber), 1g pro. **Diabetic exchanges:** 1 fruit.

APPLE PIE TARTLETS

These adorable mini apple pie pastries make a delightful addition to a dessert buffet or snack tray. The recipe calls for convenient frozen phyllo shells, so they're surprisingly easy to prepare. The lemon curd filling adds a unique flavor twist.
—*Mary Ann Lee, Clifton Park, NY*

- -

Prep: 15 min. • **Bake:** 20 min.
Makes: 2½ dozen

- 1 cup finely chopped peeled apple
- ¼ cup lemon curd
- 2 pkg. (1.9 oz. each) frozen miniature phyllo tart shells

TOPPING
- ½ cup all-purpose flour
- 3 Tbsp. sugar
- ½ tsp. ground cinnamon
- ¼ cup cold butter
  Confectioners' sugar

1. In a small bowl, combine apples and lemon curd. Spoon into tart shells.
2. In another bowl, combine the flour, sugar and cinnamon; cut in butter until mixture resembles fine crumbs. Spoon over apple mixture. Place on an ungreased baking sheet.
3. Bake at 350° for 18-20 minutes or until golden brown. Cool on wire racks 5 minutes. Dust with confectioners' sugar. Serve tartlets warm or at room temperature. Refrigerate any leftovers.
1 tartlet: 57 cal., 3g fat (1g sat. fat), 6mg chol., 22mg sod., 7g carb. (3g sugars, 0 fiber), 1g pro. **Diabetic exchanges:** ½ starch, ½ fat.

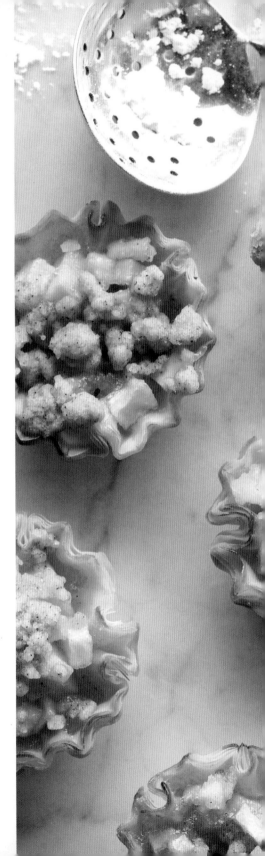

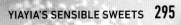

CITRUS GINGERBREAD COOKIES

Orange and lemon zest give these cutouts a refreshing twist. A honey glaze on top adds a subtle shine and extra sweetness.
—*Monique Hooker, DeSoto, WI*

Prep: 40 min. + chilling
Bake: 10 min./batch + cooling
Makes: 6 dozen

- ¾ cup sugar
- ½ cup honey
- ½ cup molasses
- ½ cup unsalted butter, cubed
- 1 large egg
- 3½ cups all-purpose flour
- ¼ cup ground almonds
- 2 tsp. baking powder
- 2 tsp. grated lemon zest
- 2 tsp. grated orange zest
- 1 tsp. each ground cardamom, ginger, nutmeg, cinnamon and cloves

GLAZE
- ½ cup honey
- 2 Tbsp. water

1. In a large saucepan, combine sugar, honey and molasses. Bring to a boil; remove from heat. Let stand 20 minutes. Stir in butter; let stand 20 minutes longer.

2. Beat in egg. In another bowl, whisk flour, almonds, baking powder, lemon zest, orange zest and spices; gradually beat into sugar mixture. Refrigerate, covered, 8 hours or overnight.

3. Preheat oven to 375°. On a lightly floured surface, divide dough into 3 portions. Roll each portion to ¼-in. thickness. Cut with a floured 2-in. cookie cutter. Place 2 in. apart on baking sheets coated with cooking spray.

4. Bake 7-8 minutes or until lightly browned. Cool on pans 1 minute. Remove to wire racks to cool completely. In a small bowl, mix glaze ingredients; brush over cookies. Let stand until set.

1 cookie: 66 cal., 2g fat (1g sat. fat), 6mg chol., 13mg sod., 12g carb. (7g sugars, 0 fiber), 1g pro.

MAKEOVER ITALIAN CREAM CAKE

This lightened-up version of a classic cake ensures a happy ending to any meal.
—*Joanne Brininstool, Austin, TX*

Prep: 30 min. • **Bake:** 25 min. + cooling
Makes: 18 servings

- ½ cup butter, softened
- 1½ cups sugar
- ½ cup unsweetened applesauce
- 3 large egg yolks, room temperature
- 1 tsp. vanilla extract
- 2 cups all-purpose flour
- 1 tsp. baking soda
- ½ tsp. salt
- 1 cup buttermilk
- 5 large egg whites, room temperature
- ½ cup sweetened shredded coconut
- ½ cup chopped pecans

FROSTING
- 1 pkg. (8 oz.) reduced-fat cream cheese
- 2 Tbsp. butter, softened
- 1 tsp. vanilla extract
- 2½ cups confectioners' sugar
- ¼ cup chopped pecans, toasted

1. In a large bowl, beat butter and sugar for 2 minutes. Stir in applesauce. Add egg yolks and vanilla; beat for 1 minute. Combine the flour, baking soda and salt; add to butter mixture alternately with buttermilk.

2. In another bowl, beat egg whites until stiff peaks form. Fold into batter. Fold in coconut and pecans. Transfer to a 13x9-in. baking pan coated with cooking spray. Bake at 350° for 25-30 minutes or until a toothpick inserted in center comes out clean. Cool on a wire rack.

3. For frosting, in a small bowl, combine the cream cheese, butter and vanilla. Gradually beat in confectioners' sugar. Spread over cake; sprinkle with pecans. Store in the refrigerator.

1 serving: 338 cal., 15g fat (7g sat. fat), 62mg chol., 291mg sod., 48g carb. (35g sugars, 1g fiber), 5g pro.

FROSTY WATERMELON ICE

Love watermelon? You'll enjoy this make-ahead frozen treat. It's so refreshing on a summer day...and you don't have to worry about seeds while you're eating it.

—*Kaaren Jurack, Manassas, VA*

- -

Prep: 20 min. + freezing • **Makes:** 4 servings

1 tsp. unflavored gelatin
2 Tbsp. water
2 Tbsp. lime juice
2 Tbsp. honey
4 cups cubed seedless watermelon, divided

1. In a microwave-safe bowl, sprinkle gelatin over water; let stand 1 minute. Microwave on high for 40 seconds. Stir and let stand until gelatin is completely dissolved, 1-2 minutes.
2. Place lime juice, honey and gelatin mixture in a blender. Add 1 cup watermelon; cover and process until blended. Add remaining watermelon, 1 cup at a time, processing after each addition until smooth.
3. Transfer to a shallow dish; freeze until almost firm. In a chilled bowl, beat with an electric mixer until mixture is bright pink. Divide among 4 serving dishes; freeze, covered, until firm. Remove from freezer 15-20 minutes before serving.
¾ cup: 81 cal., 0 fat (0 sat. fat), 0 chol., 3mg sod., 21g carb. (18g sugars, 1g fiber), 1g pro.
Diabetic exchanges: 1 fruit, ½ starch.

ALMOND-PECAN DATE TRUFFLES

My daughter and I came across a date candy recipe when she was learning about ancient Egypt. We changed some of the spices and nuts to suit our taste.
—*Lori Daniels, Beverly, WV*

Prep: 20 min. + chilling
Makes: about 1½ dozen

⅓   cup apple juice
1   pkg. (8 oz.) chopped dates
1   cup finely chopped pecans, toasted
1¼   tsp. ground cinnamon
¼   tsp. ground nutmeg
1   cup ground almonds, toasted

1. In a microwave, warm apple juice. Stir in chopped dates; let stand 5 minutes to soften, stirring occasionally. Remove the dates from apple juice; discard liquid. Transfer dates to the bowl of a food processor fitted with the blade attachment; process until smooth. Add pecans and spices; pulse just until combined (mixture will be thick).

2. Shape mixture into 1-in. balls; place on a waxed paper-lined baking sheet. Refrigerate, covered, 30-60 minutes.

3. Roll date balls in almonds.

1 date ball: 109 cal., 7g fat (1g sat. fat), 0 chol., 0 sod., 12g carb. (9g sugars, 2g fiber), 2g pro.

(5i)

STRAWBERRY-ROSEMARY POPS

We planted strawberries a few years ago. These tangy-sweet frozen yogurt pops are my favorite treats to make with them. The options are endless. Try using other yogurt flavors like lemon, raspberry or blueberry. You may also substitute your favorite herb for the rosemary, or simply omit it.
—*Carmell Childs, Clawson, UT*

- -

Prep: 20 min. + freezing • **Makes:** 6 pops

- 1 **cup chopped fresh strawberries**
- 2 **Tbsp. balsamic vinegar**
- 2 **Tbsp. strawberry preserves**
- 2 **fresh rosemary sprigs**
- 1½ **cups (12 oz.) vanilla yogurt**
- 6 **freezer pop molds or paper cups (3 oz. each) and wooden pop or lollipop sticks**

1. In a small bowl, mix strawberries, vinegar, preserves and rosemary. Let mixture stand 30 minutes; discard rosemary.
2. Spoon 2 Tbsp. vanilla yogurt and 1 Tbsp. strawberry mixture into each mold or paper cup. Repeat layers. Top molds with holders. If using cups, top with foil and insert sticks through foil. Freeze until firm.
1 pop: 81 cal., 1g fat (0 sat. fat), 3mg chol., 42mg sod., 16g carb. (15g sugars, 1g fiber), 3g pro. **Diabetic exchanges:** 1 starch.

⑤ⓕ

STRAWBERRY-HAZELNUT MERINGUE SHORTCAKES

In early summer, when the strawberry farms in our area open to the public for picking, I love to serve those big, juicy berries over a scoop of low-calorie frozen yogurt on a crunchy hazelnut meringue cookie.
—*Barb Estabrook, Appleton, WI*

- -

Prep: 25 min. • **Bake:** 45 min. + cooling
Makes: 8 servings

- 2   **large egg whites**
- ½   **cup sugar**
- ¼   **cup finely chopped hazelnuts**
- 6   **cups fresh strawberries, hulled and sliced**
- 4   **cups low-fat frozen yogurt**

1. Place egg whites in a small bowl; let stand at room temperature 30 minutes.
2. Preheat oven to 250°. Beat egg whites on medium speed until foamy. Gradually add the sugar, 1 Tbsp. at a time, beating on high after each addition until sugar is dissolved. Continue beating until stiff glossy peaks form.
3. Using a measuring cup and spatula or an ice cream scoop, drop meringue into 8 even mounds on a parchment-lined baking sheet. With the back of a spoon, shape into 3-in. cups. Sprinkle with hazelnuts. Bake until set and dry, 45-50 minutes. Turn off oven (do not open oven door); leave meringues in oven for 1 hour. Remove from oven; cool completely on baking sheets. Remove the meringues from paper.
4. Place 3 cups strawberries in a large bowl; mash slightly. Stir in remaining strawberries. Just before serving, top meringues with frozen yogurt and strawberries.

1 serving: 212 cal., 4g fat (1g sat. fat), 5mg chol., 74mg sod., 40g carb. (36g sugars, 3g fiber), 7g pro.

NO-BAKE PEANUT BUTTER TREATS

This quick and tasty dessert is perfect for a road trip. The treats won't stick to your hands, so you'll crave more than one. Keep them on hand in the fridge for an easy snack.

—*Sonia Rohda, Waverly, NE*

Takes: 10 min. • **Makes:** 15 treats

- ⅓ **cup chunky peanut butter**
- ¼ **cup honey**
- ½ **tsp. vanilla extract**
- ⅓ **cup nonfat dry milk powder**
- ⅓ **cup quick-cooking oats**
- 2 **Tbsp. graham cracker crumbs**

In a small bowl, combine the peanut butter, honey and vanilla. Stir in the milk powder, oats and graham cracker crumbs. Shape into 1-in. balls. Cover and refrigerate until serving.

1 serving: 70 cal., 3g fat (1g sat. fat), 1mg chol., 46mg sod., 9g carb. (6g sugars, 1g fiber), 3g pro. **Diabetic exchanges:** ½ starch, ½ fat.

BAKLAVA WITH HONEY SYRUP

Baklava is a sweet, buttery Greek treat. The honey syrup gives it a distinctive flavor. This is a favorite treat among my group of friends.
—*Trisha Kruse, Eagle, ID*

Prep: 50 min. • **Bake:** 35 min. + standing
Makes: 2½ dozen

Butter-flavored cooking spray
1 pkg. (16 oz., 14x9-in. sheet size) frozen phyllo dough, thawed
2 cups finely chopped walnuts, toasted

SYRUP
¾ cup sugar
¾ cup water
⅓ cup honey
¾ tsp. grated lemon zest
¾ tsp. vanilla extract

1. Coat a 13x9-in. baking pan with cooking spray. Unroll thawed phyllo dough; trim to fit into pan.
2. Layer 2 sheets of phyllo dough in prepared pan; spritz phyllo with cooking spray. Repeat 3 times. (Keep remaining phyllo covered with a damp towel to prevent it from drying out.) Sprinkle with 3 Tbsp. nuts. Top with 2 sheets of phyllo; spritz with cooking spray. Repeat layering with nuts, phyllo and cooking spray 10 times. Top with the remaining phyllo dough, spritzing every other sheet with cooking spray.
3. Using a sharp knife, cut the dough into 30 triangles. Bake at 350° for 35-40 minutes or until golden brown. Meanwhile, in a small saucepan, combine syrup ingredients. Bring to a boil. Reduce heat; simmer, uncovered, for 10 minutes, stirring occasionally. Pour over warm baklava. Cool completely on a wire rack. Cover and let stand for several hours or overnight.
1 piece: 136 cal., 7g fat (0 sat. fat), 0 chol., 67mg sod., 18g carb. (9g sugars, 1g fiber), 3g pro.

PEAR TART

My sister-in-law brought this fruity dessert pastry to dinner one night, and we all went back for seconds. It looks like it came from a bakery.
—*Kathryn Rogers, Suisun City, CA*

Prep: 15 min. • **Bake:** 25 min. + chilling
Makes: 12 servings

3 Tbsp. butter, softened
½ cup sugar
¾ tsp. ground cinnamon
¾ cup all-purpose flour
⅓ cup finely chopped walnuts

FILLING
1 pkg. (8 oz.) reduced-fat cream cheese
¼ cup plus 1 Tbsp. sugar, divided
1 large egg, room temperature
1 tsp. vanilla extract
1 can (15 oz.) reduced-sugar sliced pears, drained well and thinly sliced
¼ tsp. ground cinnamon

1. Preheat oven to 425°. Beat butter, sugar and cinnamon until crumbly. Beat in flour and walnuts. Press onto bottom and up sides of a 9-in. fluted tart pan with a removable bottom coated with cooking spray.
2. For filling, beat cream cheese and ¼ cup sugar until smooth. Beat in egg and vanilla. Spread into crust. Arrange pears over top. Mix cinnamon and remaining sugar; sprinkle over pears.
3. Bake 10 minutes. Reduce oven setting to 350°; bake until filling is set, 15-20 minutes. Cool 1 hour on a wire rack. Refrigerate at least 2 hours before serving.
1 piece: 199 cal., 9g fat (5g sat. fat), 36mg chol., 112mg sod., 25g carb. (18g sugars, 1g fiber), 4g pro. **Diabetic exchanges:** 2 fat, 1½ starch.

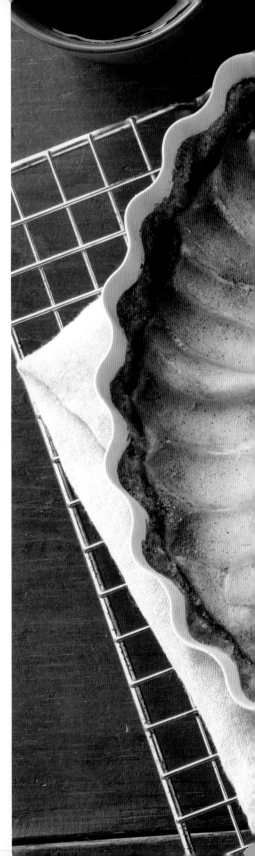

FRUIT & ALMOND BITES

With big handfuls of dried apricots, cherries, almonds and pistachios, these are some seriously tasty and satisfying no-bake treats. You can take them anywhere.
—*Donna Pochoday-Stelmach, Morristown, NJ*

- -

Prep: 40 min. + chilling
Makes: about 4 dozen

- 3¾ cups sliced almonds, divided
- ¼ tsp. almond extract
- ¼ cup honey
- 2 cups finely chopped dried apricots
- 1 cup finely chopped dried cherries or cranberries
- 1 cup finely chopped pistachios, toasted

1. Place 1¼ cups of the sliced almonds in a food processor; pulse until finely chopped. Remove almonds to a shallow bowl; reserve for coating.

2. Add remaining 2½ cups almonds to food processor; pulse until finely chopped. Add extract. While processing, gradually add honey. Remove to a large bowl; stir in dried apricots and cherries. Divide mixture into 6 portions; shape each into a ½-in.-thick roll. Wrap in plastic; refrigerate until firm, about 1 hour.

3. Unwrap and cut rolls into 1½-in. pieces. Roll half of the pieces in reserved almonds, pressing gently to adhere. Roll remaining half in pistachios. If desired, wrap individually in waxed paper, twisting ends to close. Store in airtight containers, layered between waxed paper if unwrapped.

Note: To toast nuts, bake in a shallow pan in a 350° oven for 5-10 minutes or cook in a skillet over low heat until lightly browned, stirring occasionally.

1 piece: 86 cal., 5g fat (0 sat. fat), 0 chol., 15mg sod., 10g carb. (7g sugars, 2g fiber), 2g pro. **Diabetic exchanges:** 1 fat, ½ starch.

WINE PAIRING

Moscato. This sweet, fruity and fun-to-drink wine tastes delicious with apricots. And its hint of fizziness will be an interesting textural counterpoint to the rich, buttery nuts.

⑤j

SWEET POTATO FROYO POPS

After I had a child, I got creative in the kitchen with meals and decided to keep plenty of healthy foods on hand. These frozen treats turned out to be a favorite in our house.
—*Jenn Tidwell, Fair Oaks, CA*

- -

Prep: 10 min. + freezing • **Makes:** 6 servings

- 2 cartons (6 oz. each) honey Greek yogurt
- 1 cup mashed sweet potatoes
- ¼ cup fat-free milk
- ½ tsp. ground cinnamon
- 6 freezer pop molds or paper cups (3 oz. each) and wooden pop sticks

Place first 4 ingredients in a food processor; process until smooth. Pour into molds or paper cups. Top molds with holders. If using cups, top with foil and insert sticks through foil. Freeze until firm.

1 pop: 129 cal., 5g fat (3g sat. fat), 14mg chol., 51mg sod., 18g carb. (11g sugars, 1g fiber), 3g pro. **Diabetic exchanges:** 1 starch, ½ fat.

ALMOND ESPRESSO BARS

If you like coffee, you'll love these mocha morsels dressed up with toasted almonds. Save a few bars for afternoon snacktime or even breakfast.

—Taire Van Scoy, Brunswick, MD

Prep: 15 min. • **Bake:** 20 min. + cooling
Makes: 4 dozen

- ¼ cup butter, softened
- 1 cup packed brown sugar
- ½ cup brewed espresso
- 1 large egg, room temperature
- 1½ cups self-rising flour
- ½ tsp. ground cinnamon
- ¾ cup chopped slivered almonds, toasted

GLAZE

- 1½ cups confectioners' sugar
- 3 Tbsp. water
- ¾ tsp. almond extract
- ¼ cup slivered almonds, toasted

1. In a large bowl, cream the butter, brown sugar and espresso until blended. Beat in egg. Combine flour and cinnamon; gradually add to creamed mixture and mix well. Stir in chopped almonds.

2. Spread into a greased 15x10x1-in. baking pan. Bake at 350° for 18-22 minutes or until lightly browned.

3. In a small bowl, combine the confectioners' sugar, water and extract until smooth; spread over warm bars. Sprinkle with slivered almonds. Cool on a wire rack. Cut into bars.

Note: As a substitute for 1½ cups self-rising flour, place 2¼ tsp. baking powder and ¾ tsp. salt in a measuring cup. Add all-purpose flour to measure 1 cup. Combine with an additional ½ cup all-purpose flour.

1 bar: 68 cal., 2g fat (1g sat. fat), 7mg chol., 55mg sod., 11g carb. (8g sugars, 0 fiber), 1g pro. **Diabetic exchanges:** 1 starch, ½ fat.

BLACKBERRY LEMON MUFFINS

These tender muffins make me think of spring. Garnish with grated lemon zest for added color and a greater punch of flavor.
—*Vicky Palmer, Albuquerque, NM*

Prep: 20 min. • **Bake:** 15 min.
Makes: 1 dozen

- 2   cups all-purpose flour
- ½   cup sugar
- 2   tsp. baking powder
- ½   tsp. salt
- ¼   tsp. baking soda
- 2   large eggs, room temperature
- 1   cup fat-free milk
- ⅓   cup butter, melted
- ⅓   cup lemon juice
- 1   cup fresh blackberries

GLAZE

- 1   cup confectioners' sugar
- 1   Tbsp. butter, melted
- 1   to 2 Tbsp. lemon juice
      Grated lemon zest, optional

1. Preheat oven to 375°. In a large bowl, whisk the first 5 ingredients. In another bowl, whisk eggs, milk, melted butter and lemon juice until blended. Add to the flour mixture; stir just until moistened. Fold in the blackberries.

2. Fill greased or foil-lined muffin cups about three-fourths full. Bake 15-18 minutes or until a toothpick inserted in the center comes out clean. Cool 5 minutes before removing from pan to a wire rack.

3. In a small bowl, mix confectioners' sugar, melted butter and enough lemon juice to reach desired consistency. Drizzle over warm muffins. If desired, sprinkle with lemon zest.

1 muffin: 226 cal., 7g fat (4g sat. fat), 52mg chol., 255mg sod., 37g carb. (20g sugars, 1g fiber), 4g pro.

HONEYDEW GRANITA

Make this refreshing summer treat when melons are ripe and flavorful. I like to garnish each serving with a sprig of mint or a small slice of honeydew. It's a refreshing dessert to enjoy after a spicy meal.

—*Bonnie Hawkins, Elkhorn, WI*

Prep: 10 min.
Cook: 5 min. + freezing
Makes: 5½ cups

- 1 cup sugar
- 1 cup water
- 6 cups cubed honeydew melon
- 2 Tbsp. sweet white wine

1. In a small saucepan, bring sugar and water to a boil over medium-high heat. Cook and stir until sugar is dissolved. Cool.

2. Pulse honeydew, sugar syrup and wine in batches in a food processor until smooth, 1-2 minutes. Transfer to an 8-in. square dish. Freeze 1 hour. Stir with a fork. Freeze, stirring every 30 minutes, until frozen, 2-3 hours longer. Stir again with a fork just before serving.

½ cup: 107 cal., 0 fat (0 sat. fat), 0 chol., 17mg sod., 27g carb. (26g sugars, 1g fiber), 1g pro.
Diabetic exchanges: 1½ starch, ½ fruit.
Honeydew Sorbet: After processing the honeydew mixture, pour into the cylinder of an ice cream freezer; freeze according to manufacturer's directions. Transfer to a freezer container; freeze for 4 hours or until firm.

RASPBERRY PEACH TART

There's no shortage of fresh peaches and raspberries where I live. I use the fruit I grow to bake up this sweet and special fruit tart.
—*Mary Ann Rempel, Southold, NY*

- -

Prep: 15 min. + standing
Bake: 25 min. + cooling • **Makes:** 8 servings

2⅔ cups sliced peeled peaches
     (about 4 medium)
  1 cup fresh raspberries
  1 Tbsp. lemon juice
  ½ cup sugar
  5 tsp. quick-cooking tapioca
  ½ tsp. ground cinnamon
  1 sheet refrigerated pie crust
  1 Tbsp. butter
  1 large egg white, lightly beaten
  1 Tbsp. coarse sugar

1. Preheat oven to 425°. In a large bowl, combine peaches, raspberries and lemon juice. In another bowl, combine sugar, tapioca and cinnamon. Gently stir into fruit mixture; let stand 15 minutes.
2. Unroll pie crust onto a parchment-lined 15x10x1-in. baking pan. Spoon filling over crust to within 2 in. of edge; dot with butter. Fold crust edge over filling, pleating as you go and leaving a 6-in. opening in the center. Brush folded crust with egg white; sprinkle with sugar. Bake for 25-30 minutes on a lower oven rack or until crust is golden and filling is bubbly. Transfer tart to a wire rack to cool.
1 slice: 227 cal., 9g fat (4g sat. fat), 9mg chol., 119mg sod., 36g carb. (20g sugars, 2g fiber), 2g pro.

5j

MARBLED MERINGUE HEARTS

Pretty pastel cookies are a fun way to brighten any special occasion. Replace the vanilla with a different extract for a change of flavor.
—*Laurie Herr, Westford, VT*

- -

Prep: 25 min. • **Bake:** 20 min. + cooling
Makes: about 2 dozen

3	**large egg whites**
½	**tsp. vanilla extract**
¼	**tsp. cream of tartar**
	Food coloring, optional
¾	**cup sugar**

1. Place egg whites in a large bowl; let stand at room temperature for 30 minutes. Line baking sheets with parchment.
2. Preheat oven to 200°. Add the vanilla extract and cream of tartar to egg whites; beat on medium speed until soft peaks form. Gradually beat in sugar, 1 Tbsp. at a time, on high until stiff peaks form. Remove ¼ cup and tint pink. Lightly swirl the pink mixture into remaining meringue. Fill pastry bag with meringue. Pipe 2-in. heart shapes 2 in. apart onto prepared baking sheets.
3. Bake until set and dry, about 20 minutes. Turn oven off; leave meringues in oven until oven has completely cooled. Store in an airtight container.
1 meringue: 27 cal., 0 fat (0 sat. fat), 0 chol., 7mg sod., 6g carb. (6g sugars, 0 fiber), 0 pro.

WINE PAIRING

Prosecco. The Italian bubbly would feel festive with these crisp and delicate cookies. Want to make this light duo even more special? Use berry extract instead of vanilla in the cookies and add fresh raspberries or sliced strawberries to the wine.

LIME & SPICE PEACH COBBLER

This was my grandmother's favorite recipe when peaches were in great abundance. Now I bake it often for my family and friends.
—*Mary Ann Dell, Phoenixville, PA*

Prep: 25 min. • **Bake:** 35 min.
Makes: 8 servings

- 3 **Tbsp. sugar**
- 3 **Tbsp. brown sugar**
- 2 **Tbsp. minced crystallized ginger**
- 4 **tsp. cornstarch**
- 2 **tsp. ground cinnamon**
- ½ **tsp. grated lime zest**
- 8 **medium peaches, peeled and sliced (about 5 cups)**
- 1 **Tbsp. lime juice**

TOPPING:
- 3 **Tbsp. butter, softened**
- ¼ **cup packed brown sugar**
- 2 **Tbsp. sugar**
- 1 **cup cake flour**
- ½ **tsp. baking powder**
- ¼ **tsp. salt**
- 2 **Tbsp. cold water**
- ¼ **cup chopped pecans**
- 1 **large egg yolk**
- 2 **Tbsp. buttermilk**

1. Preheat oven to 375°. Mix the first 6 ingredients; toss with peaches and lime juice. Transfer to an 8-in. square baking dish coated with cooking spray.

2. For topping, beat butter and sugars until blended. Whisk together flour, baking powder and salt; beat into butter mixture. Beat in water just until crumbly. Stir in pecans; crumble over filling.

3. Whisk together egg yolk and buttermilk; brush carefully over crumb mixture. Bake until topping is golden brown and filling is bubbly, 35-40 minutes. Serve warm.

1 serving: 287 cal., 8g fat (3g sat. fat), 35mg chol., 152mg sod., 53g carb. (33g sugars, 3g fiber), 4g pro.

ORANGE DREAM ANGEL FOOD CAKE

A basic angel food cake becomes a heavenly indulgence thanks to a hint of orange flavor swirled into every bite. The orange color makes slices of the cake look so pretty when arranged on individual dessert plates.

—*Lauren Osborne, Holtwood, PA*

- -

Prep: 25 min. • **Bake:** 30 min. + cooling
Makes: 16 servings

- 12 large egg whites
- 1 cup all-purpose flour
- 1¾ cups sugar, divided
- 1½ tsp. cream of tartar
- ½ tsp. salt
- 1 tsp. almond extract
- 1 tsp. vanilla extract
- 1 tsp. grated orange zest
- 1 tsp. orange extract
- 6 drops red food coloring, optional
- 6 drops yellow food coloring, optional

1. Place the egg whites in a large bowl; let stand at room temperature for 30 minutes. Sift flour and ¾ cup sugar together twice; set aside.

2. Add the cream of tartar, salt and extracts to egg whites; beat on medium speed until soft peaks form. Gradually add remaining sugar, about 2 Tbsp. at a time, beating on high until stiff glossy peaks form and sugar is dissolved. Gradually fold in flour mixture, about ½ cup at a time.

3. Gently spoon half of the batter into an ungreased 10-in. tube pan. To the remaining batter, stir in the orange zest, orange extract and, if desired, food colorings. Gently spoon orange batter over white batter. Cut through both layers with a knife to swirl the orange and remove air pockets.

4. Bake on the lowest oven rack at 375° for 30-35 minutes or until lightly browned and entire top appears dry. Immediately invert pan; cool completely, about 1 hour.

5. Run a knife around side and center tube of pan. Remove cake to a serving plate.

1 slice: 130 cal., 0 fat (0 sat. fat), 0 chol., 116mg sod., 28g carb. (22g sugars, 0 fiber), 4g pro. **Diabetic exchanges:** 2 starch.

READER RAVE

"Oh, my—delicious! My mom made this for Easter and the recipe is a keeper. It doesn't need any topping or sauce. It rose up beautifully, the color was nice with the top slightly caramelized, and the flavor was to die for. Can't wait to make it at my house!"

SMALL BATCH BROWNIES

Here's the perfect chocolaty treat when you only need a small batch. For a pretty accent, dust the tops with confectioners' sugar.
—Taste of Home *Test Kitchen*

Prep: 15 min. • **Bake:** 15 min. + cooling
Makes: 6 servings

2	Tbsp. butter
½	oz. unsweetened chocolate, chopped
1	large egg, room temperature
¼	tsp. vanilla extract
⅔	cup sugar
⅓	cup all-purpose flour
¼	cup baking cocoa
¼	tsp. salt
¼	tsp. confectioners' sugar, optional

1. In a microwave, melt butter and chocolate; stir until smooth. Cool slightly.

2. In a small bowl, whisk egg and vanilla; gradually whisk in sugar. Stir in chocolate mixture. Combine the flour, cocoa and salt; gradually add to chocolate mixture.

3. Transfer to a 9x5-in. loaf pan coated with cooking spray. Bake at 350° until a toothpick inserted in the center comes out clean, 12-16 minutes. Cool on a wire rack. Cut into bars. Dust with confectioners' sugar if desired.

1 brownie: 179 cal., 6g fat (3g sat. fat), 45mg chol., 138mg sod., 30g carb. (23g sugars, 1g fiber), 3g pro. **Diabetic exchanges:** 2 starch, 1 fat.

5i · ⏱

GINGER-GLAZED GRILLED HONEYDEW

If you've never grilled fruit before, you're in for a surprise. I enjoy cooking everything from appetizers to desserts on the grill. These honeydew skewers are a sweet way to get a boost of vitamin C and potassium.
—*Jacqueline Correa, Landing, NJ*

- -

Takes: 25 min. • **Makes:** 6 servings

¼	cup peach preserves
1	Tbsp. lemon juice
1	Tbsp. finely chopped crystallized ginger
2	tsp. grated lemon zest
⅛	tsp. ground cloves
1	medium honeydew melon, cut into 2-in. cubes

1. In a bowl, combine the first 5 ingredients. Thread honeydew onto 6 metal or soaked wooden skewers; brush with half the glaze.
2. On a lightly oiled rack, grill honeydew, covered, over medium-high heat or broil 4 in. from the heat just until melon begins to soften and brown, 4-6 minutes, turning and basting frequently with remaining glaze.
1 skewer: 101 cal., 0 fat (0 sat. fat), 0 chol., 18mg sod., 26g carb. (23g sugars, 1g fiber), 1g pro. **Diabetic exchanges:** 1 fruit, ½ starch.

MULTIGRAIN CINNAMON ROLLS

This recipe is sure to become a favorite. Perfect for dessert or a coffee break, the bakery-style cinnamon rolls will fill your kitchen with an irresistible aroma.
—*Judith Eddy, Baldwin City, KS*

- -

Prep: 30 min. + rising • **Bake:** 15 min.
Makes: 1 dozen

1	pkg. (¼ oz.) active dry yeast
¾	cup warm water (110° to 115°)
½	cup quick-cooking oats
½	cup whole wheat flour
¼	cup packed brown sugar
2	Tbsp. butter, melted
1	large egg, room temperature
1	tsp. salt
1¾ to 2¼	cups all-purpose flour

FILLING

3	Tbsp. butter, softened
⅓	cup sugar
2	tsp. ground cinnamon

GLAZE

1	cup confectioners' sugar
6½	tsp. half-and-half cream
4½	tsp. butter, softened

1. In a large bowl, dissolve yeast in warm water. Add the oats, whole wheat flour, brown sugar, butter, egg, salt and 1 cup all-purpose flour. Beat the ingredients on medium speed until smooth. Stir in enough remaining flour to form a soft dough (dough will be sticky).

2. Turn onto a lightly floured surface; knead until smooth and elastic, 6-8 minutes. Place in a bowl coated with cooking spray, turning once to coat the top. Cover and let rise in a warm place until doubled, about 1 hour.

3. Punch dough down. Roll into an 18x12-in. rectangle; spread with butter. Combine sugar and cinnamon; sprinkle over dough to within ½ in. of edges.

4. Roll up jelly-roll style, starting with a short side; pinch seams to seal. Cut into 12 slices. Place cut side down in a 13x9-in. baking pan coated with cooking spray. Cover and let rise until doubled, about 45 minutes.

5. Bake cinnamon rolls at 375° until golden brown, 15-20 minutes. For icing, in a small bowl, beat the confectioners' sugar, cream and butter until smooth. Drizzle icing over warm rolls.

1 cinnamon roll: 240 cal., 7g fat (4g sat. fat), 35mg chol., 251mg sod., 40g carb. (20g sugars, 2g fiber), 4g pro.

Cinnamon Pull-Apart Loaf: Follow method for cinnamon rolls but do not roll up jelly-roll style. Instead, cut dough into thirty-six 3x2-in. rectangles. Make 2 stacks of 18 rectangles. Place, cut sides up, in a 9x5-in. loaf pan coated with cooking spray. Cover and let rise until doubled, about 45 minutes. Bake at 375° until golden brown, 25-30 minutes. Cool for 10 minutes before removing from pan to a wire rack. Make glaze; drizzle over warm bread. Makes 1 loaf (12 slices).

Twisted Cinnamon Ring: Follow method for cinnamon rolls and roll up jelly-roll style, starting with a long side. Cut roll in half lengthwise. Place doughs side by side on a baking sheet coated with cooking spray. Twist together, cut side up, and shape into a ring. Pinch ends together. Cover and let rise until doubled, about 45 minutes. Bake at 375° until golden brown, 20-25 minutes. Remove from pan to a wire rack. Make glaze; drizzle over warm bread. Makes 1 ring (12 slices).

GRAPEFRUIT, LIME & MINT YOGURT PARFAIT

Tart grapefruit and lime are balanced with a bit of honey in this cool and easy parfait.
—*Lois Enger, Colorado Springs, CO*

Takes: 15 min. • **Makes:** 6 servings

- 4   **large red grapefruit**
- 4   **cups reduced-fat plain yogurt**
- 2   **tsp. grated lime zest**
- 2   **Tbsp. lime juice**
- 3   **Tbsp. honey**
  Torn fresh mint leaves

1. Cut a thin slice from the top and bottom of each grapefruit; stand fruit upright on a cutting board. With a sharp knife, cut off peel and outer membrane from grapefruit. Cut along the membrane of each segment to remove fruit.

2. In a large bowl, mix yogurt, lime zest and juice. Layer half of the grapefruit and half of the yogurt mixture into six parfait glasses. Repeat layers. Drizzle with honey; top parfaits with mint.

1 parfait: 207 cal., 3g fat (2g sat. fat), 10mg chol., 115mg sod., 39g carb. (36g sugars, 3g fiber), 10g pro.

ITALIAN ORANGE-FIG COOKIES

I love these bites because they're gluten-free. But they're so tasty, they'll be enjoyed by all!
—*Suzanne Banfield, Basking Ridge, NJ*

- -

Prep: 20 min. • **Bake:** 25 min./batch
Makes: about 3 dozen

- 2 pkg. (8 oz. each) almond paste
- 1 cup sugar, divided
- 1 cup confectioners' sugar, divided
- 2 Tbsp. apricot preserves
- 3 large egg whites
- ½ cup dried figs, finely chopped
- 1 Tbsp. grated orange zest

1. Preheat oven to 325°. Place almond paste, ½ cup sugar and ½ cup confectioners' sugar in a food processor; pulse until fine crumbs form. Add preserves and 1 egg white at a time, pulsing after each addition to combine. Transfer almond mixture to a large bowl; fold in figs and orange zest (dough will be sticky).

2. Place remaining sugars in separate shallow bowls. Drop tablespoonfuls of dough into sugar. Gently coat and shape into 1¼-in. balls. Repeat in confectioners' sugar. Place 1 in. apart on parchment-lined baking sheets. Bake 24-28 minutes or until tops are cracked and bottoms are golden brown. Remove to wire racks to cool.

1 cookie: 96 cal., 3g fat (0 sat. fat), 0 chol., 6mg sod., 16g carb. (14g sugars, 1g fiber), 1g pro.

WINE PAIRING

Vin Santo. Grapes for this dessert wine are harvested late in the season, when they are very ripe. Then the grapes are dried into raisins to make the sweet elixir. Vin santo, which means "holy wine" in Italian, is tasty with simple fruit desserts and Italian baked goods.

ALPHABETICAL INDEX